Conversations with Walker Percy

Literary Conversations Series

Peggy Whitman Prenshaw
General Editor

Conversations
with Walker Percy

Edited by
Lewis A. Lawson
and Victor A. Kramer

University Press of Mississippi
Jackson

Books by Walker Percy

The Moviegoer. New York: Alfred A. Knopf, 1961.

The Last Gentleman. New York: Farrar, Straus and Giroux, 1966.

Love in the Ruins: The Adventures of a Bad Catholic at a Time Near the End of the World. New York: Farrar, Straus and Giroux, 1971.

The Message in the Bottle: How Queer Man Is, How Queer Language Is, and What One Has to Do with the Other. New York: Farrar, Straus and Giroux, 1975.

Lancelot. New York: Farrar, Straus and Giroux, 1977.

The Second Coming. New York: Farrar, Straus and Giroux, 1980.

Lost in the Cosmos: The Last Self-Help Book. New York: Farrar, Straus and Giroux, 1983.

Copyright © 1985 by the University Press of Mississippi
All rights reserved
Manufactured in the United States of America
88 87 86 85   4 3 2 1

Library of Congress Cataloging in Publication Data

Percy, Walker, 1916–
    Conversations with Walker Percy.

    (Literary conversations series)
    Includes index.
    1. Percy, Walker, 1916–   —Interviews.   2. Novelists,
American—20th century—Interviews.   I. Lawson, Lewis A.
II. Kramer, Victor A.   III. Title.   IV. Series.
PS3566.E6912C6   1985   813'.54   84-40715
ISBN 0-87805-251-8
ISBN 0-87805-252-6 (pbk.)

Contents

Introduction

For many of us, there are always at least two stories in a Walker Percy novel. The story that we read, the verbal expression, delights and instructs us, because it satisfies our hunger for artifice and reveals new beauties and truths in our shared world. Yet there is another story—a story that we intuit, and it haunts us, for it confronts us with the mystery of personality, the private world of Walker Percy. It seems almost like a confession. But that isn't the end of our response: perhaps we are haunted, really, not so much by the revelation of Percy's experiences as by our own, suddenly illuminated by his. Surely some such psychology explains the extraordinary feeling that readers have for Percy's books.

It may be for such a reason that many readers also wish to be close to the man himself. Of course, since he lives near New Orleans and used to be listed in the telephone book, he can be expected, as a public person, to get some of those wild and agonized calls that have, in the secular city, been substituted for prayer. (Sometimes the call is not to the Guru, but to Information: while Philip Carter was visiting, a caller reading *Love in the Ruins* wanted a definition of "satyriasis.") Beyond these spontaneous seekers—who sometimes even tell him that they called him because a preferred seer's line was busy—there have been, from the beginning, those whose reading of his work caused them, in a phrase that he has frequently used, "to come to themselves." And when that has happened, all too often, they have also come to Covington. Robert Coles[1] must be forgiven a bit of Biblical hype when he says that "a host of undergraduates, graduate students, and interviewers . . . have made the trek" to Covington, Louisiana, Percy's "pleasant non-place,"[2] where he has lived since 1950.

Once an interviewer is there, imagine that Percy opens the door. Henry Kisor notes: ". . . with gulf-blue eyes, a tanned, furrowed face and white hair, he could be a Southern lawyer or doctor—which he was once. He greets the stranger at his door with grave courtesy, but a quick and generous laugh punctuates his conversation." Edmund

Fuller reports pretty much the same man: ". . . a relaxed, lanky frame, strong interestingly seamed face, and close-trimmed white hair." Philip Carter adds: ". . . a quiet man, spare, courtly, and gray. . . ." Barbara King catches just a little more quietness: "He is lean and graying and has milky blue, transparent eyes that, if not sad, seem somehow inviolably internal." "He [is] taller than I'd imagined," thinks John Jones, "with the quick, nimble movements of a boy." James Atlas also detects qualities from an earlier time: ". . . he displays the reserve, good manners and genial modesty one would expect from a white-haired Southern gentleman of 66, tempered by the shy, awkward uncertainty of a child eager for reassurance." The oft-noted slenderness hints at a younger self never lost—the eyes betray the sadness which haunts consciousness.

Now imagine that the iced tea has been served and that the tape starts. Martin Luschei[3] observes: "Though he does not much like the distraction of interviews, I [find] him very cooperative, seemingly a little puzzled as to what all the fuss [is] about." Luschei concludes that Percy has "a genuine modesty with no visible literary pretensions."

But things don't go all that well—time snags on the tape head of the present, as Lancelot puts it. Carlton Cremeens is aware of the erratic shape that the interview seems to be taking: "Walker Percy is outwardly friendly, curious, full of questions one moment, introspective the next. His deep eyes work with a penetrating glance, and one gets the impression of seeing an image recorded and then watching through frosted glass the internalizing process of its development. A moment of silence. And then he asks another question. He had rather interview than be interviewed." Barbara King has the same initial frustration: "He had rather ask questions than be asked them. . . ." Alfred Kazin[4] once wondered (and this suggests a lot about many of the interviews): "He is easy to talk to, a great listener but no very enthusiastic talker himself. . . ." Does subjectivity instinctively avoid objectivity?

Yet what can be done but go on? Barbara King perseveres: ". . . though it's often difficult to draw him out, I [am] struck by the ease with which his mind [moves] over complex and subtle subjects." Ah, if both look at an idea, then neither looks at the other. Or if both look at the landscape which borders Percy's house. Ashley Brown re-

cords: "In his country one can sit outdoors late in the year, and in the
November sunshine the visitor is delighted to find himself looking
over a bayou . . . at ease in this setting, [Percy] talks with the utmost
care and precision about his work." Charles Bunting remembers the
same combination of landscape and ease: "Frequently looking out
over the Bogue Falaya River, which flows at a distance of about sixty
yards from his house, Dr. Percy carefully and precisely [forms] his
replies to my questions." Inside, something else will serve, as Alfred
Kazin may or may not detect: "It is somehow typical of a certain
shyness, reserve, a charming gift in his nature for not bearing down
too hard in personal conversation, that he likes to keep the television
picture on without the sound. He has cultivated the art of restful
sitting and lounging, of looking easy, in a way that keeps conversation with him as casual as drifting through a summer afternoon."
Bradley Dewey is caught by the same perfected gesture: "Percy's
relaxed and unassuming manner [has] put me at ease, so that the
next two hours of our 'interview' [become] conversation." In Percy's
role-acceptance is there an echo of Dr. Gamow's evaluation of Will
Barrett: ". . . a Southern belle, . . . a good dancing partner, light on
his feet and giving away nothing"?

Granted, Percy has given away all that his interviewers have asked
of him. And by now we know a great deal, far more in truth than we
will ever know about many another writer. We know that childhood
was spent in Birmingham (though we must read the novels to taste its
pleasures and pains: Eden as a golf course and the Fall as a father's
death). We know more about the adolescence in Greenville, Mississippi, in the house of William Alexander Percy, his father's cousin. We
know of his undergraduate education at Chapel Hill and his medical
education at Columbia. We know of his psychoanalysis and his bout
with tuberculosis. We know that he spent a brief period in New Mexico before returning to marry, become a Catholic, and settle in Louisiana. In the physical itinerary, there are few of the *Lücken* that Will
Barrett has.

In like manner, the mind has been tracked. Percy has acknowledged with great appreciation the opportunities that growing up in
Uncle Will's house gave him. He has spoken of the eminent visitors,
of the love of literature and music awakened by his adoptive father's
passion. His exploration of the southern Stoicism that animated his

Percy ancestors sheds light on that theme in southern history. His description of the worldview that he accepted as a science major and a young physician (with its usually unnoted similarity to romanticism) is useful to anyone who reads his novels or ever has to deal with that kind of educated mind which seems to be immune to facts. He has repeatedly expressed his indebtedness to the Catholic philosophers, the Russian novelists, and the existentialists. He has often revealed his interest in the relationship of religion and literature, in contemporary culture, and in the fate of the south.

In matters more specifically literary, he has always been very willing to discuss the craft of fiction and his "little knack for writing," as he calls it. His recurrent description of fiction-writing as discovery offers a specific test to distinguish serious novels from those written to formula. He has stated his kinship with the modern French novelists and lack of appetite for the modern English. He has spoken of his fondness of the American Jewish novel and writers such as Bernard Malamud and of his unexpected distance from much of the southern school, including the sole owner and proprietor, Faulkner himself. He has spoken, with especial warmth, of Flannery O'Connor and Thomas Merton.

As time has gone on, the interviewers have exhausted many of these topics and have been led by his novels and essays into new areas of questioning. More and more, Percy's study of semiotics and language theory has been the spice of an interview. And, given the concept of anthropology that Percy has, discussion of these subjects—conventionally only regarded "scientifically"—often leads into philosophical, even religious reflections, and then leads back to the current cultural situation. But, be it understood, that he speaks of philosophy and religion, not as casual certainties, but as the straws of faith that a drowning man may find. And even if they get him to shore, the man must then start from nothing, which is, after all, what coming to oneself really means. No wonder that Percy so often illustrates man's predicament by referring to Robinson Crusoe, not the hardy utilitarian Crusoe of the economic myth, but the lonely and depressed human being that such a shipwreck victim would really be. Because Percy sees the human situation this way, he is frequently interested in talking about the larger cultural situation.

Walker Percy has, in short, satisfied every protocol of the interview.

Our grandsire Adam was the first person to be interviewed, and Percy may have accepted the institution as his particular burden of original sin. There is just a possibility, though, that he is drawn to the encounter. The etymology of the word, "to see each other," suggests the primary human experience that, to judge from his fiction, is never out of his mind. Thus he may need the interview to keep fresh that fundamental relationship. After all, this is what, he tells us over and over, is most important in his fiction.

It seems, moreover, that Percy uses the interview as a direct communication to parallel his indirect communications in fiction. There is, indeed, a hint of confession at times, an answer to a question not asked. The need to state how it is with him ultimately became strong enough in 1977 for him to publish "Questions They Never Asked Me." It should be noted that the novel published the same year, *Lancelot,* is one long interview, sought but then scorned by Lancelot. Percy must think that the interview is essentially salutary, helps to ward off that "shutupness" of which Kierkegaard speaks and from which Lancelot suffers. Thus we can expect more of these "conversations," certainly to answer the questions of his readers, but, more urgently, to answer the questions that they can't ask.[5]

And now to the "conversations" that we do have. Extremely brief interviews, such as those to be found in *Publishers Weekly* (March 22, 1971) or *The Christian Science Monitor* (June 9, 1971), which really derive from press conferences, and material based on interviews, such as the chapter in Paul Binding's *Separate Country* (1979) or Albert Murray's *South to a Very Old Place* (1971), which are incorporated into their books, are here excluded. We have sought to include nearly every significant interview or profile based on an interview, whether it appeared in a newspaper, a literary quarterly, or another kind of journal. The twenty-seven interviews selected for inclusion reflect the development of interest in Percy. As the momentum of his career has built up, it has become more commonplace for interviews to appear in journals with a wider readership. Thus early pieces reflect an interest in Percy as a "southern" writer. Subsequently, national publications and interviewers from countries such as France, Hungary, and Denmark have reflected what is clearly becoming an international reputation.

These interviews are reproduced just as they first appeared in print, in order of publication. No deletions have been made; and while we realize that this may result in some slight repetition, the cumulative picture will prove to be of value to scholars. It should be clear, however, that Percy has been extremely kind to his interviewers over the years and, therefore, he has answered similar questions many times. We hope that readers will find this book a valuable resource, and that the book may also help scholars to prepare to ask still more questions of Percy—whether it be in print or in the pleasant leisurely atmosphere of his home looking out over the Bogue Falaya River. As Percy reveals in his comments about Thomas Merton, heretofore unpublished, there are many topics waiting to be discussed.

Our sincere gratitude is extended to Walker Percy, his interviewers, and the publishers of books or journals in which the following interviews originally appeared.

LAL
VAK
December 1984

Notes

1. *Walker Percy: An American Search* (Boston: Little, Brown and Company, 1978), p. 146.
2. In "Why I Live Where I Live," *Esquire,* 93 (April 1980), 35–36, Percy comments on the missing elements that once graced Covington.
3. *The Sovereign Wayfarer: Walker Percy's Diagnosis of the Malaise* (Baton Rouge: Louisiana State University Press, 1972), p. 8.
4. "The Pilgrimage of Walker Percy," *Harper's Magazine,* 243 (June 1971), 86.
5. Any quotation not documented is to be found in this text, in the interview conducted by the person being quoted.

Chronology ·

1916 28 May, birth, in Birmingham, Alabama

1929 9 July, suicide of father

1930 Residence in Athens, Georgia, with mother's family

1931 Residence in Greenville, Mississippi, with father's first cousin, William Alexander Percy

1932 2 April, death of mother, in an automobile accident

1937 Graduation from University of North Carolina, with a major in chemistry

1937 Beginning of three years of analysis

1941 Graduation from Columbia University with M.D.

1942 21 January, death of William Alexander Percy from stroke

1942 Onset of three-year bout with tuberculosis

1945 Residence in New Mexico with Shelby Foote

1946 7 November, marriage to Mary Bernice Townsend

1947 Conversion to Catholicism

1947 Residence in New Orleans, Louisiana

1950 Residence in Covington, Louisiana

1954 Beginning of publication in learned journals

1961 Publication of *The Moviegoer*

1962 National Book Award for *The Moviegoer*

1966 Publication of *The Last Gentleman*

1971 Publication of *Love in the Ruins*

Conversations with Walker Percy

First Novelists—Spring 1961

Judith Serebnick/1961

Reprinted from *Library Journal*, 86 (February 1, 1961), 597.
Published by R. P. Bowker Company (a Xerox company).
Copyright © 1961 by Xerox Corporation. Permission granted
by Ms Judith Serebnick.

An illness which forced WALKER PERCY, of Covington, Louisiana, to abandon his career as a doctor, led to his novel-writing: "The years of education were by no means wasted, however, since my first writings were on scientific subjects and were published in scholarly journals. Later my interest veered toward the existentialist movement in European thought and articles on the subject were published in literary quarterlies like *Partisan Review* and *Thought*. Oddly enough, it was precisely this interest in philosophy which led directly to the writing of a novel, 'The Moviegoer' [Knopf—May]. Let me explain. Although philosophy is usually regarded in this country as a dry and abstract subject, it is one of the features of modern European thought that it focuses on concrete life-situations rather than abstractions. In particular, of course, it is mainly interested in the *predicament* of modern man, afflicted as he is with feelings of uprootedness, estrangement, anxiety and the like. It is quite natural, therefore, for philosophers like Sartre and Marcel to write plays and novels. It also seemed natural to me to express my ideas in a novel. And, to give a more practical reason, people would rather read a novel than an article. My novel is an attempt to portray the rebellion of two young people against the shallowness and tastelessness of modern life. The rebellion takes different forms. In Kate, it manifests itself through psychiatric symptoms: anxiety, suicidal tendencies and the like. In Binx it is a 'metaphysical' rebellion—a search for meaning which is the occasion of a rather antic life in a suburb of New Orleans (the action spans one week, Mardi Gras week, in New Orleans). The antecedents of this book are European rather than American: Dostoevski, Rilke, and especially Albert Camus." Binx uses the movies as a "narcotic refuge": thus the title, "The Moviegoer."

Walker Percy: He Likes to Put Protagonist in Situation

Harriet Doar/1962

From *The Charlotte Observer* /Charlotte, NC/, 30 September 1962, p. D6. © 1962 by *The Charlotte Observer.* Reprinted by permission of Mrs. Harriet Doar.

Interviewer: Where did the idea for the book come from? Did you start with the person. . . ?

Percy: "The Moviegoer" was begun first by putting the protagonist in a situation—something like Graham Greene's idea in writing "The Burnt-out Case." Greene said he liked the idea of a man turning up at a lepers' colony on the Congo. I liked the idea of putting a young man down in a faceless suburb.

Caroline Gordon wrote me recently that Jack Bolling is something like the monks of the third century: where they sought the desert, Jack sought the wasteland of a suburb. Having set down a certain sort of person in a certain sort of place, the action followed. (I wouldn't recommend this as a formula.)

The interviewer asked a series of questions on the writer's work and its connection with the South.

Percy: No, I don't write short stories or poems. The novel, moreover, is relatively a new form for me. My usual mode of expression is the essay, written for literary, philosophical and psychiatric quarterlies.

Yes, I think the novel is a completely satisfying form and far from exhausted as a form. I am working on a second novel and a nonfiction work on a semi-psychiatric and religious subject.

I work three hours in the morning on fiction (less rather than more) and a couple of hours in the afternoon on non-fiction. I've always liked the French tradition of a man trying to express himself in the two forms, art and philosophy, and one serving the other, art illustrating ideas and ideas in turn fecundating art.

My over-all plan in both fiction and nonfiction is the study of man, anthropology in the European sense, and I regard myself as more akin to the European existentialists than to the American novel. But I aim to Americanize the movement.

As for the South, love Her though I do (the capital is Percy's), I am a Southern writer insofar as a writer must write about the regional and the particular to say anything at all. It was somewhat disconcerting to hear "The Moviegoer" called a Southern novel, whatever that is.

Interviewer: What writers have particularly influenced or interested you?

Percy: The following writers have meant most to me and in this order: Dostoievski, Kierkegaard, St. Augustine, Lawrence, Joyce, Gerard Hopkins, Marcel. Yes, I read a great deal as a child, everything from Tom Swift to Jean-Christophe.

The only thing I can pass on to a younger writer is that: read.

The interviewer asked several questions about the writer's early life and education.

Percy: My parents died early and I, with my two brothers, was adopted by a cousin, William Alexander Percy . . . I was heavily influenced by him, the most extraordinary man I've ever known . . .

I got from medicine to writing by contracting tuberculosis while working as a pathologist on the TB side at Bellevue. This was partly an excuse, however. I always liked to write, wrote for the Carolina magazine at Chapel Hill. As for courses in creative writing, I cannot say since I never took one. Spent most of my school hours in the laboratory.

Education for writers? No idea.

The interviewer brought up the widely-publicized remarks of A. J. Liebling, the New Yorker writer, and others at a seminar in connection with the Book Awards this year. Briefly, Liebling said it was "sheer chance" that "The Moviegoer" had come to the judges' attention at all; that he read it because he was interested in the Longs and was reading everything from Louisiana, then recommended it to his wife Jean Stafford, who was on the judges' panel with Herbert Gold and Lewis Gannett. Several remarks were made on the publisher's lack of attention to the book, and one person attributed the neglect to Knopf's personal dislike of the book.

Percy: I only learned of Liebling's story, as you call it, after I had

gotten home from the National Book Award . . . As to what I think of
it: it appears that, if Knopf didn't dislike the book and neglect it as
Liebling suggested, they certainly gave it no more than a perfunctory
first-novel treatment. I know nothing of the publishing business, however, and it is difficult to make a judgment.

After the award, however, all three judges wrote me to assure me
that each had reached his own independent decision on the book . . .
As for winning out over Salinger, that was not as gratifying as beating
Heller's "Catch-22," since the latter was very good (I thought) and
"Franny and Zooey" wasn't much.

The comparisons of The M with Salinger or "To Kill a Mockingbird" don't make much sense. I admire "Catcher in the Rye," but
don't think much of "To Kill a Mockingbird."

Interviewer: A Carolina professor was quoted as saying "The
Moviegoer" is good reading, but 'sick' writing . . ."

Percy: I cannot argue with an esthetic judgment. My intention was
otherwise. I should say it was sick writing in the sense that a textbook
of pathology is sick. It is about sickness. It attempts to name the
modern sickness. The epigraph, in fact, is taken from Kierkegaard's
"Sickness unto Death."

Yes, some people have had uneasy reactions to the book; some
have been outraged. I suppose that it is not a bad thing that people
are not neutral about it. They either like it and identify with it immediately, or they are repelled. As well they might be, since the book
is mainly an assault.

Interviewer: One reader asked me, "Did he love the girl or didn't
he?" She obviously felt that and the protagonist are one and the
same . . .

Percy: Did he love her? Yes, as much as he could love anybody.
She? She leveled out probably at a fairly low neurotic level, never
getting past what Kierkegaard would call the sphere of the esthetic.
They probably made out pretty well.

No, Jack (Binx) and I are not the same, except that I like movies.

Walker Percy Talks of Many Things
Don L. Keith/1966

From *Delta Review*, 3 (May–June 1966), 38–39. Reprinted by permission of Don L. Keith.

Walker Percy stood on the sun-bleached pier at the edge of Bogue Falaya and pitched a wood chip into the bluegreen water. Tiny circles rippled through the surface, chasing larger ones, and the author spoke.

"It's a natural thing to go from thinking about persons in a psychiatric sense to presenting them as characters in fiction. Fiction becomes, in this light, more advantageous than expository writing."

The author of "The Moviegoer" and 1962 winner of the National Book Award was referring to his own writing, which will have its second example of the fiction form when his new novel, "The Last Gentleman," appears this June.

Previous to the publication of his first book by Alfred A. Knopf, the nephew of beloved Mississippi author William Alexander Percy had specialized in articles following philosophical and psychiatric lines, in addition to literary criticism, in such periodicals as the Partisan and Sewanee Review, the Journal of Psychiatry and Forum.

His interest in psychiatry possibly stems from his medical degree (from Columbia) and current participation in a research project conducted with clinical tape recordings regarding schizophrenia, but it was not until he reached his middle-forties that Percy sought to translate these notions into fiction.

"I felt that it would be a fascinating idea to start out with a young man whose life was free of all ordinary worries, one with a good family, fair financial stability and things with which he should be aesthetically satisfied, but who, somehow, finds himself as one of the 'outsiders' about which existentialists talk," Percy said in reference to "The Moviegoer."

The book was actually written twice, with the second version correcting weaknesses which became apparent especially in the last third of the book. Its author admits that he was not, and is not, completely

7

satisfied with the novel as a whole, but looks more optimistically toward his upcoming product which features a displaced Southerner in New York. Eventually, the character is led through bouts with amnesia, and geographically South through Virginia, the Carolinas, Alabama and finally to Santa Fe, New Mexico. "The Last Gentleman" is written in the third person, while "Moviegoer" was presented in first person.

Percy is a writer who actually looks like a physician in collegiate clothes, his greying hair contrasting his sweater and sneakers. He spends about three hours in the morning at his typewriter, and sometimes a couple of hours in the afternoon. Most of his work is done in his handsome home on the banks of the Bogue in Covington, Louisiana. "The woman who built this house wanted a French chateau, but couldn't resist the Louisiana influence," he said as he shuffled through the leaves and into the screened porch to the rear of the house.

He took up a cup of strong coffee, prepared by the family maid, Ida Mae, who watched with caution the affectionate year-old German Shepherd, "Lady."

"I've heard," she remarked, "that those dogs can be mighty mean if you're not good to 'em. So I'm being specially friendly."

The work hours of Walker Percy, unlike many authors, are not filled with joy and rapturous thanksgiving at the completion of every paragraph. He writes and rewrites, over and over. On occasion, he has been known to junk as many as 200 or 300 pages once he realizes the story line is unacceptable.

"I usually am not acutely aware of the logic at the beginning, but as the work goes along, it becomes more apparent. By following a predestined plan with outlines, like some writers, I could foresee the action and likely it wouldn't go veering off on another path. But I can't work like that. When I realize my logic is off base, I have to go back and begin again at the point where the interior logic took the wrong turn."

Sometimes, he says, the point of departure is a couple or three hundred pages back.

"And as I go along again, things shape up and I'm on the right route. There are times when I'm amazed. Sometimes I think it's luck."

Percy says he starts a novel with a concrete situation and lets the action proceed through a combination of circumstances and people. "The trick is to preserve the spontaneity and freshness, while keeping unity and coherence."

While watching his 12-year-old daughter, Ann, as she took art instructions near the edge of the woods surrounding the family home (his other daughter, Mary Pratt, is a freshman at Trinity College in Washington, D.C.), Percy explained his concept of novels and his approach to a successful rapport with readers.

"As I see it, the function of fiction is to tell someone something about himself he already knows, but doesn't know he knows. It gives a reader a sensation of recognition.

"If the subject or situation is all too strange, then the message goes unrecognized and loses its point.

"If the reader finds the matter too familiar, then it automatically becomes redundant and trite; there's no fascination.

"The 'in-between' area is the target and must be successfully hit for fictional accomplishment."

Although much of Percy's fiction has Southern overtones, he denies that he should be considered a student of the "Southern School," and asserts that he has no intention of trying short stories because of their limitations.

"I think of myself as being more in the European group than the American or Southern. I use the fiction form as a vehicle for incarnating ideas, as did Jean Paul Sartre and Gabriel Marcel. I long ago decided that my philosophy is in the vein of the existentialist, as theirs were. Both said that fiction is not just recreation. In my case, it is the embodiment of ideas of both philosophy and psychiatry into a form through which the reader can see a concept which otherwise might not be recognized. I would hope it is an authentic attempt at art."

Walker Percy slapped at the wall with a rolled-up magazine. "It looks like this summer will be a bad one for mosquitoes," he said.

An Interview with Walker Percy
Ashley Brown/1967

From *Shenandoah*, 18 (Spring 1967), 3–10. © by Washington and Lee University, reprinted from *Shenandoah:* The Washington and Lee Review with the permission of the editor and of Ashley Brown.

Walker Percy lives in Covington, Louisiana, a small town which lies across Lake Pontchartrain from New Orleans. In his country one can sit outdoors late in the year, and in the November sunshine the visitor is delighted to find himself looking over a bayou—technically a river, the Bogue Falaya, which Walker Percy explains is Choctaw for "river of mists." Although he is at ease in this setting, he talks with the utmost care and precision about his work.

Brown: Does your interest in writing novels go back to your childhood—meaning, did you always have the impulse to tell stories? Or did you arrive at this literary form in some less direct way?

Percy: No, when I was a boy I had no interest whatever in telling stories. Eudora Welty said the other day that most Southern writers were produced by a society in which people talk into the night and tell stories. My literary career came about in a different way. My education up to the age of thirty was almost entirely scientific. When I went to the University of North Carolina I majored in chemistry. In fact I read very few novels in those days. I did read Faulkner in high school. When I got to North Carolina I took the qualifying English test in Faulknerian style (I had been reading *The Sound and the Fury*). I wrote one long paragraph without punctuation. The result of that was that I was put in a retarded English class.

Then I went on to Columbia Medical School, and after graduation I contracted pulmonary tuberculosis while I was working as an intern in the pathology section of Bellevue Hospital. Then followed a couple of enforced years in the Adirondacks. That was when I became interested in existentialism. I read Dostoevsky's *Notes from Underground* and then went on to Kierkegaard, some of whose books were being translated at the time. So I began to be interested in other things besides science. My devotion to science is still with me—I like its elegance and precision. It is simply that I became aware of some of its shortcomings, and Kierkegaard helped me to see them. He said, "Hegel told everything about the world except one thing: what it is to be a man and to live and to die." As a novelist I'm interested in the same phenomena that I would be as a scientist, but I no longer see them the same way. About telling stories: I've learned to do that! My first novel, which was unpublished, didn't have a story. Allen Tate said, "This is dreadful—you've simply got to put some action in it!" But I abandoned that one.

Brown: Living here in the South, how do you feel about the so-called Renascence of the last forty years? Have you profited from the examples of Faulkner and the other members of that generation?

Percy: Whatever Renascence there was has just about shot its bolt, don't you think? The Renascence of the '20s and '30s and '40s has been supplanted by the Jewish novelists—Bellow, Malamud, Heller, and the others. Doesn't a Renascence last just about thirty years? We still have lots of "white-lady" novelists around, but the best members of the older generation are inactive nowadays, and Flannery O'Connor is dead.

As for Faulkner, he never meant as much to me as he did to some other writers. In Greenville, Mississippi, where I grew up, we had a kind of literary society. It was a very enlightened town. Will Percy, my uncle, used to have Faulkner over for tennis, but he often arrived dead drunk and couldn't play. Actually I knew David Cohn, who lived in Greenville, better, and I remember that Langston Hughes and Carl Sandburg used to drop in now and then. It was a good place to grow up in.

Brown: I suppose your training in psychiatry has been useful to you as a novelist.

Percy: I'm still very interested in psychiatry and I still do research in it. Right now, for example, I'm in on a national project which is concerned with schizophrenia. But insofar as its relation to novelwriting goes, psychiatry is only indirectly useful. I am, as novelist, concerned with the dislocation of man in the modern age, and I may well use a neurotic or psychotic man as a character who represents this dislocation, but note that it is an *individual* neurotic man.

Brown: I'm curious about one phase of this. Does a psychiatrist tend to see people as *predictable,* fulfilling a single function? John Bayley in his new book on Tolstoy says that most novelists regard their characters in this way.

Percy: Do psychiatrists push their observations in the direction of typology? Yes, the tendency is for medical men to do that. But a novelist had damn well better beware. Incidentally, a small knowledge of psychiatry is useful. It's a science still in a state of infancy. Much can still be speculated on. In *The Last Gentleman,* for instance, Barrett's amnesia cannot be altogether accounted for in a scientific way, and I tried to put it to dramatic use for that reason. As for Tolstoy: if his characters do seem to move more freely, that's simply the measure of his greatness.

Brown: You seem to me to be one of the first American novelists to write deliberately in the existentialist mode—that is, you have affinities with Kierkegaard (who supplied the epigraphs for your novels) and Dostoevsky and Camus, and you have occasionally touched on these writers in your essays. Has Camus been useful to you in working out a point of view?

Percy: Not only Camus. In somewhat this order I have read Kierkegaard, Heidegger, Gabriel Marcel, then Sartre and Camus. These writers were a revelation to me. They fulfilled a tremendous gap in my view of the world, indeed they seemed to take it over at one time. In one way or another they all dealt with this important question: What is it like to be a man in a world transformed by science? They have put tremendous stress on the *concrete* predicament of a man's life. How is this related to my novelwriting? Perhaps a novel is the best way to render this concreteness. The writing of novels should be a very serious business, and I think it has a future. In some ways we are (as novelists) at a point in history like the revolution in physics which occurred around 1900. The existentialists have their flaws. One of them is their contempt for science.

Brown: Caroline Gordon and others have mentioned Dostoevsky's Idiot in commenting on *The Last Gentleman.* Do you think that a Prince Myshkin is difficult to make convincing? Must he have some physical or psychic flaw? Your Will Barrett is certainly one of the few "good" characters to turn up in recent fiction. Why is he the *last* gentleman?

Percy: He bears a conscious kinship to Prince Myshkin. He is a device with considerable potentialities. I wanted a young man who could see things afresh, both the Northern and Southern culture. A slightly addled young man. His amnesia allows him to be a blank tablet, and that is what I mean by putting it to dramatic use. As you know, he is mixed up about time. His disorientation in time has to do with a theory of Professor Eric Voegelin's about two senses of time. In his book Voegelin contrasts the unhistoric cyclical time of the Greeks and Orientals with the historic linear time of Israel—historical time began when Israel emerged. Barrett's amnesia suggests a post-Christian shakiness about historic time. Anyway, his transplantation to New York City causes him to have a temporal dislocation, and working in Macy's sub-basement at night doesn't help things. He becomes almost Oriental in his abstraction from time. Covington, by the way, is a theosophical center. People are always sitting on the post-office steps here and arguing with me about theosophy.

Brown: Is Barrett developed to some extent from Binx Bolling in *The Moviegoer?* He is far more daring in his movements out of routine (an existentialist "leap"?) and of course you take him across a larger scene.

Percy: He certainly is developed from Bolling. The chief difference is that he's a good deal sicker. In the conventional view of things he's very sick. His symptoms of epilepsy, *déjà vu,* and so on. Binx is more relaxed. Both of them are alienated, but Binx enjoys his alienation. He is happy in what Kierkegaard calls the aesthetic mode—he lives in a place like Gentilly to savor its ordinariness. Barrett, on the other hand, has a passionate pilgrimage that he must follow, and he is looking for a father-figure. His symptoms are ambiguous, however, and he could go in various directions. The ambiguity is deliberate. The reader is free to see him as a sick man among healthy business men or as a sane pilgrim in a mad world.

Brown: I believe several reviewers have been slightly disappointed by what they think are Barrett's values—willingness to settle for a Chevrolet agency and a house in the suburbs. Do you accept the premise that a hero has to defy the contemporary social order?

Percy: This question goes to the nub of my intention. Barrett is consciously placed in Kierkegaard's religious mode. He is what Gabriel Marcel calls a *wayfarer*—like an old-fashioned pilgrim on a serious quest. He is not merely content to do what everybody else does—be satisfied with a consumers' paradise. As I was saying, he is looking for a father-figure. He thinks Sutter knows something he doesn't know, but Sutter won't tell him. What happens in the end? Does he quit his quest and compromise himself? In the big scene near the end, when Jamie is dying, Sutter is *aware* of what goes on at Jamie's baptism. Barrett isn't; he misses the import of this event. It doesn't follow that becoming the personnel manager of Confederate Chevrolet compromises him: his values are more complicated.

Brown: Why do you have Sutter, the psychiatrist in *The Last Gentleman,* confide so much to his casebook? Is this a sign of his failure of communion with other people, a kind of Cartesian split?

Percy: It was, I confess, a possible weakness in the book, but this technical device has certainly been used well before, in *Herzog* for one instance. Sutter is a very pivotal character in the book—he is the object of Barrett's quest, and he must seem very substantial. The alternative to the casebook was long Dostoevskian conversations. I was damned if I'd do that. Sutter's relationship to Jamie must be established, too. And then there are his sister Val, and Rita the humanist (who is both good and bad). They're all after Jamie. But it's Barrett who is the instrument of the boy's salvation.

Brown: *The Last Gentleman* is not a satire, but it seems to me to contain a high satirical component. Do you find this is about the best way of dealing with our highway culture?

Percy: Yes, I'd go as far as to call it a satire. I do indeed find this to my liking. As a matter of fact, a good deal of my energy as a novelist comes from *malice*—the desire to attack things in our culture, both North and South. Some reviewers, including John Wain, said *The Last Gentleman* was too satirical. Maybe something got satirized that he didn't want satirized.

Brown: Do you, as novelist, find that American life, as it steps up its rate of change, is becoming more difficult to bring to focus?

Percy: I don't know whether this is more true than it was in Henry James's day. The homogenization of the American scene is a thing that is certainly happening. But to me this is not a handicap. The notion of the American city as an alien place is exactly what I think it is. Gabriel Marcel has based his criticism of modern society upon this truth. The lostness of the American in America is a paradigm of the existentialist or even the Christian view. James McBride Dabbs, a very fine man, has written of the South as though it used to be a paradise, but it is now almost as broken a world as the North, and we must learn to live in it. No, I don't find this an impossible subject for fiction. And, to be truthful, I wouldn't have our highway culture otherwise now.

Brown: Do you have any comments on current developments in American fiction?

Percy: I don't read much fiction, to tell you the truth; I average about a novel a month. I'm very much in sympathy with the renascence of Jewish writers. My own writing is very much akin to theirs— I'm closer to them than to the Southerners. What I admire most, though, is the modern French novel. I like its absolute seriousness in its investigation of human reality. A novel like Sartre's *La Nausée,* for instance, is a revolution in its technique for rendering a concrete situation, and it has certainly influenced me.

Brown: What about the newer French novelists, for instance Beckett?

Percy: I liked his first books, but he seems to repeat himself.

Brown: I don't suppose you've read *Anguish,* by the Brazilian novelist Graciliano Ramos. It was written even earlier than *La Nausée;* it's a very powerful "existentialist" rendition of psychic life, and it deserves to be better known than it is.

Percy: No, the only Brazilian novel I've read is *Epitaph for a Small Winner* by Machado de Assis. It's amazing the way he anticipates modern developments in fiction, and he's one of their old writers, isn't he?

Brown: What are your immediate plans for novel-writing?

Percy: No comment. I have an idea, but it is giving me a hard time. Somebody compared novel-writing to having a baby, but for me it is the conception which is painful and the delivery which is easy.

Walker Percy, The Man and the Novelist: An Interview

Carlton Cremeens/1968

From *The Southern Review*, NS4 (Spring 1968), 271–90. © 1984 by Carlton Cremeens. Reprinted by permission of *The Southern Review* and Carlton Cremeens.

Before this interview, I had never met Walker Percy. He was a pleasant baritone voice on the telephone, speaking from his home in Covington, Louisiana. We had mutual acquaintances. But they could tell me little about Walker Percy. A shy reserved man, they said, living at the end of a quiet street and beside a bayou called Bogue Falaya— "river of mists" or "river of ghosts."

We met. Walker Percy is outwardly friendly, curious, full of questions one moment, introspective the next. His deep set eyes work with a penetrating glance, and one gets the impression of seeing an image recorded and then watching through frosted glass the internalizing process of its development. A moment of silence. And then he asks another question. He had rather interview than be interviewed. He wanted to know about the big news stories relating to social issues and to politics. The conversation continued for some time before I decided that his interest in social and political issues was one way of starting the interview, in which I wanted to create a portrait of Walker Percy, the man and the novelist.

Q: In October, 1965, *The Atlantic* published an article by Eudora Welty entitled "Must The Novelist Crusade?" In the article Miss Welty took issue with some journalist who had written that Faulkner would have to be reassessed because "he was only a white Mississippian." This statement by the journalist, of course, followed several murders in the Mississippi racial conflict. Miss Welty gave the journalist a good verbal spanking and then took the position that the novelist and the crusader both have their own place, separate and apart, with a different function to perform. How do you feel about this?

16

Percy: I read the article. I think she wrote that someone called her up in the middle of the night and demanded to know what she was going to do about all the trouble there in Mississippi, which meant that the caller thought Eudora Welty, as the leading writer of Mississippi, should at least have taken a stand on it.

Actually, this is a question that bothers me a great deal. I can't say whether I think Eudora Welty is wrong and that I know what the right answer is because I think it would be a mistake for a creative artist of any kind to get so embroiled in a local politic or social issue that he stopped his creative work. But, on the other hand, I don't quite agree with her. I think her point in the article was that a creative writer ought to tend to his knitting, that if he does his work well, if he studies the human heart and the motions of the human heart, he is still doing what he is supposed to do, and the politic and social issues are not his concern. I can see what she means, but I still think a writer, with his peculiar position of being a communicator, and particularly a prominent writer like Eudora Welty, who is influential, highly respected, can do a great deal of good, can have a great deal of influence without compromising her creative endeavors. My own feeling is: I don't mind saying or writing what I think on the social issues or the race issue in the South.

Q: Within the framework of a novel?

Percy: Anywhere. In a novel. In an article. In this interview. I'm not an activist, a racial activist. I don't march in picket lines, but I am completely convinced of the rightness of the Negro struggle for civil rights. My writings I think reflect this, and I don't mind saying so. I don't see how anybody, any serious writer living in the South, or in America, for that matter, who is writing novels, can avoid the social issue of race because, particularly in the South and recently in the whole country, it is the number one issue of this society. In the South it always was. And when any writer in the South pretends he can write a novel and ignore the social issue of the Negro, something is wrong.

Q: But, at the same time, don't you agree the journalist was wrong when he suggested a reassessment of Faulkner simply because, as he put it, "Faulkner was, after all, only a white Mississippian?"

Percy: Yes, of course.

Q: I presume the statement was made because Faulkner hadn't, in the opinion of the journalist, dealt squarely with the race problem. I think Faulkner was very conscious of the race problem in the South and that it was reflected in the body of his work.

Percy: Well, I agree that he certainly was conscious of the issue. But the interesting thing was Faulkner's ambivalence about it. For instance, in those days it was a case of the Southerners having the problem and the Northerners criticizing the Southerners. And Faulkner, when he was criticized, or when he was approached from the wrong angle on this, would react in an old-fashioned, Southern way. I'm sure you remember when he made that famous remark about not pushing the South too far or the whole thing would end up with the whites shooting Negroes in the streets? Or maybe he said it would end with Southerners shooting Northerners. I don't remember which. And then later, during the last few years of his life when he was at the University of Virginia, he came out squarely against the whole social institution of segregation, unequivocally against the whole thing. But he *was* ambivalent about it before that.

Q: I think one point of disagreement among writers who take a stand on social issues and those who don't is whether there's a danger of becoming so involved that it can affect the quality of a creative work. For instance, it appears the later works of James Baldwin are taken less seriously by a large number of people because, they say, he has become too embittered.

Percy: Yes, I see what you mean. And I think that's true. But I want to get something straight. Now, I often feel that a good deal of energy in my writing comes from a passion or strong feeling on something, for or against. And there is a good precedent for this. Dostoyevsky began several of his best novels after having read a news story in the paper, of some incident, of a murder, for instance, and he would become enflamed on ideological grounds. He was usually a conservative as against the liberals, you know. Anyway, he would write a tract, a piece of propaganda, which if anyone else had written it, would have remained a piece of propaganda. But with him, something happened, some miraculous transformation, and what began as some anti-liberal, anti-nihilist propaganda turned into a work of art. That's the way *The Possessed* started out. It was written in a rage about a certain incident that happened in Russia. And I think it works both ways. A man has to have some sort of passion, either a dislike for something or a like for something—love or malice—to have enough energy to write about it.

But, on the other hand, there has to be a fine balance, because if he is too consumed with his likes or dislikes, then his art will be overwhelmed by his own predilections. For instance, if I get extremely angry about some racial thing it often produces very bad writing. You cannot translate this anger immediately into writing. It has to undergo a transformation, it has to be sublimated into some other form.

I'll tell you a strange thing that happened to me in connection with the creative process. It was the Kennedy assassination, which happened right in the middle of my last book, *The Last Gentleman.* The assassination affected me so strongly it caused me to lose a year of work. It changed the whole direction of the book. I got off on the wrong track, wrote a long thing about Kennedy, brought Kennedy into the book, and I actually wasted a year. It was no good. I had to back up. And it took me a year. It really threw me. I ended up with about four lines referring to Kennedy in the book. He was mentioned once. And that was the residue of about three hundred pages.

Q: Do you think your effort was entirely wasted?

Percy: I don't know. But it goes to show you how rage, outrage, or shock cannot be transmuted raw into a viable art form. But, presumably, it can be transformed if you can maintain the fine balance required to do it.

Q: Are there any other inherent dangers for the creative writer who gets involved with social problems?

Percy: I suppose another danger, as Ralph Ellison pointed out in an interview with three young Negro writers, is the temptation to understand the issues of the times in terms of sociology, in terms of abstractions. Perhaps the danger here is greater than that of becoming embroiled, or getting caught up in an issue, or getting embittered. Young writers, even young Negro writers, tend too often to understand themselves in terms of what the sociologists say: that they are victims of slavery, of broken homes, of a matriarchal society, and of various other things. They begin to feel themselves as exemplars of this or that sociological theory, forgetting many of the riches of their own lives. And so, when you start writing novels to illustrate sociology you are going to write bad novels, because sociology is a simplification, an abstraction from what is the case. A novelist should be concerned with what is the case in the world, the facts, the richness, the intricacy and the variety of the way things are. And God help you if you ever start writing sociology, because it might be good sociology, but it's going to be a bad novel.

Q: Short lived, too?

Percy: Yes.

Q: Do you think we have any outstanding Negro writers in America today?

Percy: Well, I think of Ralph Ellison. And of course, there was Wright. But, as Ellison says, there seem to be fewer good Negro writers around now than there were several years ago. I don't know why that is.

Q: Perhaps we're back to what was just said about the tendency among many Negro writers to look into the sociologist's looking glass and to see an image created by the sociologists. And that, according to the thinking of some people, also brings us back to James Baldwin.

Percy: Yes, there *is* Baldwin. He was certainly first class when he was at his best. I think his first novel and then his *The Fire Next Time* were very eloquent things. But I think his last things have been simply consumed with hatred and obscenity. His last novel is a very unhappy business.

Q: Do you think discrimination is something innate in the human being? It seems to have been with us in one form or another throughout the history of the world.

Percy: Well, I guess it is. It has certainly been true in this country. Given any two cultural ethnic groups you are going to have prejudice and discrimination and a degree of oppression, depending on which one is first in the pecking order, which got to the country first and which came later. But the big problem the Negro faces is the fact that he is black. With the Irish, Italians, Jews, the Catholics—name any one—it was different. After the initial period of oppression, the second and third generations were able to break out of the pattern, and there was rather little discrimination after that. But the Negro has not been able to do that, even now, of course, because after the second, third, or fourth generation he is still black. You see him. There he is. And he's something different. Assuming that the recent discrimination takes place because of differences, that there is something innate in the human being that tends to find a scapegoat in the person who is different, then other cultural groups can overcome their differences simply by becoming acculturated. But the Negro cannot lose his blackness. He can become totally assimilated in all the other respects. In fact, if you have known many middle-class Negroes, nobody in the world is more middle-class or conventional than the middle-class Negro. But he is still black. And he still has difficulties. He has the worst of both worlds. He has his blackness which he despises and he cleaves to the more fatuous of white middle-class values. That is the trouble.

Q: There was one particular passage in your novel, *The Last Gentleman,* which said a Southerner sees a Negro twice in his life. I think you wrote that he sees the Negro for the first time when he looks up from his cradle at his Negro nurse. And then he sees the Negro for the second and last time when he looks up from his death bed and there is the Negro folding the bed clothes around him. Perhaps you were thinking of a certain type of Southerner when you wrote that, but do you think the Southerner's awareness of the Negro is so limited? That he doesn't understand the Negro?

Percy: I feel two ways about that. The passage in my book is an exaggeration, of course; it was a bit of satire on the universal feeling among Southerners that they do *completely* understand the Negro. I have seldom met one in my life who didn't claim that he knew all there was to know about them. I don't. But that is the Southerner's main argument.

Now, having said that the Southerner has this exaggerated opinion of his own knowledge and insight into the Negro I think, as a matter of fact, that both Negroes and white Southerners know a lot more about each other than white and colored people do anywhere else. They have been living together in the most intimate household relations for two or three hundred years, and there is an accumulated certain wisdom there. But I couldn't resist poking fun at this omniscient attitude Southerners have about their knowledge of Negroes.

Q: Do you think the Negroes understand us?

Percy: I think they had developed—until recently—the most exquisite intuition and natural radar, a most extraordinary courtesy, a natural intuition and manners as far as white people were concerned.

And so had the white people, the best of the white people. As James Dabbs says, the knowledgeable white Southerner tried to make up in courtesy and personal kindness for the dreadful injustice he helped inflict upon the Negro. Of course, it has been the Negro's business in the past to understand and anticipate, and I think he has been very good at it. They are a people with a most wonderful grace, not that there is anything new about that. This is a traditional item in literature. But the pity of it is, in the Negro revolution of the past ten years, this grace, which has been so long in cultivation by the Negro, has been kicked out the window. There has been a tendency to kick it out the window in the Negro's general rebellion against his subservient place in the American society. He's kicking out everything from the past. I don't blame him. But I think he's kicking out a lot of the good, too. And I believe, even now at this late date, here in the South there is still a reservoir of good will and a natural grace in the relationship between the white and colored people. I would go further than that. I would hope, and maybe even to a degree believe, that the South still, in spite of all, may ultimately have the genius in human relations to show the way to the rest of the country in solving the whole race situation. That would be my hope and dream for the South. And the tragedy would be if, in the era of bad feeling, both in the Negro revolution, the Negro rebellion, and the white right-wing reaction, the whole tradition of manners and grace and good feeling were simply kicked out, everything lost. I think we are going to need all the grace we can get.

Q: Since your feelings about the racial problem are very evident in your books, do you ever have any trouble with the racists?

Percy: No. Racists don't read novels.

Now, a writer living here does find himself in a rather curious position, which reminds me of something I've been thinking about in the last few days. I get several journals in the mail. I get one Southern journal, a rabid racist rag. I also get another journal from New York and, although it's on a lofty intellectual level, there is a peculiar parallel between it and the Southern publication. On the one hand, in this part of the country as you well know, there is so much absolutely irrational, downright political hatred and abuse of President Johnson and our foreign policy. These are the people who want to go in there and end the war by bombing Hanoi, dropping the hydrogen bomb

on North Vietnam or China, whatever it takes. This is the radical right
wing which has corrupted the whole conservative tradition. They use
the words *conservative* and *constitutional*. They have appropriated
these words and they have prostituted the whole tradition. They are
not conservatives. They are radicals. All of this is reflected in the
journal that comes out of the South.

Now, on the other hand, you will find that many intellectuals of
New York, of California, the American intellectual community, are
almost as uniform and conformist—and irrational—in their hatred of
President Johnson as the Southern right wingers. This you will find in
my journal that comes out of New York. It reflects the thinking of the
people who want to pull out of Vietnam and who ignore the sys-
tematic atrocities of the Viet Cong. It's a well-written journal, very
lively, but it's very close to the Southern racist paper in its same
abuse and hatred of President Johnson. There's not much difference.
And it's almost as scurrilous in its distortion of the war.

So, you have two extremes, two radical groups, and the extremes
have got so far apart they have almost met again. They are remark-
ably alike in their distortions and hatreds and fantasies. I think it's a
change, this converging of the Northern intellectual and the Southern
right winger. It's an unprecedented position for a Southern writer to
be in. Twenty years ago my natural sympathies would have been
with the liberal tradition in the North and against any resurgence of
hatred and violence. But the recent changes are complicated by how
close the wild-eyed have come to the high-browed. The Southern
writer now finds himself in the middle of somewhere and not quite
knowing where. He's caught between the right in the South and this
intellectual herd in the North who profess to be free creative spirits,
and yet, all conforming to the same lines, the same hatred and abuse
of the things they oppose. So where *does* the Southern writer stand?
It may be an advantage—living in the South. I don't know. Most
writers in the North seem to be caught up in this intellectual community, while most Southern writers, who are any good, simply won't
have anything to do with this business of hatred and abuse.

Q: What, in your opinion, is your main function as a novelist?

Percy: I would hope to be close to the function of all art. My
theory is that the purpose of art is to transmit universal truths of a
sort, but of a particular sort, that in art, whether it's poetry, fiction or

painting, you are telling the reader or the listener or the viewer something he already knows but which he doesn't quite know that he knows, so that in the action of communication he experiences a recognition, a feeling that he has been there before, a shock of recognition. And so, what the artist does, or tries to do, is simply to validate the human experience and to tell people the deep human truths which they already unconsciously know.

Q: Do you think most people are endowed with a creative intuition, a creative spark, but only a few, such as yourself, emerge as the communicators?

Percy: I don't know. It may be—I don't know how that works. I think a great many people have it, because I think the reception of a creative work is close to the creation of it. There has to be a kinship of spirit there in order for the communication to take place. But what makes the artist—the writer or painter—I don't know. It may be a question of a great deal of it having to do with luck. In my case I started out in one profession and got sick and had to quit. So, I had time. I did a lot of reading. I had wanted to write, and I began to write. I don't know how these things happen, however, or why they happen.

Q: After reading both *The Moviegoer* and *The Last Gentleman* I got the impression that your novels start with an idea or theme, rather than with a character. Is this true?

Percy: I would rather say they start with a situation. *The Moviegoer,* for instance, was conceived by putting a young man in a certain situation, not with the idea of a preconceived story line or certain roster of characters, but with the idea of a young man put down into the world under certain circumstances. In this case, the place was Gentilly, a middle class suburb of New Orleans. I'm not primarily concerned with plotting a story. I'm concerned with a certain quality of consciousness put down in a certain place and then seeing what kind of reaction takes place between a character and his environment and the people he meets.

Not long ago, John Barth said it was no longer possible to write nineteenth-century novels, a novel which has the usual characters where the characters interact, where there is a story line, a development of plot, a resolution—a classical novel. I'm not sure I agree with him. But, I think I would agree with him to this extent:

that, insofar as a novel reflects the life of its time, I think that the nineteenth-century novel would reflect a rather intact society, an intact culture, where people understood who they were and what they were doing; whereas, now, the world is much more fragmented, people don't understand themselves as well or what they are doing as well. And to the degree that a novel reflects life, I think that the modern novel has become much more fragmented, without a strong and conventional plot and all that.

Q: Would you say there is a tendency toward less emphasis on character?

Percy: Maybe it's not so much a question of *emphasis* as a question of *numbers.* Instead of having a large cast of characters, like Tolstoy in *War And Peace,* the tendency now—at least my feeling is—to write from one point of view of one consciousness located in a certain place at a certain time. Maybe it's because of a breakdown in communications you hear so much about now. Maybe writers, both poets and novelists, are much more locked into themselves, and because of that, perhaps a creative work is more apt to be written from the perspective of a single consciousness seeing the world around him. The classical novel took place on a great stage which the reader watched more or less unselfconsciously. In the modern novel, the perspective backs up. What is being presented now is not so much the action on the stage as the experience of the spectator in the privacy of his box.

Q: Since your novels begin with the conception of a situation, do you have any problem with characters, such as giving them life, dimension?

Percy: I don't know. I don't think about that. I don't think I have any difficulty along that line. My characters are all fairly recognizable. And the settings are recognizable. My novels are not like the French anti-novels where there is a complete de-emphasis on the characters. Actually, the writers of the anti-novelist school in France are more interested in objects and things. They spend five pages describing a tea cup, or at least how a man sees a tea cup, all the details of his consciousness of a cup. So, I certainly don't place myself in that school.

Q: We spoke earlier of James Baldwin, and I believe you mentioned the obscenity of his later books. This reminds me that there

were no graphic sexual scenes in either of your two novels, the kind
of thing a number of people have come to expect these days and, I
suspect, the kind of thing a great many writers feel they have to give
the public in order to sell novels. How do you feel about that sort of
thing?

Percy: Of course, that's the trouble. My own feeling is that you
can put anything into a novel. There are no taboos. It all depends on
how you do it and why you do it. As you say, so many novels now
are obscene in two senses. We have the novel where the writer cyni-
cally contrives to be lascivious and to arouse sexual feelings in a
reader simply to sell his book, which has nothing to do with writing at
all. Pornography is a different activity from writing. And then there
are many writers who are under the impression that good writing
consists of being free, in quotes, which to them means being
rebellious, simply contravening the mores of the times, including as
much sexual activity as possible. And that doesn't make good novels.
You can do it. You can do anything you want to as long as you do it
right. But novels have nothing to do primarily, with the physiology of
sex or exciting the reader. They have to do with, as Faulkner said,
the fundamental and eternal movement of the human spirit. And to
the degree that sex is a symbol for that, it's perfectly valid. But, no
one would want to write forty pages on the mechanics of eating and
chewing and swallowing. So, why all the mechanics of sexual intercourse? It has nothing to do with the fundamental structure of novel
writing.

Q: Have you found that the arduous application required to become a medical doctor and then a writer has, to any degree, lessened
the problem of discipline with which so many writers seem to be
bothered?

Percy: I hadn't thought of that. I don't know. But that does bring
up a favorite subject of mine, and that is the importance of a knowledge of science to any serious writer. Maybe I wasted my years
studying chemistry, physics, biology, zoology and premedical sciences, but my first enthusiasm was science, the scientific method, and
I think it was a valuable experience. I wouldn't have had it otherwise.
I think too often there is a feeling among artists, the creative people,
that science represents the unpleasant, or the cold, the unemotional
side of life, and that art represents the emotional or warm side. I think

that is a mistake. In the first place, we are living in a culture which is completely saturated by the whole scientific ethic, the whole scientific outlook, and anybody who pretends he is not affected by science and doesn't benefit by science is simply deceiving himself. I am convinced of the value of the scientific vocation, of the practice of the scientific method.

Now, in changing to writing, to creative work, I am equally convinced of the absolute seriousness of that in much the same way. I think that serious novel writing, that serious art, is just as important, and just as cognitive; it concerns areas of knowing, of discovering and knowing, just as much as any science. In fact, in art, particularly in the modern novel, you are dealing with areas of life which cannot be reached in any other way. So, on the other hand, I am opposed to the idea current in many circles, that science is knowing, that science is fact, and that art is play, art is emotion. I deny that completely. I think that the serious novelist is quite as much concerned with discovering reality as a serious physicist. And that tends to connect with the question you asked me concerning the conception of my work. That's why my primary concern is not in telling a story and putting characters together so that something is going to happen, but in using the fictional situation, a man in a concrete situation, exploring reality in a way which cannot be done any other way. It cannot be done with science, a microscope, or with sociology or psychology, however refined it is.

Q: Do you think it's possible to establish truth?

Percy: I think you can *discover* the way things are, what is the case and what happens when you put a man in a certain situation. What you are doing is exploring the quality of a particular consciousness of a particular time—and at a time when the contemporary consciousness is fragmented and imperiled.

Q: In a way which cannot be done by the historian or sociologist?

Percy: Certainly. How is the historian or sociologist or social scientist of any kind going to deal with the subject of personal alienation? Take the situation of a young man, a college student, a graduate student, or a young man in business. There he is in an American city, working at an American job, and by a psychological or sociological theory, he has everything he is supposed to have. He has fulfilled his needs. He has his wife and children, his house and car and plenty to eat, his art, television, everything. Now, suppose in spite of all that this man experiences a deep unrest, feels a deep sense of estrangement?

Q: Like The Moviegoer?

Percy: In a way, like The Moviegoer, not that there is anything unique about The Moviegoer. Alienated man is a fairly common subject of modern literature, as you well know. In fact, by now it has become modish. But when you write about this particular kind of consciousness people know what you are talking about, because a lot of other people have it. Now, what is that? It's a quality of consciousness which a novelist is concerned with. He writes about it. You can't measure it with a psychological device, with a physical device, but it's something that's there, it's part of reality, and so the novelist is concerned with it.

Q: What's the origin of all this unrest, this deep sense of estrangement?

Percy: (Laughing) Well, that's a big subject. Actually, I think the whole subject of alienation has become exaggerated and overdone. It has become a hobby horse now, a fashionable thing where the protagonist in most novels is supposed to be the alienated man. In fact, I would almost go so far as to say that one of the conditions of becoming a modern writer is that the writer must start off with a very unhappy young man in the conventional suburb, you know, that sort of thing. And I don't think that tells the truth. A good bit of The Last Gentleman and The Moviegoer had to do with the positive values and the beauties of the very things that are made fun of in so much of alienated literature. So many people ask me why I didn't write about the French Quarter in New Orleans instead of Gentilly. Who cares about Gentilly? Gentilly looks like any other place. All the alienated writers say it's anonymous. Well, that's what my main character, Binx Bolling, liked about it. He liked the quality of the sky out there in Gentilly. He liked the new parochial school across the street, made of brick and aluminum and glass. He had an appreciation for these mass manufactured objects. It's very easy to sneer at mass society or the American suburb, but there are many beauties there. So, this business of alienation can certainly be overdone. But, of course, alienation, after all, is nothing more or less than a very ancient, orthodox Christian doctrine. Man is alienated by the nature of his being here. He is here as a stranger and as a pilgrim, which is the way alienation is conceived in my books. It's the orthodox sort of alienation, but expressed, I hope, in an unorthodox or fresh language.

Q: Do you think there are any outstanding writers in America today?

Percy: I have a lot of respect for current Jewish writers. People like Saul Bellow, Singer, and Joe Heller. And there is Bernard Malamud. He's one of the Jewish writers I greatly admire.

Q: In what way do the current Jewish writers interest you?

Percy: There is a parallel with the situation of the Southern writer, and the problem of universalizing the particular. They are deeply concerned with Jewish culture, American Jewish culture, and I think that a man has to write about his own background, his own culture. Good Jewish writing about Jewish culture is valid for the whole society, for American culture. Maybe the moral is that the only way to write about America in general is to write about America in particular. There are some who say the Jewish writers are excessively concerned with their culture, that they seem to have great difficulty in getting out of it. So what? You are aware, for instance, when reading a book like *Herzog* that it is saturated, supersaturated with Jewish culture, almost to the exclusion of anything else. And yet, Saul Bellow wrote a book called *Henderson the Rain King,* almost as if to demonstrate that he wasn't limited to Jewish themes and Jewish characters. This is a book which, if I recall, didn't have a Jew in it. It's an amazingly successful and funny book. It's really an amazing triumph of the creative imagination.

Q: I noticed that the locale in your last book shifted from New York, down the Atlantic Seaboard, across the South, and then all the way to New Mexico. Was there any particular reason for this?

Percy: I suppose the physical travels of my main character were the physical analogue of his spiritual odyssey. He was on the move geographically and spiritually at the same time. It seemed appropriate for him to be moving. He is *Homo viator.*

Q: It appears a great many Southern writers are now trying to avoid the regional tag. I thought that may have been one of your reasons for writing about so many sections of the country.

Percy: Well, not really. I think the country as a whole is rapidly

becoming so completely homogenized that there is not a great deal
of difference between the South and other parts of the country, between a Northern city and a Southern city. *The Moviegoer,* as I mentioned, dealt with a part of New Orleans not particularly indigenous
to New Orleans. It could have been a suburb of Memphis, Atlanta, or
even Cincinnati. And then, in *The Last Gentleman,* the Southern
scenes were mostly laid in what is called the New South, a Southern
city which is relatively new, a place like Birmingham, which is different from other Southern cities in many ways, bustling and indus-
trialized. So nowadays, I think a writer, unless he goes out of his way,
or goes back and deals with rural themes like Faulkner, with small
towns, or sagas, or long recollections, that sort of thing, he's pretty
much looking at the same sort of reality in New Orleans or Birmingham or Atlanta as his counterpart in Cincinnati or Los Angeles. The
similarities are much greater than the differences.

Q: Do you think environment has anything to do with writing?
Let's take this particular spot. Do you think you write better here, or
can you write equally as well anywhere?

Percy: I don't know. Sometimes I write better in a motel than
anywhere else.

Q: Regardless of where it may be?

Percy: Well, maybe in spite of where it is. There is something so
faceless and rootless about a motel that it may be a good place to
write. In fact, I wonder if Nabokov didn't write *Lolita* in a motel. It
sounds like he did.

Q: Do you think an association with other writers is beneficial?

Percy: I don't know. I don't associate with other writers. As you
can see, I live in a country town in Louisiana of about 10,000 people, and my friends are local business men here. I have a couple of
writer friends, but I don't see them often. It may be that a society of
other writers and artists would be stimulating, would provoke more
thought and more energy than my own writing. I've often wondered
about that. I would say that I have more medical friends than writer
friends. I have retained doctor friends from the time I was a doctor.
But, as I said, I've never been thrown with writers except for one or
two good friends. So, I don't know what it's really like.

Q: Maybe it's because writers, as a rule, are not inclined to seek
each other out?

Percy: That could be. I suppose writers are an ornery lot.

Q: How about your reading and the books that may have influenced you?

Percy: I was strongly influenced by the Russian novelists, much more strongly than by the English novelists. I would be ashamed to tell you how few English novels I've read. I read Russian novels primarily and then the French. More so than the American novelists even. I guess it's because the Russians, to begin with Dostoyevsky, and then later the French, were interested in a radical new novelistic form earlier than the Americans were. And the French always had this notion of union of philosophy and literature, of using art forms to either express ideas or to discover ideas, to explore reality. I think the European novelist is much more metaphysically oriented than the American novelist; that is, he has much more interest in the nature of reality, what reality is like. I always was closer to Frenchmen like Sartre or Camus or Marcel.

Q: Have you always wanted to write? From a very early age?

Percy: Yes. I can remember a time when I couldn't have been over ten or twelve, during the days when the old magazine *Liberty* was being published. They used to have something called the short short story. Anyway, I must have been about ten years old when I decided to write a short short story. I wrote it and sent it to *Liberty,* and I didn't even get a rejection slip.

Q: Did you get an acceptance?

Percy: (Laughing) No. Nothing. I probably didn't even get the address right. But it seemed like a good way to live, to sit down and write something and send it off to a magazine.

Q: Do you have any interest now in writing the short story?

Percy: No. No interest at all.

Q: Never will?

Percy: Never will. I would feel like a fool trying to write a short story because I wouldn't know how to do it, no more than I would know how to sit down and write a play. I think it goes back to what we were talking about earlier. I don't conceive my own writing to be according to the traditional artistic forms of short stories and classical novels. I see it as an exploration of reality. And, in that respect, I would be a fool to sit down and try to write a short story. With that objective in mind, I would no sooner get squared away with the first

situating of a character than it would be over. It wouldn't make
sense. A short story has to be a small perfect form, and I don't have
the faintest notion of how to go about it.

Q: Then you will continue writing novels? Are you working on
another one now?

Percy: Yes, I suppose it's a novel. It's very difficult trying to get
set—all important that you get the right point of view, what perspective you are writing from, and getting started in such a way that the
whole thing carries. I often think, and I even have the feeling and
attitude that if you can get the first sentence right, the whole rest of
the book follows that first sentence.

Q: Once you are started, do you always know in what direction
you're going?

Percy: Just vaguely. But, as I say, it's an exploration. It may be
that it's written mainly to entertain myself, and if I had it laid out in
outline form, prearranged, I would be bored stiff and would never
finish it. I meant it literally when I said *discovery* and *exploration*
because it's a discovery for me.

Now, I don't want to give the impression that it's a haphazard sort
of thing where anything can happen because that's not true. I write
straight through. But I often have to back up half way, throw away
two hundred pages which don't work. My writing involves many false
starts, many blind detours, many blind passages, many goings ahead
and backing up where something has been tried and doesn't work.
Sometimes, the first half will be all right and the second half doesn't
work at all. You don't know why it doesn't work, it doesn't swing, it
doesn't cook, it doesn't go; so, you just back up. It's mysterious, this
thing of not knowing why it doesn't work. All you know is that when
it *does* work, you know it. So, it's not a case of my rambling all over
the place, although some of the reviewers accuse me of doing that. It
rambles to significant purpose, I hope.

Q: Do reviews bother you?

Percy: Honestly, they don't. I've been lucky. I haven't got any
really destructive reviews. I imagine it would be painful to be made
mincemeat of, like some reviewers can do in good style. But even the
worst reviews usually have a few good things to say.

Q: How do you feel about reviews generally?

Percy: Reviews are not very interesting. Out of a hundred reviews there might be four or five that will be original or perceptive, and this includes the bad ones as well as the good. A bad review can often be interesting because it is perceptive enough to see the weaknesses. But so many reviews are simply repeats. They say the obvious or summarize too much. And the early reviews are usually the least interesting. The best are usually published months later in perhaps an obscure quarterly or journal. Some fellow has had a chance to read the book and to think about it for a long time. He has his own ideas about it, and he cuts loose. That can be very interesting.

Q: After you have finished a book, do you have any vivid memories of how you did it?

Percy: No I don't. The only thing I can say is that it takes place— or the best of it takes place—in a sort of vacuum. On the worst of mornings. On the least likely of mornings. When you expect nothing to happen. When the page is blank. When the mind is blank. Even in a state of depression or melancholia. And then, only with good luck. I sometimes get the feeling that the slate has to be wiped completely clean, that there can be no prospects, nothing pending, nothing coming in the afternoon or the next day, that there has to be some sort of vacuum in order for something else to come out. But I don't know why it happens. And conversely, at times when you think you have a lot of things to say, a lot of good ideas, nothing good takes place. It's a contrary process that seems to happen in spite of all the best reasons you can think for it.

Q: Do you ever suffer from creative paralysis or writer's block?

Percy: Oh, sure.

Q: Do you get worried when this happens?

Percy: No. I remember something Franz Kafka wrote. He had a motto, *"Warte,"* written on the wall over his bed. *Wait.* You don't have to worry, you don't have to press, you don't have to force the muse, or whatever it is. All you have to do is wait. And that's true.

Q: Do you think it's harmful to try to force it?

Percy: It doesn't work.

Q: I suppose I was trying to tie force in with the discipline most writers impose upon themselves.

Percy: Oh, don't misunderstand me. I think you have to be sitting there. You have to "wait" in good faith. You have to go to work like anyone else, or I do anyway. I have to go to work at nine o'clock. And in that sense you force it. You've got to start in some way. Someone told me the other day that before he started to write he wrote anything, a page from the telephone directory, the dictionary, anything. Everybody has his own way. But yes, I do think you have to have a routine and live up to it and then hope for the best.

Q: Then, you maintain a certain schedule?

Percy: Yes. I try to write three hours every morning.

Q: And whether or not anything comes, you stay right there?

Percy: I try to.

Q: Which means that you probably have trouble controlling your frequent desire for a cup of coffee, tea, or a drink of water?

Percy: (Laughing) Oh, yeah. Anything to avoid getting with it, you know. There's always the pencil sharpening routine, closing a window, or opening a window. Anything at all.

Flannery O'Connor used to say that she spent three hours a day working and the rest of the day getting over it. This meant, of course, that she worked very hard. You know, she had a fatal disease during the last ten years of her life—during her entire writing career—and when she was dying—or during the last six months of her life when she was in the hospital—she asked the doctor what she could do, what she was allowed to do. She still had some strength left. You know what he told her? He said, "Well, you can't do any work, but you can write all you want to." She thought that was funny.

My wife tells me she always knows when I've had a good morning because I come out of that room smelling bad. Unfortunately I've been smelling very good recently.

Q: Did you serve a long apprenticeship in becoming a writer?

Percy: Well, I wrote a couple of bad novels which no one wanted to buy. And I can't imagine anybody doing anything else. Yes, it was a long apprenticeship with some frustration. But I was lucky with the third one, *The Moviegoer;* so, it wasn't so bad, I guess.

Q: Had you rather be a writer than a doctor?

Percy: Let's just say I was the happiest doctor who ever got tuberculosis and was able to quit it. It gave me an excuse to do what I wanted to do. I guess I'm like Faulkner in that respect. You know

Faulkner lived for a while in the French Quarter of New Orleans where he met Sherwood Anderson, and Faulkner used to say if anybody could live like that and get away with it he wanted to live the same way.

Oh, You Know Uncle Walker

Philip D. Carter/1971

From *The Washington Post*, 17 June 1971, pp. C1, C4 Reprinted by permission of *The Washington Post* and Philip D. Carter.

LeRoy ran the family plantation out from town. Phinizy taught law in New Orleans. But Walker, the mysterious other Percy brother from my town of Greenville, Miss., was sort of a remittance man, it seemed, a "doctor-who-never-practiced-and-turned-Catholic," a semi-recluse, self-exiled (with his wife and daughters) to a Louisiana bayou where he wrote books he never seemed to publish and essays nobody seemed to read.

"Oh, you know Uncle Walker," his nephew Billy said once when the topic came up. "Now get your head down, boy, here comes some mallards . . ."

COVINGTON, La.—"I think people admire Walker Percy," Carol Harrison was saying. "But there's this element that doesn't understand him at all. I wish a nice, strong little Klan writer would come along as far as the success of my bookstore is concerned."

She wasn't really complaining. "Love in the Ruins," the third novel by "Covington's own Walker Percy," was sold out, all 35 copies, and autographed paperback copies of his first two books, "The Moviegoer," and "The Last Gentleman," seemed to be selling at least as fast as "Chariots of the Gods."

"All this notoriety, you just can't turn it off. I think people are taking a second look at their local author," Mrs. Harrison said.

So is the world at large. "The Moviegoer" sold less than 10,000 copies while winning the National Book Award in 1962, but a half-million copies have since sold in paperback. "The Last Gentleman" has also done well, and now "Love in the Ruins" is in a big first printing of 30,000 copies.

Alfred Kazin, writing in the June Harper's magazine, pronounced Percy "a philosopher among novelists," "a natural writer, downright

subtle, mischievous," a Southern "seeker" on a pilgrimage of faith
"far off the beaten track" of New York letters.

And out on Bogue Falaya, the molasses-brown bayou that meanders through the heart of Covington, Percy's phone is ringing again.

The caller, who is in the midst of "Love in the Ruins," asks Percy
what "satyriasis" means, and then hangs up, leaving the author and
his visitor to one of those elliptical Southern conversations about the
region and its people and the reasonable strangeness of things.

Percy is a quiet man, spare, courtly and gray, and he renders the
most optimistic and the most apocalyptic observations with a noncha-
lant calm.

"Things, are pretty bad, sure," says Percy. "But take a little town
like Covington—which certainly is a conservative town if there ever
was one—and still the schools are integrated. The teachers seem
hopeful. They know they have a real problem, but they're going to
make it.

"The country is racist; so is the South. But there is a residue of
civility in the South—usually between blacks and white conservatives. A lot of it is still paternalistic, sure, but in spite of all there is a
modus vivendi. They do know how to get along. . . ."

All of Percy's novels have dealt in part with the cost and hardship
of some kinds of "getting along" and in his conversation, as in his
books, one mood generates its opposite before a tentative, experi-
mental synthesis finally emerges.

"People talk about how beautiful Covington is, how beautiful the
houses are—but they don't think about 27th Avenue (a black slum
area) . . . what constantly amazes me is that with conditions like this,
you don't have more rage. But time is running out; the young blacks
are different.

"Before Mardi Gras in New Orleans this year there were dire predictions of all sorts of trouble, both racial and with the hippies. Nothing happened in New Orleans, but they had a race riot here in
Covington. Whites started it. Several people were injured and they
called in cops from all around the state. . . .

"Politically and in matters of race, I guess I'm what you'd call a
liberal. But I'm usually out of sympathy with many of the militant
movements, the drug cults and that sort of thing."

Percy's new book is set in a Southern suburb called Paradise sometime in the near future when things are grievously falling apart racially, spiritually, generationally, politically, and even physically. There are snipers along the stairways and grassy cracks in the interstate highway and Howard Johnson's is tumbling down. The locale, as local readers have noted, is not unlike Covington—a town of 10,000 or so connected with New Orleans by a 27-mile causeway across Lake Pontchartrain.

The Percy home, set beneath oaks and pines at the sheltered end of a gravel road by the bank of the bayou is a perfect writer's retreat. But Percy's reasons for settling here remain mysterious.

His parents died when he was young, and he moved with his brothers from Birmingham to the home of his cousin, "Uncle Will," Greenville's planter-poet-lawyer, William Alexander Percy. Greenville is a writing town. Percy's high school contemporaries included Charles Bell, a poet and novelist, and Shelby Foote, a novelist and Civil War historian to whom Percy dedicated "Love in the Ruins." By one count Greenville has produced 64 published authors (or perhaps it is books), and David Cohn, one of the ablest of the local literary offspring, use to remark fondly that "every white lady in Greenville keeps a thesaurus under her mattress."

Percy left Greenville for the University of North Carolina and medical school in New York. He contracted tuberculosis while an intern at Bellevue, forsook medicine, took to philosophy, and eventually wound up in Covington, where a friendly bartender helped him find a house.

Walker Percy's first published article was a piece in Commonweal on Stoicism in the South. He made $25, he says, and decided to write full-time, but tore up two novels before he published "The Moviegoer," which Knopf somehow assigned to its religion editor. "When 'The Moviegoer' came out I asked my wife, 'What did I do for 15 years before that?' "

Now, at 55, Percy has been so thoroughly discovered that back in Greenville, where the patrician Percy tradition still runs deep, the town's leading conservative Republican has seen fit to send copies of "Love in the Ruins" to President Nixon and Vice President Agnew, who should take some comfort in one of Percy's versions of the novel's message:

"Don't give up, New York, California, Chicago, Philadelphia! Louisiana is with you. Georgia is on your side." One suspects all sorts of ironies. But you know Uncle Walker. Like the rest of the family, he is an excellent shot.

An Afternoon with Walker Percy

Charles T. Bunting/1971

From *Notes on Mississippi Writers*, 4 (Fall 1971), 43–61. Reprinted by permission of *Notes on Mississippi Writers* and Charles T. Bunting.

The following interview took place on a warm but pleasant Thursday afternoon, May 27, 1971, on the screened back porch of Walker Percy's home in Covington, Louisiana. Frequently looking out over the Bogue Falaya River, which flows at a distance of about sixty yards from his house, Dr. Percy carefully and precisely formed his replies to my questions. The sounds of tinkling ice cubes in our tea glasses, crying marsh birds, and roaring motor boats from the river occasionally punctuated our conversation—and were picked up by the tape recorder which lay on the arm of the couch between us.

Q: In William Barrett's *Irrational Man: A Study in Existential Philosophy* the author states: "The decline of religion in modern times means simply that religion is no longer the uncontested center and ruler of man's life, and that the church is no longer the final and unquestioned home and asylum of his being." In *Love in the Ruins* the narrator says, "The center did not hold." Is he expressing your concern for religion and the religious institutions in this country?

Percy: Well, I think I had a couple of things in mind. One is the fact that the political center did not hold. Overtly it's a satire about the polarization between left and right, liberal and conservative, but there's also a deeper meaning of the word "center" as applying to man's psychic center, and in that sense, I suppose, the religious connotation would probably hold true, mainly not that the Christianity or Catholic religion is any less true but that it is less meaningful for modern man, and in the sense that the decline of religion, decline of belief, it could apply to the center not holding.

Q: If one believes in the Christian concept of God, doesn't he recognize that the origin of man's despair must come from God, even if it is by way of Free Will?

Percy: You mean must come from the loss of God? Yeah, I suppose that's the theme of this novel as well as the others: that it's not so much of God being dead as of man's, modern man's, loss of God, loss of belief in God, and this theme of despair which I use, particularly in *The Moviegoer*, where I remember, I think, the epigraph talks about one of Kierkegaard's definitions of despair, the worst kind of despair being that kind of despair which is not aware of the stuff of despair. So I see a close connection between despair and the loss of God.

Q: Flannery O'Connor once commented, "If the Catholic writer hopes to reveal mysteries, he will have to do it by describing truthfully what he sees from where he is. A purely affirmative vision cannot be demanded of him without limiting his freedom to observe what man had done with the things of God." What difficulties are imposed upon you as a writer who is a Catholic?

Percy: Difficulties in what way? You mean writing about—

Q: In considering the theme of redemption and the theme of salvation that seems apparent in your novels.

Percy: The main difficulty is that of language. Of course the deeper themes of my novels are religious. When you speak of religion, it's almost impossible for a novelist because you have to use the standard words like "God" and "salvation" and "baptism," "faith," and the words are pretty well used up. They're old words. They're still good words, but the trick of the novelist, as the Psalmist said, is to sing a new song, use new words. You mentioned Flannery O'Connor. She got around the difficulty through grotesquerie and exaggeration and bizarre writing. As I recall, she said that for people who can't see plainly or can't see clearly you have to draw in caricatures—something like that—so the so-called Catholic or Christian novelist nowadays has to be very indirect, if not downright deceitful, because all he has to do is say one word about salvation or redemption and the jig is up, you know. So he has to do what Joyce did: he has to practice his art in cunning and in secrecy and achieve his objective by indirect methods.

Q: Father Boomer, the priest who baptizes Jamie Sutter in *The*

Last Gentleman, reminds me of Father Flynn in Flannery O'Connor's "The Enduring Chill." The presence of Sutter Vaught in this scene from your novel would parallel Asbury Fox's skepticism of the priest. What intention did you have in your portrayal of Father Boomer? It seems that the priest comes out to be a rather foolish character in modern literature. Can we consider him to be serious anymore? Can we portray a serious priest?

Percy: Oh, sure. I used Father Boomer on purpose to avoid the stereotype. It would have been very easy to create an intellectual, a sympathetic Hollywood priest, or even somebody like Teilhard de Chardin, but you can't get away with that. The idea is to create somebody like Father Boomer because, after all, the whole point is that the sacrament of baptism works whether it's Father Boomer or anybody else. So Father Boomer was made a rather ordinary priest but with deliberate intent in mind: namely, that it makes no difference.

Q: In other words, he is an Apostle, no matter what else he is.

Percy: Yeah. And you mentioned Sutter. A curious thing about that scene in Sutter, although he is a skeptic, in a way an unbeliever, Sutter was aware of exactly what was going on, you see. He was aware of the importance of it. And Will Barrett was not. All Will Barrett was aware of was that Sutter was aware of the importance of it. Afterwards he asked Sutter what was going on in there: "I could tell from the way you looked that something was going on." And Sutter answered his usual, "I'm not going to tell you what was going on. That's your business to find out."

Q: At the end of Camus' *The Stranger* Meurseult opens himself to "the benign indifference of the universe." What prevents Sutter from doing the same thing?

Percy: I suppose the fact that Sutter was closer to being a believer that Meurseult in *The Stranger.* Particularly at that stage of Camus' writings, he was a flat unbeliever and attributed no significance whatsoever to any sort of theism, whereas Sutter was a—. The possibility is left open that Sutter may have become a believer at the end, later. In any case, Sutter was not the one to have any benign indifference to anything. He was a more passionate man. He would have had no use for Meurseult's flat indifference to things. Sutter is not an indifferent man.

Q: I suppose that's what I like about him: his seeming indifference where he really cares. It's probably a hangover from the idea of being "cool" in the face of adversity.

Percy: Yeah, and, after all, I guess it was Camus who said that all philosophy springs from the possibility of suicide. And to that extent Sutter was true to Camus' philosophy; however, I think Meurseult didn't believe any such thing. He simply lived a flat life without affect or without much protest, except at the end when he railed at the priest, you remember.

Q: Norman Mailer once remarked that "the war between being and nothingness is the underlying illness of the twentieth century." Would you agree with him?

Percy: I never know what Mailer—when Mailer starts talking about existentialism—I never know what he's talking about. I'm not sure he knows. He throws around words, like "being" and "nothingness" and those words have been given so many different meanings and used in such loose ways that you'd have to—I'd have to—have it defined what we're talking about, whether we're talking about Thomas Aquinas or Sartre or what.

Q: I would assume it would be a reference to Sartre's *Being and Nothingness.*

Percy: Well, Sartre has been of value to me, not because of his philosophy, because I think his philosophy is self-contradictory; namely, that his philosophy has been atheistic existentialism with the implication that life and existence are without meaning and presumes that if it is without meaning, therefore, that communication is impossible or at least unnecessary. And yet Sartre's whole vocation is that of a writer: communicating—and communicating a lack of meaning to people meaningfully, but I think his own vocation contradicts his philosophy. If what he says were true, then he should be consistent at least. I remember what the philosopher Wittgenstein said: "Whereof one does not know, thereof one should not speak." And when Wittgenstein believed that, he actually stopped teaching and moved to the coast of Ireland for seven years and said nothing. So Sartre, if what he says had been true, he should have shut up, but he kept writing at a great rate. And far from being the case that his life was meaningless, he still kept communicating meaning and writing and actually having a better time in spite of his talk about absurd, absurdity, and the misery of human existence. He was actually enjoying himself more and making more money by writing in his French cafes than his characters actually seem to be, you see. I was influenced by Sartre in his first novel, *Nausea*, which is to me very good and very well done. It influenced me because the idea of having a certain belief and then trying to communicate it through a novel, through a concrete situation—a man set down in a certain situation—was very exciting. I liked his technique, but later when he began to—when he became a Marxist—I think his novels became too political. And his later trilogy, the Mathieu trilogy, was heavily politicized. I think not nearly as good as his first novels.

Q: Have you raised any religious or political questions in your novels that trouble you because you can't answer them?

Percy: No. It doesn't work that way. I'm really interested in seeing how the characters react in certain situations, and I use the novels also as a way of exploring the way things are as a discovering process. It works the opposite way for me. It's not something troublesome; it's a discovering process. To the extent that the novel succeeds or the writing succeeds, it helps me toward my own understanding of things. I know what I believe, and my problem is the craft of novel writing, how to write the novel. There's the agony. I mean the agony is not with me a religious agony. The agony is the agony of the craft, of getting it right.

Q: William Faulkner once remarked during an interview that "An artist is a creature driven by demons." What Muse or demon compels you to write?

Percy: I don't know. I write because it's what I want to do. And sometimes it goes very well and sometimes very badly. When it goes badly, it's bad indeed. But when it goes well, it's very good, you know.

Q: Your philosophical essays are geared toward a particular audience. Do you have an audience in mind when you write your novels?

Percy: No, not really. Actually I'm always faintly surprised later when actually somebody—when I see somebody reading [my book]. I never really think of somebody sitting down to read the book, and I'm always amazed when somebody reads it and really understands it. And the most unlikely people do. Often they say that only women buy novels. That's not quite true. Some people will call me or write me. I got a letter from a businessman from North Louisiana who had read this novel [*Love in the Ruins*]. He spoke of it with great understanding. I never know who's going to read it and get it.

Q: So you just write the best way that you can.

Percy: Sure.

Q: I wonder if you have any trouble with your narrators. In Ken Kesey's *One Flew Over the Cuckoo's Nest* the narrator, Chief Bromden, is a schizophrenic Indian. Considering the mental state of your narrator-protagonists, do you have much difficulty making your point of consciousness credible?

Percy: Yeah, well, there was a very real difficulty with this last book because—really with the last two—because in both cases the protagonist is, sometimes, mentally ill, so the trick was to present the narrative faithfully, that is, in a disjointed way that would be true to the disjunction in the narrator's mind, and yet to do so without confusing the reader. In several cases the editor said to me, "Why did you repeat such-and-such?" The answer was that Doctor More didn't remember. He was in a kind of a fugue state, and he had certain themes that would recur in his own mind, in his own dreams, and the things that he would see. And these repetitions were deliberate in my case, but it bothered the editor, and so actually I eliminated some of them.

Q: Why did you choose to write a futuristic novel? It's certainly a departure from your other two books?

Percy: It's a good way to do satire. It gives you a chance to speak to the present society from a futuristic point of view. Then you can exaggerate present trends so that they become noticeable and more subject to satire. Increase the polarization, increase the mannerisms or the psychic upsets, the anxieties of the liberals and the constipation of the conservatives. You know, that's really the business of the satirist and the futurist: to exaggerate so that things will become more noticeable. Also, I always liked science-fiction. The third reason is that I'm a lazy writer as far as doing research is concerned. And if you do science-fiction, you can make up your own state of the world or your own science or your own psychiatry or your own—in this case—the lapsometer.

Q: Another Southerner, William Styron, remarked in an interview:

"Only a great satirist can tackle the world problems and articulate them." Particularly in the opening pages of *Love in the Ruins* you use a kind of literary scattergun to satirize some of the foibles of our time. Did you, or do you, feel that you might have been talking too much?

Percy: You mean too many subjects or—

Q: Too many subjects.

Percy: Maybe so. I don't know. Somebody asked me what the book was about. I said it was about everything. Maybe you can't do that. I was enjoying myself. I had a good time. Here I can only hope that the reader does too. That's the good thing about satire. With satire you can fire at will. So whether or not I got away with it, I don't know. Maybe not.

Q: I just thought that if you had intended to pinpoint some of the difficulties and the adversities of our times, maybe you have to focus more, but perhaps there's just so much wrong with our times.

Percy: That's right. It was supposed to be a serio-comic review of the state of the world, throwing in everything at once, you know: race, religion, neurotic complaints, and so on. I don't know. It might have been too much.

Q: Is the title derived from Robert Browning's poem, "Love Among the Ruins?"

Percy: Not particularly. In fact I've been told also that there was a book by Evelyn Waugh called *Love Among the Ruins,* which I hadn't been aware of, although I've read most of Waugh. I think that Browning was "Love *Among* the Ruins."

Q: In your essay "Metaphor as Mistake" you make reference to "the authority and intention of the Namer." Aside from the fact that your protagonist, Dr. Thomas More, and the English statesman, Sir Thomas More, share a vision of a Utopian society, what other parallels between the two men did you intend? Did you give consideration to other historical or contemporary figures?

Percy: No. The main thing was the fact that Saint, Sir or Saint, Thomas More was English. That was the main object. Also one of my favorite saints. What this was deliberately supposed to do was to establish an Anglo-Saxon, English-American, Roman Catholic point of view. It was a rather overt attempt to de-Irish the American Catholic Church. I think a lot of novels, so-called Catholic novels, American-

Catholic novels, are usually Irish Catholic. Some of them are very well done indeed. Like Edwin O'Connor. And then there's Flannery—although she's a Georgia fundamentalist. But I thought it might be interesting to do something from rather a fresh point of view, in this case an Anglo-Saxon, Roman-Catholic point of view. Therefore, Thomas More. He is both the most English of Englishmen and the most Catholic of Catholics.

Q: How far did you intend the allegory to go in the novel? For example, how seriously should the reader consider Art Immelmann as Mephistopheles and Dr. More as Dr. Faustus?

Percy: Yes. To the degree indicated, it is a—There again, this was a deliberate attempt to place the novel squarely in the Western tradition. The fact that, I suppose, the novel could be looked on as what might be called the Western counter-attack against certain Orientalizing and other influences. The use of the Faust theme was deliberate. Dr. Thomas More represents a deliberate attempt to place the novel squarely in the Western tradition of Dante, Don Quixote, Henry IV, and so on. That's why the Faust theme was used, also the Don Giovanni theme, Dr. More—Was Dr. More Doctor Faustus, or Don Giovanni? He is both.

Q: How important is music to your novels? Considering Don Giovanni, I am reminded of the fugue state of Will Barrett and the musical-erotic state of Dr. More induced by the lapsometer.

Percy: Well, in the case of this novel, *Love in the Ruins,* music is given, is used, in the Kierkegaardian sense of music being the highest state of the so-called aesthetic sphere. That is Kierkegaard's phrase. It's his. And he uses Mozart and Don Giovanni as the highest attainment of the musical-erotic. So when Dr. More makes his deal with the devil, the devil gives him the best possible deal: namely, the highest state of what Kierkegaard would call aesthetic damnation, namely, the musical-erotic, so Dr. More combines the two, a very real love for music and a very real love for his three girl friends. And there's a lot of good to be said about all of them, the music and the girls. Yet it remains what Kierkegaard called it, aesthetic damnation. The devil knows how beautiful music and women are. So the best way to get Dr. More is to enshrine them as idols.

Q: Each of your three principal protagonists, Binx Bolling in *The Moviegoer,* Will Barrett in *The Last Gentleman,* and Dr. More in

Love in the Ruins, either marry or plan to marry at the end of the
novel in which they appear. Kierkegaard, whom you have mentioned
elsewhere as having an influence upon your thinking, has stated in
his *Works of Love* that "to love human beings is the only true sign
that you are a Christian." Do you consider that your characters have
fulfilled themselves as Christians and have reached some final resolution at the ends of the novels?

Percy: Well, in a way. Although to different degrees. Which is not
to say that marriage is the highest state of the Christian. Since you
mention Kierkegaard, I think that Kierkegaard regarded marriage as
the highest state of the ethical existence, which doesn't preclude the
sanctity of celibacy of many of the saints, but it was different in all
three. In the case of the first two, Binx Bolling and Will Barrett, these
were two young men who engaged in various kinds of pilgrimages. I
mean they experience various losses of identity and lack of belief and
alienation, and they were seeking one thing or another. They were
different. Will was a lot sicker than the other one, and I think probably Binx Bolling came to a happier end than Barrett, Will Barrett.
Will Barrett, of course, was a very sick young man. He probably
didn't turn out too well. Of course he married Kitty Barrett, and I
think maybe he lived tolerably. But who knows?

Dr. Thomas More was entirely different. These first young men
are, as I say, rather conventional types in current American fiction in
the sense of being lost young men, in search of one thing or another,
and maybe finding it in one degree of what they are looking for. But,
you see, Dr. More is different. From the beginning he knows exactly
who he is and what he needs. He has no doubt at all. There's no
identity crisis here. He knows exactly. The only problem facing the
reader is who is crazy, whether it's Dr. More or the rest of the world.
The problem is posed for the reader: whether More is right or the
world is right, whether Paradise Estates is right or Dr. More is right.
So his marriage at the end is not a philosophical or religious solution.
It's a moral solution. With him, his crisis is not philosophical or psychiatric. At the beginning of the book he sets out exactly who he is,
what his belief is, and where he stands, so that neither he nor the
reader has any doubt about that.

Q: Each of your narrator-protagonists undergoes a spiritual odyssey. Do you feel that the quest for the self has become the dominant American theme?

Percy: Of course the point of my book is that the quest for the self is probably self-defeating. I mean if religion has any validity at all, then the quest for the self is nonsense, you know. It's the quest for God, or as Kierkegaard, I think, said: the only way the self can become self is by becoming itself transparently before God. So, to answer your question, I suppose a good deal of my novel-writing could be a satire on the theme of the so-called quest for the self, or self-fulfillment, et cetera, et cetera. A great deal of bad novel writing is about searching for one's self.

Q: Do you think that the individual, in attempting to achieve coherence and unity in his life has failed to adjust to the chaos and absurdity of the world in which he finds himself?

Percy: (Laughing) I don't know. That's too big a question for me. I don't know how to answer that. I think everybody is responsible for himself. Everybody does the best he can. And that's all I'm trying to do in writing the novels, you know.

Q: On page 19 of *Love in the Ruins* you have a paragraph beginning, "American literature is not having its finest hour." Henry Steele Commager has said that "the historian of the future who chronicles this decade will be puzzled by the depth, strength, and prevalence of our anti-intellectualism." Are you concerned with the lack of an intellectual atmosphere in which to write?

Percy: Oh, no. Not really. Truthfully, I think the novel is fairly healthy. There are some good things being written. My novel, as I say, is satire and was written not really to prophesy, but to show how the predictions can be avoided. I don't think we'll come to that: that the writers fifteen years from now will be Jacqueline Susann and Harold Robbins and that Gore Vidal will be our grand old man of American letters, because we have a lot better writers than them now. I was really drawing a bead on the popular taste: the fact that *Love Story* sells four-and-a-half million copies and Jacqueline Susann's and Harold Robbins's printing of best-sellers. It doesn't speak to the fact that a hundred thousand people buy a Bellow novel.

Q: But the all-time best-selling piece of fiction is *Peyton Place.* That's what I meant by anti-intellectual climate.

Percy: To tell you the truth, that doesn't have anything to do with good writers. I mean there are good writers, and they needn't be bothered. It's just that one sometimes get discouraged by popular tastes, although I think the novelists never had it so good as they have it now. Particularly, I think maybe Jewish novelists have it best of all because when the Jewish novelist writes a good novel, he has a ready-made audience, I mean a readership of a hundred thousand, just like that. Of course I think Jews buy books more than any other group. I don't think novelists can complain. If it's good, it can get published, and it can get sold. I don't know any other time when novelists had such a wide market. There are some really good people writing, too. I just read Saul Bellow's last book the other day—I hadn't read it before—*Mr. Sammler's Planet.* It's really extraordinary.

Q: Do you think, as some critics say, that Bellow is the intellectual's novelist?

Percy: I don't know. I just know he's a damn good novelist. He's very, very fine.

Q: Is it true that *The Moviegoer* is going to be filmed, or is that just a rumor?

Percy: (Laughing) That is a perennial situation. It's been going on for years. Several people have had options on *The Moviegoer,* and the options run out, and the money runs out. This is a chronic situation. Twenty years from now somebody will be talking to me about filming *The Moviegoer.*

Q: Which novel do you think is most adaptable to the films?

Percy: I don't know. Certainly there's more interest in this novel *(Love in the Ruins)* for the films than the other two. My only question is whether—even if somebody wants to buy it—whether I should sell it, because I try to imagine how it could be filmed, and it's hard to imagine. It's a word story, not a picture show. I never write with the movies in mind. It would seem to me difficult to do *The Moviegoer,* which is about going to the movies.

Q: On page 19 of *Love in the Ruins* the protagonist says, "I've stopped going to the movies." Are the movies that bad?

Percy: Filmmakers have gone crazy. Really, they've gone crazy. I think they've lost their minds.

Q: Have you seen any films lately?

Percy: I haven't seen any good ones recently. I go to see movies, and they're either skin flicks, or something worse, or else foolishness. I've only seen one good movie in the last two years, and that was *Five Easy Pieces*. It had its points.

Q: Did you experience any particular problems of technique in writing *Love in the Ruins?*

Percy: I had a lot of trouble, if that's what you mean. I got half way through it a couple of times, read it over, and tore it up, and started over again. Which is not uncommon with me. It happens that it just doesn't look right or doesn't sound right, so I tear it up and start over. I could have done this one again. I could have taken it and rewritten it and done a better job. But I suppose there has to be the end of this somewhere. After a couple of years, you have to let go of it.

Q: Did you consider an alternative ending, such as a total apocalypse?

Percy: No, not really. I wanted a hopeful novel. It wasn't supposed to be a Vonnegut black ending. That's too easy: to put everything down. I like the idea of a new beginning, to try again. Somebody said that I am a Benedictine because the Benedictines are always flourishing, becoming corrupt, and being renewed. And the abbey goes to pot, and the vines grow in the ruins, and then is re-established.

Q: In *The Moviegoer* Binx remarks: "Though I do not know whether I am a liberal or a conservative, I am nevertheless enlivened by the hatred which one bears the other." The politicalization and polarization of the American people have obviously been a major influence in your writing in *Love in the Ruins.* Are you at all optimistic that our factions and frictions can be healed?

Percy: Yeah, sure. In the first place I wouldn't be bothering to write about it if I hadn't been. On the whole I'm optimistic. The task of a satirist is to put something down so that it can be made better. I do believe in reconciliation. I think you can see signs of hope now. Strangely enough, I think the best things that are happening are happening in the least likely places. I think probably the best hope for peace for race relations is small towns in the South, like this town, Covington. God knows, it's a conservative town, but the schools are integrated, massively integrated, and they work pretty well. I know some of the young teachers, some of the young students. They do their jobs and by and large people are getting along with each other. So if the center holds, I'm hopeful.

Q: What about the increasing black militancy?

Percy: Sure. What else can you expect? After four hundred years of white racism, the black backlash had to come. A black girl gets murdered in Drew, Mississippi, yesterday. Nothing new about that. It's been going on for a long time—in Mississippi. But eventually what else happens: white cops get shot in the back in New York. There's nothing surprising about it. Of course the danger's there of further polarization, the danger of guerrilla warfare. Maybe it's up to the South to save the Union this time. It may come to that. I've talked to liberals, old-style liberals, from New York, Detroit, and Boston. They've almost given up; they've thrown in the sponge. They're less hopeful than the segregationists on the local school board, who at least are obeying the law and trying to make it work.

Q: In the latest issue of *Harper's* (June, 1971) Alfred Kazin speaks of your "growing concern with symbolism." How do you assess the use of symbols in your novels?

Percy: Actually, Kazin was probably talking—because I never spoke to him about it—I was using the word "symbol" in a very particular way, not in the usual literary sense. We were talking about a philosophy of language, and I was talking to him about some work that I was doing, about the theory of language, in which words are regarded as symbols rather than as signs. That's the old argument between the theory of words as signs, and words as symbols. The buzzer or the bell to which dogs salivate. My conviction is that words are not signs like Pavlov's buzzer and bell; they are symbols—in other words, they name things. I've been writing on this subject for some years. So I think that when Kazin spoke of my interest in symbols, he was talking in that context, not in the usual sense of literary symbols. So if you ask me about literary symbols, I'm not particularly concerned one way or the other. If they're there, well and good. If they're not, I'm not interested. People often write papers about my fiction, about such and such a symbolism. I usually don't know what they're talking about, but maybe that's the way it's supposed to be.

Q: I would like your comments on the matter of style. Is there any one particular problem that you encounter?

Percy: Nothing that I can define—from the point of view of a proper literary style. You see, I didn't get an education in English; I got an education in medicine. All I know is that after I write something, I can read it after a while and tell that it's not right. So I sit down with it and try to get it right. I can see a sentence is bad, a paragraph is bad by looking at it, although I can't really say exactly why it's bad, except that it doesn't sound right.

Q: Professor Kazin calls *The Moviegoer* an "unseizable sort of book." Honor Tracy, in reviewing *The Last Gentleman* in *The New Republic* commented, "It is difficult indeed to see what the author is at. . . . The strength of the book is in the detail."

Percy: Well, that's their problem, not mine. If they can't seize it, than either it's seizable and they don't get it and they're at fault, or there's nothing to seize or it's badly written and the book's at fault. So I can't comment.

Q: Is there any particular critical gauge by which to evaluate your novels for someone who is reading them for the first time? Should one read some of the existentialists as a background, for example?

Percy: Oh, no. God forbid if we have to read philosophy in order to read a novel. No, I would say that the novels do something which is maybe not traditionally American, something more akin to the European, particularly the French and Russian tradition, than it is to the American tradition: that is, in the former of which the author used the novel form to convey his own feeling about the way things are, the way a man is in the world. This is not what Americans have ordinarily been interested in. They're interested in the novel as a form, the novel as literature, the novel as tract, the novel as sociology. Strangely enough, although I regard Faulkner as one of our greatest novelists, I'm probably least influenced by him than anyone else. I guess the only American novelist who influenced me at all would be Mark Twain—*Huckleberry Finn.* So in a way *The Last Gentleman,* particularly, was a kind of Huckleberry Finn journey, not down the river, but from the Eastern seaboard all the way to the South to the West. The use of travel, moving. Incidentally, this theme was discussed in some length in an article in *Partisan Review:* the idea of rotation, the idea of seeing around the bend, seeing something new.

Q: Frank O'Connor once said, "A novel is something that's built around the character of time, the nature of time, and the effects that time has on events and characters." To what extent would you agree or disagree with this statement? It seems to me that you are very preoccupied with the matter of time in your novels.

Percy: I don't think that I'm engaged with time as a character or a theme. As Heidegger was interested in time as philosophical theme. My main interest in time is really from a psychiatrist's point of view more than anything else: seeing a person in time, using time well or badly, being bored or being excited, a thing which only humans do. I mean in *The Moviegoer* the character speaks of what he calls "everydayness." In this book there's Monday morning. Anything is better—war is better—than going through an ordinary Monday morning in an ordinary way.

Q: And Will *(The Last Gentleman)* has to get by Wednesday.

Percy: Yes, well, maybe so, Maybe it's Wednesday. The thing that fascinates me is the fact that men can be well-off, judging by their own criteria, with all their needs satisfied, goals achieved, et cetera, yet as time goes on, life is almost unbearable. Amazing! So here's the strange phenomena of alienation and boredom in the face of an affluent life and all needs satisfied. Conversely, the phenomenon of the transformation under the conditions of ordeal. In *Love in the Ruins* Dr. More prescribes ordeal for one of his patients, Ted Tennis, who flounders around in the swamp for five hours and is a lot better off as a result. This is not something I made up. It is the commonest of phenomena. When the subway stops in New York—breaks down—and the lights go out, that's the best of times. And the worst of times is an ordinary Wednesday afternoon. For me this is fascinating.

Q: Ted Tennis. How do you go about naming your characters?

Percy: I don't know. I can't imagine where that one came from. It's tough. Names are an interesting problem in itself. What makes a name good?

Q: Dr. More is constantly reading Stedmann's *World War I.* Is this for the same reason that he drinks Early Times?

Percy: Well, this has to do with his preoccupation with what makes the best of times, what makes the worst of times. And the strange paradox of the twentieth century is that one of the best of times has been times of war, of all things. This has been a century of the greatest catastrophes of the human race. Of course some ethologists, like Lorenz and Ardrey, would find no great mystery to that. Of course man loves war. War is man's greatest pleasure. The thing is what to do now we're in the cold war. You can't have a world war now because everyone will get killed. But what substitute are you going to find that's half as much fun as war?

Q: There's been a five year interval between the publication of each of your three novels. Will we have to wait another five years for your next?

Percy: (Laughing) It may be forever. I don't know. I may have quit.

An Interview with Walker Percy

John C. Carr/1971

From *The Georgia Review* 25, (Fall 1971), 317–332,
© John C. Carr. Reprinted by permission of John C. Carr and
The Georgia Review.

Walker Percy's first novel, The Moviegoer (1961), *won a
National Book Award and his recent novel* The Last Gen-
tleman *has received wide critical attention. A native of
Alabama, he was educated at the University of North
Carolina and the Columbia University School of
Medicine. He gave up his medical practice for a career in
literature.*

Carr: Shelby Foote dedicated *Shiloh* to you. Did you grow up together in Greenville?

Percy: Yes, from the age of about . . . I moved to Greenville when
I was, I think, 13 or 14. He was maybe one year younger. I remember we started out at the same study hall at Greenville High School.
At the time, I was writing poetry, verse, for a high school class. I got
very proficient. The teacher would assign sonnets, and I would crank
out a sonnet and sell it for 50 cents. Everybody had to write a sonnet, so . . . Shelby saw me writing poetry, so I really take credit for
launching Shelby on his literary career.

Q: In *The Last Gentleman,* you say the town was named Ithaca
because the man had a fondness for the classical world and had had
enough of Southern Baptists, or words to that effect. Shelby has
named Greenville Ithaca in his novels. Is this a kind of an in-joke?

A: No. I liked the name. I wanted to use it, and I told Shelby I
hoped he didn't mind. He said he didn't. It wasn't a joke.

Q: You characterized Greenville in your novel as having a degree
of culture that the rest of Mississippi did not. Do you think that was
true then and is now?

A: I think it was very much true then. Mainly because of my uncle,
who was also my adoptive father. When my parents died, we went to

live with him. Of course, he was a remarkable man. He certainly had
a powerful influence on me. The whole idea of the Greek-Roman
Stoic view, the classical view, was exemplified in him more than in
any other person I ever knew.

Q: In another interview, you described the ambience pretty well,
with Faulkner coming to play tennis and showing up too drunk to
play, and so on. Did Mr. Percy, your uncle that is, influence your
decision to write?

A: I think he did. Most certainly he did because he had an extraordinary quality which only a few good teachers, as you know, have,
and that's the quality of making you see a poem or a painting the
way he sees it. And he could read poetry aloud, which very few
people do well, and he could make you see the beauty of a passage
in Shakespeare; Shakespeare and Keats were his two favorites, and I
could see it exactly the way he read it. He could turn you on. And
music, too. He owned a Capehart, a huge monstrous thing. And it
was the first time I had seen anybody play classical music. And so we
were exposed to all these good things—literature and music—for ten
years. Not only that, but he had a great influence in the town itself.
He was quite influential, affecting other people like David Cohn and
Hodding Carter.

Q: You started writing late, and you have said elsewhere that you
were a scientist until you were in your thirties, when you caught TB
at Bellevue. There's a question in my mind as to whether you're a
philosopher who exemplifies his philosophy in his writing, or a writer
who perfected his craft writing philosophical essays. How do you feel
about that?

A: All I can say is that I was interested first in philosophy, in writing
essays, although I never took a course in philosophy at Chapel Hill.
As I told you earlier, I spent most of the four years in the chemistry
lab, biology lab, and so on. But later I began to read philosophy and
got interested and developed violent agreements and disagreements.

Q: I've noticed that.

A: I've always found . . . my main motivation, the wellspring of my
writing, I hate to say it, is usually antagonism, disagreeing with somebody and wanting to get it right. Somebody provokes you and that's
good, you like something, you don't like something else. I remember
I read Susanne Langer's book *Philosophy in a New Key,* which was

for me a very, very exciting book. But I thought it went wrong at the
end. And so I just thought I would write and say how it went wrong,
and I wrote a long review and sent it to *Thought Quarterly,* and lo
and behold, it was published.

Q: Was that the first thing?

A: It was the first thing I had *ever* published.

Q: Let's go back for a moment. Not in time, though. How do you
react now, now that you're about the age he was when he was publishing, to Will Percy's *Lanterns on the Levee?*

A: Well, as I told you before, I think it's a minor classic in its way.
That and the W. J. Cash book that came out at the same time, expressing two very different points of view. I was greatly influenced by
it, of course, and sympathetic to much of it. In the end, there's an
ideological division between the way he saw it and the way I see it. A
lot of it may have to do with time. The times are different now. In
those days, believe it or not, he was considered a liberal. But now it
seems that *Lanterns on the Levee* really expresses a paternalism, a
noblesse oblige, and a rather dark view which is based on stoicism,
Greco-Roman Stoicism, in which a man doesn't expect much in the
world and does the best he can and tries to make one place a little
better and knows in the end . . . knows that he'll probably be defeated in the end. I became a Catholic and accordingly I have a
different view of how things should . . . of attitudes of whites towards
blacks and blacks towards whites. I have probably, I think, more
hope.

Q: Why have writers, and both Cash and your uncle were profes-
sional writers, found it so hard to write about the South? Presumably,
people accustomed to handling the language as well as being among
the brighter minds of their region could do it, but neither book totally
convinced me.

A: The South is a very complicated place to write about. Faulkner
had Quentin Compson telling his roommate, "I don't hate the
South." And any writer, any Southern writer, is stuck with this ambivalence, I think, this hate and love. I don't know. A couple of people suggested I write a book about the South. What does that mean?
Look at the difference between Atlanta and Birmingham, between
this place here and New Orleans, or between North Louisiana and
South Louisiana. I sometimes think that some parts of the South are

more like the North than the North itself. There are more Cleveland suburbs in the South than there are in Cleveland.

Q: If you don't mind my asking, when did you become a Catholic?

A: I think it was 1946, twenty-four years ago.

Q: Was that after you'd gone through the Bellevue thing?

A: Yeah, right.

Q: Did that have anything to do with it, or is that unfair?

A: Well, it came as a result of being . . . I was ill and I quit medicine, and I was laid up for a couple of years, and I was doing a lot of reading. I could get into a long thing there. I don't know whether you want to go into it.

Q: Yeah, I'm interested.

A: Well, just in general terms, what I got interested in was anthropology, in the European sense of the word, in a view of man as such, man as man. My orientation up until that time had been strictly scientific, in the then-prevailing naturalistic scientific mode, which very much attracted me at North Carolina and also at Columbia. Later it troubled me, because it amounted almost to behaviorism.

Q: Behaviorism?

A: I remember at North Carolina that classical behaviorism in the psychology department was running very strong. And at Columbia, it was the idea of the mechanism of disease, which is very valuable, the idea that disease is a mechanism of response in the body to the disease agent. So I began to be interested in a view of man as such, man as man. And I saw one day . . . maybe it was something of a breakthrough, something of a turning of a corner, that science can say so much about things, objects or people, but by its very method, by its own definition, by its own self-imposed limitation, the scientific method can only utter a statement about a single object, a glass or a frog or a dogfish—or a man—only insofar as it resembles other things of its kind. If you want to make general statements—which scientists recognize, that's the nature of science insofar as one dogfish resembles another dogfish—that is what science is interested in, making general statements about certain kinds of things and certain kinds of responses and reactions and changes. Well, I suddenly realized that when you apply this to man, you stop short at the very point where it matters to man. Science can say everything about a man except what he is in himself.

Q: Did you become interested in existentialism through Kierkegaard and Heidegger?

A: I'm trying to remember. I think it was probably through Sartre
first, probably through reading *Nausea*. And then later going back to
Kierkegaard and then coming forward to Heidegger and Marcel.

Q: In almost every article you've written, there's a reference to
Marcel.

A: I read quite a bit of him some time ago, but Kierkegaard is
probably the one who deserves the most credit. He saw it most
clearly. Although he was speaking of Hegel, you could say the same
thing of the scientific method: that it's a quantitative thing, that science cannot utter one single sentence about what a man is himself as
an individual. Of course, it doesn't even attempt to do so. And therefore, if a man embraces this particular view of the world, he is left
with a very peculiar view of things in which he sees the world ordered in scientific constructions with himself as a great lacuna, a great
vacuum. There's all this business about identity crisis nowadays, and
I think it has a lot to do with this cultural attitude. What I was protest-
ing during so much of the time you are talking about was the view of
so many, not merely scientists, but also writers and artists, that only
scientists and only science is interested in telling the truth. Provable,
demonstrable truth, whereas art and writing has to do with play, feeling and emotions, entertainment. I've always held that art and even
novels are just as valid as science, just as cognitive. In fact, I see my
own writing as not really a great departure from my original career,
science and medicine, because, to get back to what we were talking
about, where science will bring you to a certain point and then no
further, it can say nothing about what a man is or what he must do.
And then the question is, how do you deal with man? And if you are
an anthropologist in the larger sense, interested in man, how do you
study him? And it seemed to me that the novel itself was a perfectly
valid way to deal with man's behavior.

Q: I object to philosophical superstructures which expose their
joints in a man's writing.

A: I don't believe in writing in enigmas and acrostics. I've read
novels that you have to have read some sort of handbook in order to
understand. In fact, I think if this sort of novel—the philosophical
novel or whatever it is, the sort of thing that the French pioneered—is

any good, then the philosophy is part and parcel of the novel, and there's no illustrating of theses. You don't have a thesis and then illustrate it. What you do is put a man in a certain situation and see what happens.

Q: Why weren't you influenced by American writers? I've never seen a reference to an American writer in your essays.

A: That's true. It had to do with the original reason why I began to write. The philosophy I was interested in was what was called then existential philosophy. Of course, the word no longer means much. It still means a concrete view of man, man in a situation, man in a predicament, man's anxiety and so on. And I believed this view of man could be handled very well in a novel, and I was interested in phenomenology, which is very strongly existentialist: the idea of describing accurately how a man feels in a given situation. And that's certainly novelistic.

Q: Does existentialism aim for the salvation of man, or propose the salvation of man, in your opinion? I'm thinking now about your and Marcel's peculiarly Catholic existentialism.

A: I think it would be the idea of transcending the everydayness, of transcending being so caught up in the everyday world that even religious reality, especially religion, becomes a sort of stereotype and something you go through every day. And Marcel speaks of something he calls "recollection." That is, a man recollects himself, so he can recover things anew and afresh. And, of course, here is where the great divergence comes. Both Marcel and the atheistic existentialists like Sartre will agree that there's a certain absurdity and ugliness in the world and a certain alienation of man in the world. Of course, Marcel would say this reality can be transcended by an I-to-you relationship, that it can only be transcended by authentic political action and so forth. I think Sartre already undercuts himself because, although his philosophy disallows any communication between people, still he spends most of his time writing books.

Q: You wrote in your article "Symbol as Hermeneutic in Existentialism" that "Sartre is surely mistaken in analyzing the sources of my shame at being caught out in an unworthy performance by the look of another. It is the other's objectifying me, he says, that makes me ashamed . . . No. I am exposed—as what? Not as a something—as nothing, as that which unlike everything else in the world cannot be

rendered as *darstellbar.*" And, further on, "When Matthieu stops in
the middle of Pont Neuf and discovers his freedom in his nothingness—'Within me there is nothing. I am free'—he is after all only
hypostasizing the unformulability of self. The tell-tale sign is his ela-
tion, his sense of having at last discovered his identity. He is something after all—Nothing! And in so doing, is he not committing the
same impersonation which Sartre so severely condemns in others? If
the structure of consciousness is intentional, to be of its essence directed towards the other, a being-towards, then the ontologizing of
this self-unformulability as Nought is as perverse as any other impersonation—really a kind of inferior totemism."[1] Are you referring back
here to Marcel's "Existence and Human Freedom," which Marcel
dates from February, 1946, and in which he says "There is perhaps
nothing more remarkable in the whole of Sartre's work than his
phenomenological study of the 'other' as looking and of himself as
exposed, pierced, bared, petrified by his Medusa-like stare. My subjective reactions to this form of aggression are, in the first place, fear
(the sense of being endangered by the liberty of another) and, sec-
ondly, pride or shame (the sense of being at last what I am, but a
distance from myself, for another who is over there)."[2]

A: I'm sure that I'm indebted to him. That reminds me that I remember at the time that one of my objections to Sartre was that,
although, as I say, I felt a very strong attraction, his character in
Nausea was always being revolted by some aspect of reality which
was usually described in terms of being viscid or wet or organic, particularly the idea of the home being a nest or . . . a nest where the
children are, the babies are, the birds are, and mother. These things
provoked a kind of horror in Sartre. Which is all very well, but I think
he confuses the aesthetic with the philosophical there. He has an
aesthetic revolt, but I think he allows that to become a premise for
philosophical conclusions from it.

Q: In your article "Symbol as Hermeneutic in Existentialism" you
say, "yet even Sartrean existentialism can be edifying to the empirical
mind. For whatever the sins of bad faith of an existentialism which
postulates atheism, it has been able to recover that which the empiri-
cist in his obsessive quest for reducibility and quantification has lost—
the uniqueness of human beings."[3]

A: Well, presumably I meant a philosopher has no business post-

ulating theism *or* atheism. It's arriving at one or the other, not setting
out from atheism or theism. I think Sartre begins with atheism and
erects his system on that. Not even Aquinas postulated theism. But,
of course, Sartre changed completely. He has, in so many words,
repudiated this whole period we're talking about. He's rejected that
as being bourgeois and individualistic now.

Q: He's a Marxist now.

A: He's a Marxist. He says at last he's seen the right of things. In a
way I think he's right, in the sense that he does at last see the social
dimension. It's not just one man sitting around the streets and sitting
in the cafés and being revolted by the roots of a chestnut tree. At
least he is aware of a social dimension, even though it's Marxist. Of
course, Marx was the first one I think who adumbrated alienation,
but he put it strictly on the basis of production, of a man making
something—

Q:—he had no control over. I detect in your work, though, a certain will toward theism which I suspect was there before you started
building your philosophic outlook. Do you have any feeling about
that?

A: Well, I guess we're all what we are. If you're a Marxist, you
can't help but be affected by that orientation in your writing. And I'm
a Roman Catholic, although many Roman Catholics don't understand how I could write the novels I do and be a Roman Catholic. Of
course, that's an interesting subject in itself. What is a Catholic novelist? Is he a novelist who happens to be a Catholic, or is he a novelist
who is first a Catholic before he's a novelist? All I can say is, as a
writer you have a certain view of man, a certain view of the way it is,
and even if you don't recognize it or even if you disavow such a view,
you can't escape that view or lack of view. I think your writing is
going to reflect this. I think my writings reflect a certain basic orientation toward, although they're not really controlled by, Catholic
dogma. As I say, it's a view of man, that man is neither an organism
controlled by his environment, not a creature controlled by the forces
of history as the Marxists would say, nor is he a detached, wholly
objective, angelic being who views the world in a God-like way and
makes pronouncements only to himself or to an elite group of people. No, he's somewhere between the angels and the beasts. He's a
strange creature whom both Thomas Aquinas and Marcel called

homo viator, man the wayfarer, man the wanderer. So, to me, the
Catholic view of man as pilgrim, in transit, in journey, is very compat-
ible with the vocation of a novelist because a novelist is writing about
man in transit, man as pilgrim. I think it would be a disadvantage, for
example, to be a Freudian and a novelist. I think a great many novels
have been spoiled by Freudian preconceptions. Or behaviorist preconceptions. And I think most Marxist novels are bad.

Q: I think novels that have a basis in radical thought are good. It's
just that the novels which try to take the latest "correct line" or fall in
with the latest New Left fad are so bad.

A: And by the same token, nothing is worse than a bad Catholic
novel. Nothing is worse than a novel which seeks to edify the reader.

Q: There's a constant refusal to edify anyone in any of your
novels . . .

A: This is Kierkegaard. Kierkegaard was always saying . . . he
wrote a wonderful, a very important essay called "The Difference
Between a Genius and an Apostle." It's very, very important. He said
a genius could see the word *sub specie eternitatis,* the way things are
in general, and he could tell people this—the way things are in general—but he did not have the authority to come to anybody and tell
them any news. Or if he told them the news, he didn't have the
authority to make everyone believe the news. Whereas an apostle is
precisely a man who has the authority to come and tell everybody
the news. Kierkegaard . . . well, of course, Kierkegaard had much
more claim to having authority than I do. He was a preacher. But he
was still not an apostle. A novelist least of all has the authority to
edify anyone or tell them good news, to pronounce Christ King.

Q: You reject that all the way through. You keep coming back to a
funny line, you must have read it somewhere, that "Socrates, Jesus,
and Buddha were all *mature* personalities," and I wondered if that
was from some ridiculous pamphlet or something.

A: Well, in a way I suppose it's a reaction against my Uncle Will,
whom I loved and admired, but he was always telling us about the
great ones of the earth. He would always list them, Buddha, Jesus,
Socrates, he'd always include Richard Coeur de Lion, Philip Sidney
. . . So, it's a sort of a pantheon of the sexless saints.

Q: Shelby Foote mentioned that he thought Aunt Emily in *The*

Moviegoer, who gives the speech about the broadsword virtues, is
your uncle in disguise.

A: It's very close. In that particular scene, when she tells off Binx—
and she tells him off in good style, too—that's the way Uncle Will
would have told him off. And of course he'd be partly right. People
in the South think that's the best part of the book, where Aunt Emily
tells off Binx, and they think that Aunt Emily's point of view represents my point of view!

Q: That must be kind of wild. You said at one point that Binx was
on Kierkegaard's plane of the esthetic, and that's why he lived in
Gentilly.

A: Yeah, that's true, although not at the end. Binx lives in Gentilly
as a kind of . . . as a conscious cultivation of a certain kind of experience, whereas anybody else who comes to New Orleans or wants to
live the free life in New Orleans would naturally go to the French
Quarter and get an apartment in the proper dilapidated style with a
balcony and so on, but just as a reaction he does the opposite. But
Binx goes in to Gentilly. This appeals to him simply because it's not
like the French Quarter. He doesn't want to be down in the French
Quarter with a lot of guys who are artists and writers.

Q: The hip young set.

A: They are exactly the kind of people he's trying to avoid. There's
also a rather conscious parallel between Binx going to Gentilly and
Phillip going to the Gaza Desert. A man goes to the desert to seek
something. Gentilly is a desert if ever there was one. The same thing
happened in *The Last Gentleman.* They end up in the Western desert.

Q: It occurred to me that *The Moviegoer's* two main characters
escaped alienation by confirming each other's alienation, and *The
Last Gentleman* showed a man escaping alienation by rotation.

A: Well, they overlap and interweave, but they are different. Binx
lived almost entirely in what Kierkegaard calls the esthetic mode of
consciously cultivating certain experiences, of living in a certain place
with a certain feeling to it and having sensations about being there
. . . you walk across the street to the parochial school, and sit there in
the evening looking in the papers for the movie schedules, very
much aware of how it feels, and very much aware of getting on the

bus and going ten miles to Algiers, across the river, to see a movie. This is to oversimplify what Kierkegaard calls the esthetic mode of existence. But in the end—we're using Kierkegaardian terminology— in the end Binx jumps from the esthetic clear across the ethical to the religious. He has no ethical sphere at all. That's what Aunt Emily can't understand about him. He just doesn't believe in being the honorable man, doing the right thing, for its own sake. But at the end, a couple of hints are dropped; for instance, the end is also a commentary, or gloss, on the end of *The Brothers Karamazov*. He goes out to the car. Lonnie's brothers and sisters are in the car, and they ask him about Lonnie, and Binx says, "Well, he's dying" or "He's dead," I've forgotten. One little boy jumps up and says, "Is it true, Binx, that Lonnie will rise up on the last day and there will be a resurrection and Lonnie will be well in the resurrection, not crippled?" And Binx says, "Yeah."

Q: And Kate's mad at him because he's so cold-blooded.

A: Well, Kate missed it, missed the whole thing. No, I think Kate said, "You were very sweet with him," and Binx just looks at her. She's missed it, you see. But Binx doesn't joke. Like Alyosha he tells the truth. He wouldn't have said, "Yeah" if he didn't mean it. The implication is that . . . you see, in *The Brothers Karamazov*, Alyosha does the same thing with those kids. One of the kids says, "Is it true we're all going to rise up on the last day and be together?" A little boy named Kolya had just died. And so Alyosha said, "Yeah, that's true. We're really going to be there." And the kids say, "Hurrah for Karamazov!" And so this was a salute to Dostoevsky.

Q: Binx always kind of disturbed me. Even knowing about the Kierkegaardian esthetic mode, I always felt that Binx was holding himself in abeyance, that he was acting in a very self-centered way.

A: It's what Kierkegaard called esthetic damnation. You mentioned *The Last Gentleman*. That was different. This young man, Will Barrett, was both a great deal worse off than Binx and better off. He was worse off because he was sick; he was really sick. He didn't know where he was. Half the time he was in a fugue of amnesia, and he'd go into a fugue and come out of a fugue, and he'd wake up somewhere, not knowing where he was yet. He really existed in what Kierkegaard would call the religious mode. He was a real searcher. He was after something. He was clinging to a piece of wood, a floating spar; he's a drowning man clutching at straws, really on the ragged edge. The abyss was always yawning at his feet. The book is nothing but a journey. The question, you see, is whether it is better to be a drowning man, or alive and well in East Orange.

Q: The journey is rotation.

A: Well first, rotation—he's wandering around through the South—but then repetition. He goes back home. He goes back to a place like Greenville, and there he stands in front of his father's house, he recovers his . . . I think Kierkegaard says, "Every man has to stand in front of the house of his childhood in order to recover himself." So Barrett is obsessed with this thing that had happened, his father's suicide. And the whole first two-thirds of the book is going back to this thing that happened, which actually had shocked him so much he'd almost become a hysteric. He was deaf in one ear.

At first, there's a repetition back to Ithaca and then he gets hold of Sutter's diary and he follows Sutter to the desert. There's an encounter where he meets Sutter in the desert which is something like the encounter of Phillip with the eunuch in the Gaza Desert. But at the end, this is different. He knows that Sutter's on to something. Sutter's got something he wants to know, and Barrett has this radar. He knows that people know something he doesn't know. So he fastens on Sutter, because he has to find out what it is. Sutter leaves him this diary which has all kinds of clues and such, but he still doesn't know exactly what Sutter's getting at. So he finally catches up with Sutter, and in the death scene a baptism takes place, with a very ordinary sort of priest, a mediocre priest. And here again, Barrett has eliminated Christianity. That is gone. That is no longer even to be considered. It's not even to be spoken of, taken seriously, or anything else. But he still has this acute radar. He knows what people are feeling. And he is aware of something going on between the dying boy Jamie and Sutter there across the room and the priest. And he is aware that Sutter is taking this seriously. So after the boy dies, they leave and Barrett catches up with Sutter and he says, he asks Sutter, "What happened there? Something happened. What happened?" And Sutter brushes him off, as usual. "What do you think happened? You were there." Well, it ends, unlike *The Moviegoer,* with Barrett missing it, like Kate missed it. He *misses* it! He says something to Sutter like, "Why don't you come back to a town in the South and make a contribution, however small?" So presumably, you see, Barrett, who existed in a religious mode of search, repetition, and going into the desert, which are all in Kierkegaard's religious mode, at the end misses it. Whereas Binx, who exists in the aesthetic mode of damnation, as Kierkegaard would call it, in the end becomes a believer, in his own rather laconic style.

Q: A real flip-out. You never look for that. I look and what has he done? This guy is now a Christian! I didn't see this coming.

A: Well, most people didn't see it at all. In fact, most people will deny it's in there. They stand me down. "That's not true. You don't baptize Binx in that book." They accuse me of copping out.

Q: Does it bother you that the death of young boys and their conversion, or at least a giving of religious significance to their deaths, occurs in both novels?

A: Susan Sontag said to me, "You've written two novels, both of which end with a philosopher bending over a dying youth." My wife said, "Enough of that."

Q: Goodman, reviewing *The Last Gentleman* in *Life,* said that you stand back from sex all the way through the novel.

A: Well, he probably means that I don't describe the physiology of sexual intercourse, which everybody does now in novels. And which I have no particular objection to, except that I don't think it's necessary. I already had physiology in medical school.

Q: You don't think anything can be learned about people from the way they approach sex?

A: Well, it's gotten to be such a formality now. The description of sexual encounters is now almost as obligatory as their avoidance in the Victorian novels. I'll be damned if I'm going to be dictated to by either style. I do it my own way . . . I take pleasure in turning Freud upside down. Instead of something being a symbol for sex in the Freudian style, I use sex as a symbol of something else. Sex here is a symbol of failure on the existential level.

Q: In the May 11, 1962, *Commonweal* you reviewed *A Dream of Mansions* by Norris Lloyd, *The Wandering of Desire* by Marion Montgomery, and *Judgement Day* by Thomas Chastain. And in that review you said, "A sense of place can decay to the merely bizarre. A sense of person can be pushed to caricature and a whole region populated with eccentrics." Do you purposely stay away from the

Southern kind of thing of peopling your novels with physical and mental eccentrics?

A: I stay away from the Southern novel in several ways. There's a certain thing everybody always says about the Southern novel. In almost any interview with a Southern writer, the writer always says something about, "Well, the reason Southerners can write good novels is that they were raised sitting on front porches listening to people tell stories, and Faulkner sat on a bench outside the court-house in Oxford and heard the people tell all these stories. And we're exposed to family sagas and all sorts of bizarre and eccentric charac-ters, also inter-relationships." This may be true. Yeah, sure it was true, but hell, it's gone, it's all over.

Q: Do you think so, really?

A: As far as I'm concerned. Whatever impetus I had towards writ-ing owes nothing to sitting on a porch listening to anybody tell stories about the South, believe me. I think that the day of regional South-ern writing is all gone. I think that people who try to write in that style are usually repeating a phased-out genre or doing Faulkner badly. I don't think that's the way it is. I think the South is sufficiently cor-rupted, or at least amalgamated with the rest of the United States, so that a young man coming back to the South is not so different from a young man coming back to Denver or San Francisco. Except the South has certain advantages. I make use of the Southern scenery, the Southern backdrop, but just as that, as a place where a young man can react. But I think it's just fifty years later than the time of family stories and sagas and histories and so on.

Q: You don't consider yourself a Southern writer, then?

A: I'm not sure of that. I do. If I were in Colorado or New York, I'd be writing something different.

Q: Really?

A: I think what we're stuck with in the South and what's of value are two things: one is religion and the other is the Negro. And Flan-nery O'Connor says there's no way you can be raised in the South without being affected by the very strong fundamentalist Christianity, usually in rebellion against it, but certainly you bear some kind of relationship to it. Compare yourself or myself with somebody grow-ing up in Shaker Heights in Cleveland. The subject never even arises. You and I have seen Jesus Saves signs. We were brought up seeing

Jesus Saves and Garrett Snuff signs. And then there is the black thing. Of course, this is a hideously complicated business, very ambivalent, a very rich source for relationships because no matter what you say, or how bad the South is, there's still a long history of viable relationships here, a long history of people getting along with each other.

Q: For one reason or another.

A: Yes, and a certain civility still exists here. And so you find yourself attacking the South and at the same time falling back on ways of communication which still exist. I can't help but think it's an advantage.

Q: There aren't any very strong women in your fiction except Rita, who is by turns strong and not so strong. Kitty is kind of pitiful and Kate is weak.

A: I write about women from the exclusive point of view of the hero or anti-hero. As such, the view of women or anyone else may be limited by the narrowness of the vision. The nature of the narrowing, however, I would hope to be significant. If Binx Bolling tends to see people oddly, then perhaps the times are such that people get seen oddly. Accordingly, there is no attempt to flesh out female characters—or any other characters—in the style of the nineteenth-century novel. It was said that Tolstoy knew exactly how it felt to be a horse five minutes after his first acquaintance with a horse. Presumably this held true of women too. Certainly I am no Tolstoy and cannot do this. But I wouldn't if I could. What interests me is not how it feels to be that particular horse or that particular woman, but how it feels to be a particular consciousness, male or female, set down in the world the way it is now.

Q: Did you read Ellen Douglas' pamphlet about you which she wrote for the Religious Dimensions in Literature, published by the Seabury Press?

A: Yes.

Q: What did you think about it?

A: I thought it was quite good in most ways. Very sharp. I thought she handled my . . . she asked me if I was still a Catholic. I told her I still was, and she sounded as if she didn't believe me. She wrote something about the Percys having a tendency to toy with Catholicism. This does a bit of injustice to both the Percys and the Catholic

Church. I may not be a good Catholic, but I hope I am not a dilettante.

Notes

1. Walker Percy, "Symbol as Hermeneutic in Existentialism," *Philosophy and Phenomenological Research,* XVI (June, 1956), p. 529.

2. The article referred to is "Existence and Human Freedom" in the book *The Philosophy of Existentialism* by Gabriel Marcel (Manya Harari translation), Citadel Press, NYC, 1968, and the passage is on page 71 of that volume.

3. Percy, op. cit., pp. 529–530

A Talk with Walker Percy

Zoltán Abádi-Nagy/1973

From *The Southern Literary Journal*, 6 (Fall 1973) 3–19, and reprinted by permission.

Editor's Note—the interview with Walker Percy that follows was conducted by Professor Nagy, of the faculty of Kossuth University, Debrecen, Hungary, with a view toward publication in Hungary. Because many of the comments are of interest to American readers as well, it is made available here.

Q: You maintain that perhaps the best way of writing about America in general is to write with authenticity about one particular part of America. By extension this means that, likewise, your attitude and reaction toward philosophical questions of universal human importance—toward the question of the human predicament, to use the term of your philosophy—will be that of an American. Is that correct?

A: I think that is true. My novels have more a European origin than American. They are so-called philosophical novels which is probably a bad word. But you know that the first half of your question is quite true. The greatest exponent of this was Faulkner who concentrated on a small village in Mississippi. It is true that I am interested in philosophical, religious issues and in my novels I use the particular in order to get at the general issues. For example, *The Moviegoer* is about New Orleans, one part in New Orleans, a young man in New Orleans. The conflict is a hidden ideological conflict involving, on the one hand, what I call Southern stoicism. I have an uncle whose hero was Marcus Aurelius. The other ideology is Christian Catholic. The third: the protagonist is in an existentialist predicament, alienated from both cultures.

Q: What in your view is it in America that makes an existentialist today? What facets of the American intellectual climate, of the American existence in general, are favorable to existentialist thinking?

A: I think in America the revolt is less overtly philosophical. It is a feeling of alienation from American suburban life, the suburb, the country-club, the business community. There is a difference between my protagonists and the so-called counter culture. Many young people revolt in a purely negative way, oppose their parents' culture; whereas the leading characters in my books are much more consciously embarked on some sort of search. I am telling you that because I would not want you to confuse the characters of the counter culture with my characters. One of their beliefs is that the American scene is phony, and their revolt is to seek authenticity in drugs, sex, or in a different kind of communal existence. The characters in my books are embarked on a much more serious search for meaning.

Q: Can you think of other contemporary American writers who have studied European existentialism as systematically as you have and who have had that philosophy in mind when writing?

A: I honestly cannot. I am sure there are some. Probably some of the Jewish writers in the Northeast like Friedman and, of course, Norman Mailer, who defines himself as an existentialist although I do not take him too seriously on that.

Q: Your view of life in your literary works is very close to the absurdist view, but the term 'absurd' and the whole Camus terminology hardly ever appears in your philosophical essays. Does this coincide with your preference for Marcel's Catholic version of existentialism as opposed to the post-Christian character of the meaninglessness of Sisyphus' situation?

A: Yes, that is correct. I identify philosophically with people like Gabriel Marcel. And if you want to call me a philosophical Catholic existentialist, I would not object, although the term existentialist is being so abused now that it means very little. But stylistically mainly two French novels affected me: Sartre's *La Nausée* and Camus' *L'etranger.* I agree with their novelistic technique but not with their absurdist view.

Q: Is not your third novel, *Love in the Ruins,* with its Layer I and Layer II—the social self and the inner, individual self—a comic attempt to solve Marcel's dilemma about this separation?

A: You are right. This is a comic device to get at what, ever since Kierkegaard, has been called the modern sickness: the disease of abstraction. I think in the novel Dr. More calls the illness angelism-bestialism. There is nothing new about this. It had been mentioned by many writers in various ways. Pascal said that man is both not quite as high as an angel and not quite as low as a beast. So Dr. More is aware of this schism in consciousness. He talks about the modern mind which, as he sees it, abstracts from the world, from itself, and manages to lose touch with reality.

Q: When I said 'comic' I did not mean that the book is a parody on this existentialist dilemma. Rather, the source of comedy seems to be your view that science is not able to cope with this task. If any-thing this, I feel, is Marcel again rather than his parody.

A: That is true.

Q: Much of it, especially in *Love in the Ruins*, seems to be a social problem viewed from an existentialist viewpoint of the human predic-ament. Actually, this is a kind of movement I notice in your works: an increasing awareness of how much the social predicament has to do with the human predicament. If Binx in *The Moviegoer* was suffocat-ing in an adverse climate of malaise which was a social phenomenon, he was not much aware of its having to do with society; he was not concentrating on things like the social self as later Dr. More is in *Love in the Ruins*. Was this an intentional change on your part or was the movement towards the concept of malaise as a social product spon-taneously developing through the inner logics of these relations?

A: It was a conscious change. *Love in the Ruins* was intended to take a certain point of view of Dr. More's and from it to see the social and political situation in America. Unlike Binx, whose difficulties were more personal, Dr. More finds himself involved in contemporary is-sues: the black-white conflict and the problem of science, scientific technology which is treated as a sociological reality today. Both the good and bad of it. I really use this to say what I wanted to say about contemporary issues. About polarization; there are half a dozen of them: black-white, North-South, young-old, affluent-poor, etc. And do not forget that at the end of *Love in the Ruins* there is a sugges-tion of a new community, new reconciliation. It has been called a pessimistic novel but I do not think it is. A renewed community is suggested. The suggestion is in the last scene which takes place in a midnight mass between a Christmas Saturday and Sunday. The Catholics, the Jews come to the midnight mass, also the unbelievers in the same community. The great difference between Dr. More and the other heroes is that Dr. More has no philosophical problems. He knows what he believes.

Q: Is it a religious reconciliation then?

A: Yes, that is the case. This was meant for Southerners in particular and for Americans in general.

Q: Binx in *The Moviegoer* and Barrett in *The Last Gentleman* do not seem to have the set of positive values needed for absurd creation as conceived by Camus to create their own meaning in meaninglessness. Is this connected with your idea of the aesthetic reversion of alienation, i.e. by communicating their alienation they get rid of it?

A: Yes, there is something there. In the case of Binx it is left open. The ending is ambiguous. It is not made clear whether he returns to his mother's religion or takes on his aunt's stoic values. But he does manage to make a life by going into medicine, helping Kate by marrying her. I suppose Sartre and Camus would look on this as a bourgeois retreat he had made.

Q: How do *you* look on it?

A: Well, I think he probably . . . as a matter of fact the last two pages of *The Moviegoer* were meant as a conscious salute to Dostoevski, in particular to the last few pages of *The Brothers Karamazov*. Very few people notice this.[1]

Q: To me the most striking difference between the European and the American absurdist view is the ability of the American to couple the grim seriousness with hilarious humor, to turn apocalypse into farce. In comparison, Beckett, for all the grim comedy which is there, is a sheer tragic affair. Can you think of some explanation for this?

A: That is a good question and I can only quote Kierkegaard, who said something that astounded me and that I did not understand for a long time. He spoke of the three stages of existence: the aesthetic, the ethical, the religious. When you pass the first two you find yourself in an existentialist predicament which can be open to the religious or the absurd. He equated religion with the absurdity. He called it the leap into the absurd. But what he said and was puzzling to me was that, after the first two, the closest thing to the third stage is humor. I thought about that for a long time. I cannot explain it except I know it is true.

There is another explanation, too, of course. Hemingway once said: all good American novels come from one novel written by a man named Mark Twain. With *Huckleberry Finn* Mark Twain established the tradition of this very broad and satirical humor. I think the American writer finds it natural to use humor both in his satire and in describing even the worst predicament of his main character. In this country we call it black humor: disproportion between the gravity of the character's predicament and the hilarity of the humor with which it is treated. Vonnegut uses this a good deal.

Q: Richard B. Hauck in *A Cheerful Nihilism* points out how Franklin, Melville, Twain, Faulkner have shown that the response to the absurd sense can be laughter. At one point Binx becomes aware of the similarity of his predicament to that of the Jews. "I accept my exile," he says. Whether we accept this as his affirmation of life in its absurdity or not, what follows is comedy. Could you agree that this comedy as well as Franklin's, Melville's and the others' could be regarded as the absurd creation of the American Sisyphus as opposed to the serious defiance of Camus' king?

A: I do not know if I would go that far. It may be much simpler. There is an old American saying that the one way to stop crying is to laugh. Binx says, "I feel more homeless than the Jews." Between him and the Camus and Sartrean heroes of the absurd there is a difference. Camus would probably say the hero has to create his own values whether absurd or not, whereas Binx does not accept that the world is absurd; so he embarks on a search. So to him the Jews are a sign. I think he said, "Lately when I see a Jew on a street I am amazed nobody finds it remarkable. But I find it remarkable. But to me it is like seeing Friday's footprint in the beach." Of course, he is not sure what it is the sign of. Sartre's Roquentin in *La Nausée* or Camus' Meursault in *L'etranger* would not find anything remarkable about a Jew, they would not be interested in him.

Q: In your philosophical essay, "The Man on the Train," you stress the speakability of the commuter's alienation and the fact that the commuter rejoices in this speakability. We can probably add: laughability. Incidentally, you do mention in the same article how Kafka and his friends were roaring with laughter when Kafka read his work aloud to them. Again if we had the answer to how alienation can become a laughing-matter, we would have the key to much of what is recently called black humor.

A: I think you are right. In "The Man on the Train" I was talking about the aesthetic reversal: the alienated commuter feeling totally alienated when reading a book about alienation feels better because there is a communication between himself and the writer.

Q: The forms of alienation you are concerned with in your fiction are all results of the objectification, mechanization of the subjective. Does not this view meet somewhere at a point with Bergson's view of the comic as the mechanical manifested in a living human being?

A: It sounds reasonable but I cannot enlarge on that. I am not familiar enough with Bergson. But to your previous question. Let me finish. It is the first time it occurs to me. You brought it up. Maybe, a person like Sartre spent a lot of time writing in a café about alienated people, the lack of communication, etc., and yet, in doing so, he became the least alienated person in France. By writing he performs a superb act of communication for which he has many readers. So you have a complete reversal. He writes about one thing and re-verses it through communication. Here we have the American writer locked in his alienation. But I can envision the American writer get-ting onto it; by seeing the possibility of communication, exhilaration, his alienation becomes speakable. There can be a tremendous re-lease from that. I have never thought of this before. Nobody knows what is going on when you communicate the unspeakable. This all-important step from unspeakability to speakability is such a triumph that in his own exhilaration the American writer finds it natural to use the Mark Twain tradition of the funny, the humorous.

Q: This emphasizes a point of departure of American black humor from traditional comedy as seen in Molière or as viewed by Bergson. The energy released, as you have just mentioned, bursts into com-edy; much of it becomes, I think, comic energy. But this comic en-ergy does not produce figures who do take their mechanistic behavior—always a comic obsession—seriously as in traditional com-edy. For all the similar tendency for objectification and toward behav-ing like a mechanism, the black humorous character, instead of having comic obsessions taken seriously, is split into a myriad of frag-mented comic gestures toward serious problems. Cannot comedy at this point, with ambiguities and only ambiguities and comic alterna-tives offered, become comedy for its own sake, a kind of nihilistic play?

A: I think it not only can but it does. That is what is wrong with the American so-called black comedy: absurd situation used for its own sake, gags, impossible situations. Like Philip Roth, who seems to have the idea that the more outrageous you make a situation the better. I deplore this. I think that using black comedy for the sake of itself defeats art. But, you know, I think I owe a good deal of the kind of humor that I use to Jewish humor, which is a very wry, self-critical sort of humor. It is funny. We Americans are very familiar with Jewish humor simply through the medium of Broadway and TV. The Jewish comedian is a stand-up comic. I think I find myself using what the Jewish comedians call the gag—a one-liner. And there again we have the same situation: Jewish humor developing from an oppressive and tragic situation. We were talking about the common fact of black humor being connected with a difficult situation. Surely there is a connection there, too, of humor in a difficult situation. Kafka's sharp, devastating humor certainly traces back to ghetto literature. I am reading Böll now. The relationship of religion and humor is interesting. He is a German Roman Catholic and uses the most devastating satirical humor, often extremely anti-clerical. I find a kinship with him. I find it perfectly natural for a Catholic writer to fall into this harsh, satirical comic technique.

Q: An interesting outward sign of the false truths these black humorous characters are surrounded with, and which they reject, is their inability to laugh amidst all the comedy. What worries Aunt Emily in *The Moviegoer* most is that "the child does not laugh"—Kate, that is. This also means—only seemingly a paradox—that they who make us laugh at everything, even at themselves, and who are unable to laugh themselves most of the time, *are* able to tell the difference between true and false laughter and the difference in attitude to the world that may kill or provoke laughter. Aunt Emily suspects Binx can make Kate laugh.

A: Yes, I think she tells him this at one point. Maybe she means that. But your analysis of humor is way ahead of me. I had not thought about these lines at all. I notice you do not mention Freudian theory. Is that because it does not interest you too much?

Q: No, it does not interest me too much.

A: I agree. I do not think his theory is true. Talking about humor we should not overlook a simple thing: humor used in the service of

satire. Swift's gallows humor is a good example. There is no more
deadly weapon. I give you an example of how effective it is. Two or
three friends of mine who are segregationists always remember one
line from *Love in the Ruins* because they think it is effective. Dr.
More describes a segregationist academy called Valley Forge
Academy. He is watching the Christian Kaydettes marching back and
forth, and describes what the school is founded on: "religious and
patriotic principles and to keep Negroes out." That sentence made a
tremendous impression on segregationists, they feel the impact of it.
You know what I mean?

Q: They did not take it as an affirmation of their attitude?

A: No. They say, you really got to us, hit us where it hurt, exposing
the hypocrisy of it. These academies are very religious, very patriotic,
American flags fly all over the place, yet blacks are not allowed. Just
a small example of how comic satire can be used as an effective
weapon.

Q: Religion reminds me of another tendency I notice in your
novels from Binx through Dr. Sutter to Dr. More: the scientist Dr.
Percy showing in the novels much more than the Catholic. How
would you comment on your religious presence in the philosophical
essays—the whole idea of the islander opening all those bottles hop-
ing for 'the message'—and on the absence of practical religion from
the novels. I know that religion is there as a theme but with no commitment of the writer in any direction.

A: Well, that is very simple. James Joyce said that an artist must be
above all things cunning and guileful and must use every trick in the
bag to achieve his purpose. In my view the language of religion, the
very words themselves, are almost bankrupt. If you are writing a
technical article on philosophy you can use the correct word for the
correct meaning. But writing a novel is something different. In my
view you have to be wary of using words like 'religion,' 'God,' 'sin,'
'salvation,' 'baptism' because the words are almost worn out. The
themes have to be implicit rather than explicit. I think I am conscious
of the danger of the novelist trying to draw a moral. What Kierkegaard called 'edifying' would be a fatal step for a novelist. But the
novelist cannot help but be informed by his own anthropology, the
nature of man. In this respect I use 'anthropology' in the European
philosophical sense. Camus, Sartre, Marcel in this sense can all be

called anthropologists. In America people think of somebody going out and measuring skulls, digging up ruins when you mention 'anthropology.' I call mine philosophical anthropology. I am not talking about God. I am not a theologian.

Q: What I meant was not the question of style and technique explicit or implicit but the religious *commitment* which is there in your philosophical writings but absent from the novels or always left open at best.

A: As it should be left open in the novel.

Q: Here is Jamie's death-bed conversion in *The Last Gentleman* as a case in point. Brainerd Cheney maintains that Dr. Sutter admits to a sort of faith here. It seems to me that to say Dr. Sutter is not going to commit suicide *because* he gained hope from Jamie's conversion would reduce a work of complexity and artistic integrity to a simple, very conventional solution which would mean the abandonment of the complex view of life the book stands for.

A: Well, it is left open. He certainly does not specify that he will be converted. The only suggestion against suicide is at the very end when Barrett shouted, "Wait." Sutter stopped and waited. The only suggestion is that he would not have stopped if he had wanted to commit suicide. But it is all left open. I am not sure what happened to Barrett. He probably went back to the South, married Kitty, and worked in the Chevrolet agency. He never knew what was going on. He kept asking Sutter what to do and Sutter refused to tell him.

Q: None of the main characters in your three books have problems in making a living. Binx is a successful broker, Barrett inherited from his father, Dr. More from his wife. Do you do this to contrast seeming affluence with emptiness under it?

A: I had not thought about it. Maybe so, maybe also to use it as a device to reinforce the rootlessness. After all if these fellows had been day-laborers working very hard they would have had no time for various speculations.

Q: Does that mean that existentialism has no comment on those who are without these economic means—and consequently perhaps in a much more serious predicament—because they have no time for speculations?

A: To that Marx would have an answer, Henry Ford would have an answer, Chaplin would have another, etc. Marx invented the term alienation. . . .

Q: He reinterpreted an older concept, he discovered a new explanation for alienation. . . .

A: But it is now transferred to a different class of society in Sartre, Camus. These desperately alienated people are members of a rootless bourgeoisie, not the exploited proletariat.

Q: Your novels demonstrate that to many questions affluence is no answer. Danger of life and the saving of lives often figure in your work as in many other black humorists', too. One can think of Barth's *The Floating Opera, The End of the Road, Giles Goat-Boy,* Vonnegut's *The Sirens of Titan, Mother Night, Cat's Cradle* and others, Kesey's two novels, Pynchon's *V.,* Heller's *Catch-22* and *We Bombed in New Haven,* etc. Do you think that this or a similar event of great moment in one's life is necessary to awaken the existentialist hero to his absurd situation and that this somehow is needed to shock him into the feeling of necessity for 'intersubjectivity' and shared consciousness as an escape from 'everydayness'?

A: I think that touches on a subject I have been interested in for a long time—a theme I use in all my novels: the recovery of the real through ordeal. It is some traumatic experience—war, Dr. More's attempted suicide—in each case. You have the paradox here that near death you can become aware of what is real. I did not invent this. Prince Andrey lying at the Battle of Borodino and looking at the clouds, makes a discovery: he *sees* the clouds for the first time in his life. So Binx is the opposite of Prince Andrey: he watches the dung-beetle crawling three inches from his nose.

Q: Correct me if I overinterpret the difference but now that you make this comparison it occurs to me that perhaps there is some irony here in the way it is an opening up of vision for Andrey towards the clouds, the sky, some magnificence suggested by these, and in the way Binx zooms down on an ugly little dung-beetle.

A: Maybe there is a little twist there. But the point is that a little creature as the dung-beetle is just as valuable as a cloud.

Q: His traumatic war experience taught Binx a great deal. He then 'saved' Kate, figuratively speaking. But is it not ironic, perhaps part of the black comedy in the book, that Barrett in *The Last Gentleman,* who is very sick and searching for something himself, and who knows nothing of the world, should be the tutor to the dying Jamie? His general distrust of commonly accepted truths may teach something to Jamie, but basically Barrett himself is a person who is in need, in actual search of a tutor.

A: Barrett is a pretty sick boy, you know. His main talent was communication. He is described as having a sensitive radar. He knew how to get on other people's wave lengths. David Riesman would say that Barrett was a typically "other-directed man" anxious to respond properly to what others were thinking. Here is what the irony is. In that death-scene Barrett acts as almost a true radar receiving set. Jamie can talk to him; Barrett can understand him. Sutter cannot, the priest cannot. Here is Barrett acting as almost a mechanical transmitter between Jamie and the priest, between Jamie and Sutter. This very important exchange takes place between these three. Barrett is used as a transmitter; yet he himself does not understand what is going on, the only one who does not understand. Later outside he asks Sutter one question: "What happened back there?" and Sutter: "You were there. Don't you know?" There is the irony.

Q: Ordeal is one existentialist solution to escape from the malaise. How effective do you think the others, rotation and repetition, can be? Is it possible that their effect can be more than temporary?

A: To use Kierkegaard's term, they are simply aesthetic relief, therefore temporary.

Q: Friedman says that distortion can be found on the front page of any newspaper in America today. It is not the black humorist who distorts; life is distorted. Does everyday American reality stir you to write with similar directness? I ask this because once in an interview you appreciated the way Dostoevski was stirred to writing by a news item in a daily paper and because once in connection with Faulkner and Eudora Welty you referred to the social involvement of the writer as useful because social likes and dislikes, you said, can be the passion and energy you write from.

A: I see what Friedman means. Right. The danger with newspapers and TV is that it is all trivial. You remember in Camus' *The Fall:* we spend our lifetime "fornicating and reading the newspapers." I think the danger is that you can spend your life reading the New

York *Times* and never get below the surface of current events; whereas in Dostoevski's case—*The Possessed*—the whole was inspired by a news story in a Russian newspaper. I would contrast the inveterate newspaper reader and TV watcher who watches and watches and nothing happens—he is formed by the media. Dostoevski reads one news story, gets angry and this triggers a creative process.

Q: Intersubjectivity is an escape for Binx from everydayness and the other forms of the malaise, he is certainly not formed by the media. But are his aunt's values—cars, a nice home, university degree—somehow recreated through intersubjectivity so that he can go back to these formerly rejected values?

A: Yes, sure. The question is, how much? And whether he did not go a good deal beyond intersubjectivity when he regained his mother's religion. Binx says at the end that what he believes is not the reader's business, he cuts the reader loose, refuses to be edifying. This is Kierkegaard going back to Socrates, "I want no disciples."

Q: But in the next paragraph he says, "Further: I am a member of my mother's family after all and so naturally shy away from the subject of religion (a peculiar word this in the first place, *religion;* it is something to be suspicious of)." This means, it seems to me, that Binx definitely objects to being edifying, especially in a religious way.

A: Yes, if you like.

Q: *The Moviegoer* was a first-person narration. *The Last Gentleman* is not. This means a greater distance between character and writer in the latter work. Was this distancing intended by you because Barrett is so much sicker and less the person that you can identify with?

A: Yes. I wanted him seen as a patient, an ill man suffering all kinds of difficulties. In the first person it would have been incoherent because he has this in and out of amnesia.

Q: You also keep referring to him throughout as 'the engineer,' which introduces further distancing, ironic possibilities.

A: Yes, he was trying to "engineer" his own life, an impossible task. But I think most of the satire here comes from a different design of the book. It is a novel of the return. A young man returns from New York to the South in a bad time—the 1960's—when the racial conflict was at its peak. There were those really wild, extreme reactions, almost paranoid reactions of segregationists to integration. A good deal of it was satire directed to events happening in the South.

Q: I wonder why it is necessary to bring the mental sickness of these characters into such a sharp focus? Is it to perplex the world with the old enigma: are these sick people in a normal world or normal people in a sick world? Or is it the interest of the medical doctor? Or both?

A: It is partly therapeutic, medical interest but also goes deeper than that. The view of Pascal and some others who were interested in the human condition was that there is something wrong with mankind. So it is always undecided in my novels. This is the main question of the novels. Here is a hero who is afflicted, shows malaise, dislocation, and he is surrounded by apparently happy and sane people, particularly Dr. More, who lives in Paradise Estates. So who is crazy, the people apparently happy or those radically dislocated characters?

Q: Dr. More's surroundings in *Love in the Ruins* is a superb achievement of satiric art, an intricate fictional structure with an amazing satirical relevance. Even the nurse from Georgia is called Miss Oglethorpe, not mentioning the beatnik called Ginsberg, the euthanasia in the federal Good Time Garden on the Happy Isles of Georgia, or Paradise Estates itself with a host of ironic illusions.

A: It is amazing how much alike some man-made paradises are. Hilton Head Island off South Carolina with its new affluent society could have been called Paradise Estates. Yet underneath there is a good deal of malaise, a despair that does not know itself.

Q: The lapsometer, Dr. More's invention, is a central satiric device. With this, he is more than his predecessors, Binx and Barrett. He not only can diagnose the malaise but can offer a cure for others. This is well in keeping with another novelty of this book: the increased interest in the absurdities of the social scene and its relation to alienation. Does Dr. More's failure suggest that mechanical devices can be no solution, or, that the best scientific device in the wrong hands can bring about disaster?

A: Sure. Dr. More was a diagnostician. He knew something was wrong but he fell victim to pride, was seduced by the devil. Immelmann was the devil, of course, who showed Dr. More how to cure. It worked for a while. You are right. The big mistake was in him, that he could believe he could treat a spiritual disease with a scientific device however sophisticated.

Q: You are a scientist yourself, so you do not have to go far to hit upon the idea of those two electrodes in the head of "the St. Petersburg Blues." May I ask you just the same if you have read Vonnegut's *Welcome to the Monkey House* with its Ethical Suicide Parlors, or a short story in the same volume, "Harrison Bergeron"? More interesting is the parallel with Vonnegut's *The Sirens of Titan.* Perhaps you can get any number of other, purely sci-fi novels with Martians with antennae in them, but it is the coupling of technical perfection and euthanasia that makes me think of the parallel with Vonnegut.

A: I had not read that Vonnegut. I am glad I did not. I would feel bad about it.

Q: At the beginning of this talk you referred to your uncle, William Alexander Percy, who was a much respected figure in the South in his time. He attracted Carl Sandburg and others to his house.

A: He was a writer and a poet and other writers would come to his house.

Q: Faulkner used to be one of your uncle's guests. What are your memories of him?

A: All I can remember is what my uncle said, that Faulkner would drink and miss the ball when he came to play tennis.

Q: Did you ever meet him in person?

A: No, I did not meet him in person. Later—perhaps I should not speak about this—when I was 16 years old going to college at Chapel Hill with my friend, he asked me why do we not stop and see Faulkner. My friend is an outgoing and extrovert type, I was not. I was shy; so I said, "No, I don't want to." When we drove up to Faulkner's house at Oxford I told him, "You can go in, I'll stay out in the car and read." He went in and talked with him a couple of hours. I have always been sorry I did not go.

Q: Although I know you have been frequently asked about the position of the writer in the South, I would like to ask you to summarize your view on this question for the Hungarian reader for whom this talk is primarily intended and for whom your view of the writer in the South will be a novelty.

A: The position of the Southern writer now, as opposed to thirty years ago when Faulkner was writing, is more and more on a level with other writers' in other parts of the country. In other words the United States is becoming more and more homogenized. America is becoming more alike. Towns in the South lose their distinctive character. And yet, I think, in spite of this, there remains and probably there will remain a unique community in the South between black and white, so that there is much more communication, strangely enough, between middle-class white and black people in the South than there is between intellectual black and white in the North. In the South they have lived in physically intimate terms for 300 years. And whatever might have been the evils of this system, there still exists a strong historical basis of communication. I think it will continue to exist.

Q: Speaking about America, it occurs to me to ask you at this point if you have ever thought of rotation in historical aspect? Of America as a historical experience in rotation? What the settlers did coming from Europe, or the pioneers did going west was, it seems to me, as exactly zone-crossing as anything in the existentialist meaning of the term—even though the term came much later. If I may go one step further, how can you comment on the effectiveness of this rotation in the light of what you say on the first pages of *Love in the Ruins:* "our beloved old U.S.A. is in a bad way." And later, "now the blessing or the luck is over, the machinery clanks, the chain catches hold . . ."?

A: I did not think of rotation in an historical aspect. But if rotation is temporary it should run out. That makes it tough. There are more suicides in San Francisco today than in other cities; that is why the rotation has run out, which may or may not be significant. That is what Kierkegaard calls aesthetic damnation—living by rotation.

Notes

1. Walker Percy in an earlier interview has detailed the salute in *The Moviegoer* to Dostoevski's *The Brothers Karamazov.* See John Carr's "An Interview with Walker Percy," *Georgia Review,* XXV (Fall, 1971), 317–32. John Carr published the same interview in a volume he has recently edited: *Kite-Flying and Other Irrational Acts: Conversations with Twelve Southern Writers* (Baton Rouge: Louisiana State Univ. Press, 1972), 34–58.

Walker Percy Prevails
Barbara King/1974

From *Southern Voices,* 1 (May–June 1974), 19–23, and reprinted by permission.

I interviewed Walker Percy on a blazing summer
afternoon in his Covington, La., home, a quietly elegant
and awesome place isolated amidst a patch of woods
along the Bogue Falaya River. One gets the sense that
this rather shy, sensitive, brooding man *belongs* here in
these curiously gothic surroundings, where ducks and
cows roam about in the backyard just outside his bedroom office window. We sat on his screened patio overlooking the river, sipping iced tea from kelly green glasses
(the kind my mother used to retrieve from oatmeal
boxes), as his wife and older daughter—there are two—
came in and out of the room. He is lean and graying and
has milky blue, transparent eyes that, if not sad, seem
somehow inviolably internal. He had rather ask questions
than be asked them and though it's often difficult to draw
him out, I was struck by the ease with which his mind
moved over complex and subtle subjects.

BK: A college professor of mine once said that your view of human-
ity and your interest in social causes have "an enchantment that be-
speaks a distance."

WP: I really don't know what he means. I certainly don't believe
there's a *distance* between me and the story or the characters. He
must have been talking about the style, which is, I suppose, a rather
flat, unemotional one. But that's simply a matter of technique.

BK: He also described you as a romantic, but went on to say that
your Catholicism has given you a very *conventional* concept of Romanticism.

WP: Now I don't think of myself as a romantic, but I *do* think
things might have been easier if I had never been a Catholic. I've
often thought—it'll probably happen after I'm dead and gone—some

guy will come along, like they always do, and say, "If this fella hadn't been a Catholic he'd have been a pretty good writer!" In truth it's the other way around. I'm a convert and I didn't really begin to write until after I became a Catholic. I would agree with Flannery O'Connor that my Catholicism is not only not a hindrance but a *help* in my work . . . it's a way of seeing the world. I don't think my writings are meant to preach Catholicism, but the novel can't help but be informed by a certain point of view—and this happens to be a Catholic point of view.

BK: When did you convert?

WP: About 25 years ago.

BK: After you finished med school, then.

WP: Yes.

BK: You became ill around that time, didn't you?

WP: Yeah, I had to quit medicine on account of my health so I did a lot of reading. You see, I had a scientific background—I hadn't taken much English in college. This was the first chance I had to read and think, so as a result of reading Dostoevsky, Kierkegaard, and the French novelists—I didn't read any of the American novelists, incidentally, except Mark Twain—well, one thing led to another. These things work out funny. I think one of the most influential books I ever read was Dostoevsky's *Brothers Karamazov,* which is bitterly anti-Catholic.

BK: What interested you in the Russian and French novelists, as opposed to the Americans?

WP: I think my interest was mainly because of the difference in the European novel as against the English and the American novels. The European novels are more philosophical, more novels of ideas. Oftentimes, especially in France, the novelist was a philosopher or engaged in things other than writing. I'm thinking of people like Sartre, who's in politics and philosophy. And of course Dostoevsky would be inspired to write a novel because of some incident or newspaper story that made him mad or got him excited and he would set out to write a tract, something ideological. In anybody else's hands it would probably be very bad. But his genius was such that what would start out as a tract would end up to be a great novel, like *The Possessed* or *Brothers Karamazov.* The classical English novelists—Jane Austen, Dickens—were not so much interested in philosophy or ideology or ideas as they were in a portrayal of life as it was at that time. The American novel was either Romantic, as you mentioned earlier, or maybe a novel of region, like Faulkner. That never interested me much. I've always been a polemicist and a moralist. I mean moralist in a large sense, of saying this is the way the world *ought* to be and not the way it is. As I got interested in philosophy and language and linguistics I began writing articles and was able to get them published. But, number one, I didn't make any money, and, number two, nobody read them. So I thought—well, you know, wouldn't it be nice to write a *novel* saying the same thing, maybe even saying it better. After writing two bad novels which I'm glad were not published, I sat down one day in New Orleans and began to write *The Moviegoer* and all of a sudden everything fell into place for me. I got on to a certain way of writing. I saw how it was possible to translate my ideas into concrete situations. But nothing would be worse than a so-called philosophical or religious novel which simply used a story and a plot and characters in order to get over a certain idea. On the other hand, a novel in which the characters are real, the situation is real, the action is real, and which also expressed a certain point of view is what I was getting at and what I think I succeeded at in *The Moviegoer.*

BK: Many people see the book as a message of despair.

WP: Yes, you're right. I never intended that. The end, I thought, was very simple, very hopeful. Binx, the protagonist, finally emerges from his peculiar life in Gentilly and discovers what he wants to do.

BK: Would you say his life in Gentilly was a calculated despair?

WP: Exactly. He simply lived there as a rather cool, detached exercise in cultivating different sensations. And his girl friends, his business, his reading, were all a kind of playacting. But the whole idea was that he got out of it. You know, you can't make these things too explicit. People seem to have a lot of trouble with the ends of my books. . . . Maybe that's because I have trouble ending them. I can get into them but I have a hard time getting out.

BK: How long did it take you to write *The Moviegoer?*

WP: That one wasn't so bad . . . two years. It gets worse and worse. *The Last Gentleman* took three, *Love in the Ruins* four. It's getting harder instead of easier.

BK: Has *Love in the Ruins* been the most successful?

WP: By far. I don't know how these things work. I think you build up an audience, but maybe it's because the last one was a little more spectacular . . . you know, the idea of the end of the world. I think that appeals to people. It was the only one on the bestseller list. *The Moviegoer* was a flop. It fell dead from the presses. The hardcover sold maybe 10,000 at the most. If it hadn't been for a fluke it wouldn't have ever done well. It was published by Alfred Knopf—the editor read it and liked it and told Mr. Knopf and he said, "Oh, yeah, Walker Percy, isn't he the nephew of my dear old friend Will Percy? Well, sure, publish it. Will's nephew's book has *got* to be all right." He *had* been a friend of Uncle Will's and in fact published his novel, *Lanterns on the Levee,* a long time ago. I was told he didn't bother to read *The Moviegoer* until he published it . . . then he read it and disliked it. And I don't know whether it was a consequence, but the editor who liked it was fired shortly thereafter. So as a result the book received no publicity. Anyway, most first novels don't do well.

BK: But you won the National Book Award.

WP: Just by accident. It wasn't because Knopf recommended it. Jean Stafford happened to get it and read it. She was one of the judges. The story I heard—I never knew if it was true or not—was that her husband was down here in Louisiana writing a book about Earl Long. He happened to see this book and wanted to read something about the local color of New Orleans. He liked it and gave it to his wife and she gave it to the judges and that way, by a stroke of luck, it happened to win the National Book Award, which was the same year *Catch-22* was published. So I was *really* lucky.

BK: You think a lot of Joseph Heller, then.

WP: Oh, yeah . . . well . . . I liked *Catch-22.* It's one of the few books I can re-read, even though I have reservations about the end of it. He has the hero copping out of the war completely, getting in a boat and rowing to Sweden. The trouble was, as Heller admitted later, he picked the wrong war. It would have made better sense in the Vietnam war. But his antiwar message in *Catch-22* doesn't really stack up too well when you consider the fact that Heller is Jewish and six million Jews were killed by the Germans. So if ever there was a justifiable war that was probably it. Still it's a very readable book. I've been waiting for his second novel but apparently he can't get out of that B24 he's been in for 25 years.

BK: Do you more or less isolate yourself here?

WP: Oh, I wouldn't say that—you're here! I don't seek publicity and I generally avoid it if I can. I seldom accept invitations to literary events, festivals, or lectures and so forth.

BK: Why is that?

WP: I'd as soon stay here and write or read. It's an awful lot of trouble going somewhere. Like Faulkner said when he was invited by President Kennedy to a dinner in Washington. "That's a long way to go to eat."

(A motor boat passes on the Bogue Falaya just outside the back porch, drowning out his voice).

WP: This goes on all summer, unfortunately. Do you water ski? (I answer no and try to return to my questioning, but his constantly probing curiosity and tendency to keep turning the interview around took over for a while as I told him a little about *myself.*)

BK: Did your uncle have a strong influence on your life? My professor kept referring to both of you as aristocrats, to him as a great patrician of the Delta.

WP: Good God, I didn't know we *had* any aristocrats in this country. In fact I do owe my uncle a great deal. He's one of the few people I ever met who . . . I don't know if you *ever* had a really great teacher; you're lucky if you have one or two in your lifetime. He was one . . . the sort of man who had this electrical quality. He loved beautiful things—art, music, literature. He could make you *see* it, see it the way *he* saw it; he could get you excited about it. As the kids say, he "turned me on" to literature, made me see what was good and what wasn't. A great deal of *The Moviegoer* and *The Last Gentleman* have to do with the differences between me and my uncle. The whole thing is a dialectic between his attitude, which *was* a Southern patrician paternalism, and the attitude of the two young men in these novels, a more detached, alienated point of view. (He pauses, contemplating, for a minute.) You know, what I envy you for is the fact that you see different people in your work. You might not appreciate that now but if you wrote fiction, you'd realize that everything you see or do, you record. People have this misconception when they read a novel: they try to recognize characters. They say, "this person is so-and-so." That's not the way it works. What happens is that when you have an experience, meet people, it gets into your unconscious. Your creative power draws on all these things and fuses them in different ways. So when these characters emerge they *do* come from past experience. Without that, you're sunk.

BK: At the same time it sharpens those powers of observation and puts you in touch with what you're experiencing.

WP: Absolutely. Journalism is nothing to sneeze at. There's nothing wrong with writing a good, clear, clean-cut news story.

BK: Where did you get your first writing experience?

WP: Oh, I used to write the gossip column, "The Man in the Moon," for the Greenville, Miss., high school paper. And I also used to write sonnets when I was a junior. We had a good English teacher and were given the assignment of composing a sonnet . . . I discovered I could write them with great facility. They weren't much good, but I could make them rhyme and come out with the right number of lines. I could do it so well, in fact, that I sold them for 50 cents apiece. Then I began writing for the high school paper. I wrote a few poems which were dreadful, and when I went to college—Chapel Hill—I wrote for their journal. You know, a friend of mine discovered I had written articles for the student magazine and dug them up and wrote an article about *them,* to my mortification. They were terrible. You know what they were about? Moviegoing, I enjoyed writing but then I got sidetracked into medicine for several years. So when I got sick it was a good excuse to start writing again.

BK: So you didn't particularly want to go into medicine?

WP: Not particularly.

BK: Did you do it for someone else? Your uncle, maybe?

WP: Yeah, my uncle wanted me to. But it wasn't his fault. He told me I could do what I wanted but everybody in my family had been a lawyer and I didn't want to do that. So I figured, well—medicine was respectable. It never occurred to me to set out to become a writer. That *wasn't* respectable, you see.

BK: That's odd, since your uncle was a writer.

WP: But he was primarily a lawyer. He went to Harvard Law School and was a planter and a poet.

BK: Were you living here on the Bogue Falaya when you started writing seriously?

WP: No, I started up in New York State, in the Adirondacks. I was reading a lot and found a book which got me excited. You know,

that's the whole secret to writing. You have to get excited about
something, either for or against it. It doesn't matter which, really.
Otherwise I don't see how anybody ever could set pen to paper. You
know, it's such hard work . . . it's really *murder*. Anyway I read a
book by a lady, a philosopher named Susanne Langer, called *Philosophy in a New Key,* which concentrates on language. I thought
she had gotten hold of something and then turned around and let it
get away from her. I wrote an article saying what was right and what
was wrong with her book. You see, to be a writer you have to be
conceited, you have to think you know more than anybody else. So I
wrote it and sent it off to a journal called *Thought* and they *accepted*
it, they *published* it. I got no money but they sent me a whole stack
of reprints, which I've still got upstairs. Anyway, I thought, "Gee, this
is great. I can write something and publish it." I then wrote several
such obscure articles for obscure journals. It really is such a great
pleasure the first time you see yourself in print—it *looks* different. It
looks better than it sounds, actually.

BK: It must be a bit frightening to see your first *book* in print,
though.

WP: You mean waiting for the reviews?

BK: Oh, no . . . the feeling that there you are, exposed, a little like
being naked in a way, vulnerable.

WP: That's true. Except I had a painter friend of mine tell me
about that. He said, "You writers are lucky. You don't expose your-
selves, really. You publish a book and there's the book and you have
to turn one page after the other to get at it. With a painting, there's
the whole thing right there at once." There you are—as you said—
exposed. So he felt painters were more vulnerable.

BK: I think perhaps they can cloak it better.

WP: Yes, but then it depends on what you're doing. There are
roughly two schools of writing. There's the modern confessional
style, where the writer simply writes a straight autobiography of what
he or she is doing or thinking. It's straight confession and that *is*
vulnerable because that's *yourself.* The other is the conventional
novel, which is presumably more objective, more at a distance.

BK: Maybe it's that the *reader* feels vulnerable, sometimes even
embarrassed—that sense of "Christ, I've been discovered, found out.
Someone knows all about me." That's the feeling with your books.

WP: That's good. Theoretically that's supposed to be a pleasure
. . . the so-called shock of recognition. That's what the writer is always aiming for. He's trying to tell you something you know, but
don't *know* you know; so that you say yeah . . . that's the way it is.

BK: What role has psychiatry played in your writing?

WP: Mainly for satirical purposes, I guess. In two novels I've used
a psychiatrist, not so much to show how much he knew or how
much can be gained from psychiatry, but to show the limitations of it.
In both cases the character is seeing a psychiatrist and either the
patient and doctor weren't communicating at all, or else the patient
had exhausted the psychiatrist, had gotten everything he could from
him and then just went on to something else. There's a tendency in
this culture to treat psychiatry as a religion—thrilling that you can get
your salvation from it, that the answer is there if you can just find the
right analyst, the right group, react to the right group dynamics. In
my case I went through two years of Freudian analysis. At the time I
thought maybe Freud was the answer, and he is indeed a great man.
I certainly don't want to put him down, but I elevated him far beyond
the point that even he would place himself. At one point he said that
when it comes to the ultimate mysteries of the human mind, the
psychiatrist must yield to the artist, to the writer. He was talking about
Da Vinci, Dostoevsky. But now there is a cult of psychiatry; it's almost
a religious thing. In fact, it's all confused with Eastern religion. So I
use it that way in my novels, and the other way is as a kind of science
fiction device. In *Love in the Ruins* Dr. Thomas More invents a machine that can diagnose anything that ails you, which he calls a lapsometer. I use a kind of superficial knowledge of psychiatry to make
this device plausible. But I can't say that psychiatry is essential to or
has a deep significance in my writing.

BK: Are you working on anything now?

WP: I've done a couple of long articles which I've been trying to
do for years . . . always going backwards. The thing that got me
excited 25 years ago was language, and I always go back to that in
between books. So I've done these pieces and now I'm through with
it—I hope forever. I'm now at work on a long novel. It's a very
strange thing. I was thinking last night—you have an idea, and if
good things happen to it, it'll begin to grow. It's kind of like pregnancy, I guess. In fact, I read an article recently by a critic who said

there's a big feminine streak in a writer because a novel has to grow like a child. And it's an organic thing—either it grows and takes on an independent existence or it doesn't work at all. You can't force your own intentions on it, you can't push it this way or that way. It has to go its own way.

BK: Do you write every day?

WP: When I'm *writing,* I do. You have to. God help you if you don't. You've got to try, you've got to sit down and follow a schedule. Everybody's different, everybody's habits are different. I have to sit down at 9 o'clock in the morning and write for three hours or at least look at the paper for three hours. Sometimes I don't do *anything.* But unless you do that—punch the time clock—you won't *ever* do anything.

BK: Are you distracted much by the noises around here?

WP: Oh, no. In fact I don't mind having *kids* around. The distractions are when you go wrong, when you try to force your creation in the direction it doesn't want to go. I can get off the track for months and write 200 pages that are not good. All of a sudden I'll read it and see how far off I am and then I have to back up six months.

BK: It must make you feel like ending it *all* right then and there.

WP: No, not really. Because you knew all along something was wrong. You have this uneasiness. It's like amputating a gangrened arm—you get rid of it and make a fresh start.

BK: Do you ever get bogged down in the most trivial problems? Should it or shouldn't it read this way? Will he do this or that?

WP: Absolutely, absolutely. In fact it's the hardest thing in the world just to get a character from one room into the other. What do you say? Does he get up and walk through the door? How will he do it? It's then I feel like a sophomore.

BK: I can often get hung up on the simplest word, even in my news stories.

WP: Yes . . . I can get at a loss for a word. Don't think I don't need a thesaurus. You can get blocked, your mind can go blank, so you use a thesaurus to free-associate in order to get different words going. But the strange thing is, nobody really knows how the creative process works. On those days or mornings when you feel worst, when you think everything is hopeless, that nothing will happen—sometimes the *best* things happen.

BK: How do you mean?

WP: Often you feel stupid for an hour, and look at the stupid page for an hour, and then something will light up.

BK: You probably have a rather scientific approach.

WP: Well, I still keep up with medicine. I write articles, mostly in psychiatric journals. Of course, having a scientific education, I figured I might as well use it. So I used it in a kind of science-fiction way in *Love in the Ruins*—more satirically, for comic-serious purposes. The good thing about knowing a little science or a little psychiatry is you realize how little is known about them at all. So then you can do whatever you like, make up anything you please.

BK: Have you ever gotten anything wrong? Your description of the telescope in *The Last Gentleman* was wonderful, but I kept thinking, "My god, what if he doesn't know what he's talking about!?"

WP: I didn't, I didn't. I just made it up. Except there *is* such a telescope. They cost $1,000.

BK: Yours was $1,900.

WP: (laughter) It was better. Sure. He could see more.

BK: I read once you said you couldn't write short stories. I empathize. I can come up with brilliant titles, but no plots to accompany them.

WP: We should collaborate—I can never think of titles.

BK: Have you ever collaborated with anyone before?

WP: I don't know how you would *do* that, because writing seems to me to be a solitary, private, miserable business.

BK: Unless it's comic material, I guess.

WP: Or musicals . . . lyrics and melodies.

BK: Do you see a kind of humor to everything?

WP: I don't see it, no. But somehow or other my writings take a sideways, ironic view of things. I'm not sure how that comes about. I guess my natural style has a certain irony or satire to it.

BK: Yes, a kind of double vision.

WP: Right. It's what the modern critics call black humor, making fun of what you're not supposed to. You know, I'm in a very peculiar position for a writer. For instance, a lot of people think of me as a Catholic writer and yet Catholics think I'm a real nut. So I usually find myself falling somewhere in between. I don't exactly know where I belong. Non-Catholics put me with Catholics and the Catholics would like to get rid of me.

BK: I've never thought of you as a Catholic writer, really. But I suppose the alienation of the characters in your books has a kind of peculiar quality. And you never deal explicitly with sex.

WP: Oh! There again I'm in trouble. Most critics say that I'm unnecessarily reserved on describing sexual behavior and they ask me why I'm so circumspect with love scenes. And yet I went to a party and some lady came up to me and said, "I read your book and you've got a dirty mind." So am I prissy or dirty-minded?"

BK: Well . . . I certainly found many of your scenes quite *sexual,* in spite of all. What do you think—as a psychiatrist, knowing of Freud—about the sexual revolution? Freud thought mores should be modified, that some values should still endure.

WP: *Love in the Ruins,* of course, is partly a satire on the so-called sexual revolution. Particularly the Masters and Johnson Clinic. There's a love clinic in the novel, where you have love and sex as a piece of objective behavior, like a rabbit going through a maze in psychology classes. The purpose of the satire was—I suppose this is ultimately a Catholic or a Judeo-Christian point of view—that sex is a mystery, that you cannot understand it as simply as a piece of over-behavior which can be studied as stimulus and response. Ultimately it's a mystery, and it's distorting to study it in that kind of clinical laboratory. That was the direction of that satire. I'm in fact getting increasingly revolted by the trend of a certain branch of the American novel, which is more and more explicit with all kinds of sexual encounters—natural, perverted, and otherwise. This can be applied to violence too. It's just that I think this was not required by the great writers of the past . . . it was not required by Aeschylus or Shakespeare or Dante or Tolstoy or Faulkner or Sartre: All this lurid sexuality and lurid violence distracts the reader from the real purpose of art. I don't mean that sex or violence should be excluded from art, but rather integrated into the whole artistic process; to have circus sex going on page after page may be psychology, but it ain't art. As Faulkner said, the one kind of writing has to do with glands and the other with art . . . which has always to do with the human heart. So it's a hard question. I think the sexual revolution is good in the sense that nothing should be suppressed. A writer should be free to say anything he wants, and free to use any material he wants for what he's trying to do. But the novel has gotten so *crazy* nowadays.

BK: Do you think there are many good Southern novelists writing today?

WP: Well, the so-called Southern thing is over and done with, I think.

BK: Because the North and South are becoming one?

WP: Yeah, right. Until recently, it was the Jewish renaissance, not the Southern renaissance. The Jewish thing seems to have run its course quicker than most. For the last 15 years most of the exciting writers have been Jewish: Saul Bellow, Isaac Bashevis Singer, Bernard Malamud. People always ask me who the best Southern writers are today. That's hard. I can't think of very many.

BK: There's still a peculiar quality—not like Faulkner, not with that kind of regionalism—but a distinct feeling about Southern writing.

WP: Particularly by a woman. If you're going to be a writer, there's a double obstacle to overcome. You have to transcend it. I don't mean stop being a Southerner, but avoid that particular *stereotyped* Southern writing. The other is being a woman writer . . . the kind of writing I call "white lady" writing, which I can recognize after the first paragraph. It's kind of bad Eudora Welty—who is very good indeed. It's very good when it's done right, but Eudora did it so well that Southern women writers are just going to have to get beyond that. There's a writer named Ellen Douglas from Greenville, Miss., who's very good, and Berry Morgan, from Port Gibson, Miss., who writes mostly short stories for *The New Yorker*.

But back to your question about Southern writing in general. There was a time when the South was really *different* from the rest of the country, being in the unique position of tragedy and defeat and romantic nostalgia for the past. But as Southern culture began to merge with the rest of American culture, Southern writers began to make their experiences universal. Of course, it started with Faulkner and Thomas Wolfe. And then 20 or 30 good writers, the agrarian poets like John Crowe Ransom, Allen Tate, Robert Penn Warren, and Cleanth Brooks, and a lot of novelists like Eudora Welty and Flannery O'Connor entered the scene. Faulkner was writing about these strange people and strange towns in Mississippi which *may* have existed at one time but they *don't* exist now. . . . Yet Faulkner was talking about universal things, about human beings. This kind of Southern writing lasted for about a generation until finally the cultures merged. The big question now is, what does a Southern writer do? That's maybe what your generation is going to have to decide. *Mine* has spent most of its time getting out from under Faulkner. . . . He was a great writer but he's also been a great burden. I can think of any number of Southern writers my age who've been cursed by him, imitating his sentences and scenes and characters. I was lucky because he never meant much to me, although he lived just a few miles away. He was a friend of my uncle, and he used to come over dead drunk and try to play tennis. . . . He'd fall flat on his face every time. But anyway, I didn't care about this so-called Southern thing, the myths, the story-telling, the complex family situations, anecdotes—I was concerned with what happens to an alienated young man who in fact was fed up with the whole Southern scene. He'd run out of it, didn't know what to do. So what becomes of him when you put him down in a place like Gentilly? Odd country characters are not the scene anymore; the scene is what to do with a big urban sprawl like Baton Rouge. How're you gonna write that? How're you gonna write about New Orleans—not the French Quarter, but Gentilly? The function of writers and novelists and poets is probably the highest in the culture, because their job is to make people understand themselves. You were saying a while ago about reading a novel and recognizing yourself—that's the purpose of the novelist and poet.

BK: Do you think there are any Southern writers besides yourself who are creating a new Southern writing?

WP: I would have said Flannery O'Connor if she hadn't died. I guess Eudora Welty is the best we've got now, although sometimes I have trouble reading even *her*. I loved *The Optimist's Daughter,* but had trouble with *Losing Battles.* We've been marking time for years now and I don't know what's gonna happen. You're probably in a better position than I am to talk about it. What do you think?

BK: I think it'll be a long dry spell. You know, I believe you can usually tell from the first paragraph of a book whether it's going to be any good. There's something about *talent.* It's like turning on a

switch and there's a kind of electric hum . . . You can *feel* it. That's
how it is with your books, particularly *The Last Gentleman*. Suddenly, in a few words, you're into the *movement* of the story.

WP: Well something's got to happen right away. I remember one
time Caroline Gordon, a wonderful writer, showed me a manuscript
one of her students turned in. The first hundred pages had to do with
the thoughts of a young man as he was lying in bed facing the wall.
And I said, "Well, this is pretty boring," and she said "yeah." I asked
her what she told the guy and she said that after the first paragraph
either you've got to get out of bed and do something or else somebody's got to get in with you. Then she quoted a poem of A. E.
Housman's, "Clay lies still, but blood's a rover." That means that the
novel has to do with *action,* with an encounter between two people.
It's an old formula, very simple but very necessary. You know, I feel
sorry for people just starting out to write. Not long ago there was a
knock on the door and a young man, a total stranger, was standing
there and he said, "Are you the writer Walker Percy?" I told him I
was and he asked if he could talk to me. "I want to be a writer," he
said, "and somebody told me you could tell me how." So he came in
and sat for a while and I realized he just wanted to "become a
writer." He wanted to be magically transformed into another category. He wanted to be what a writer *is.* Finally he said he thought it
would be a good idea to interview me and he could write *that* and
sell it, I told him I didn't think that would work; it might be a better
idea to get a job and support himself. It took me 10 years before I
made a halfway decent living. And the only way you become a writer
is the obvious: *Write.*

Walker Percy Talks about Kierkegaard: An Annotated Interview

Bradley R. Dewey/1974

From *The Journal of Religion,* 54 (July 1974), 273–98. Reprinted by permission of *The Journal of Religion,* the University
of Chicago, and Bradley R. Dewey.

The main body of this article is an interview with contemporary American novelist Walker Percy which explores some dominant religious
influences on his novels, especially Kierkegaard's central role in shaping Percy's theological and psychological perceptions. But before pro-
ceeding to the interview, a few introductory remarks about Percy are in
order.

There have been Percys in the Deep South since 1776 when
Charles Percy, a British naval lieutenant, made his fortune in the Spanish territory which is now Mississippi. Links to the landed aristocracy of
the South include Confederate leaders and a United States senator.
Into this rich heritage Walker Percy was born in 1916. His father
committed suicide when Percy was eleven, and his mother died in an
automobile accident two years later. Percy and his two younger
brothers were conscientiously raised by William Alexander Percy, the
senator's son and their father's bachelor cousin. In addition to his role
as gentleman planter and lawyer (Harvard Law School), "Uncle Will"
was a published poet and essayist. Literary figures frequented his
Greenville, Mississippi home, and Faulkner occasionally played tennis
on the Percy's court. While an undergraduate chemistry major at the
University of North Carolina, Walker Percy wrote some articles for the
campus literary magazine. In 1937 he went north to Columbia Medical
School, receiving his M.D. in 1941 and interning in pathology at Bellevue Hospital in New York. While performing an autopsy on a tubercular body he contracted pulmonary tuberculosis. During his years of
slow convalescence he engaged in serious reading and reflection
which led him to leave medicine and turn toward writing. Fortunately,
his economic independence made this possible. This major career

change followed three years of Freudian analysis during medical school and was related to his rising awareness of the limitations of mechanistic science, as well as his increasing doubts about his commitment to the practice of medicine. By his own account, the decision to leave medicine and devote himself to writing made him feel happy, liberated, and even "saved," in some sense of the word. That first rush of freedom was followed by years of hard work as he labored through challenging works of technical philosophy and European literature.

From 1954 to 1961 he wrote twenty-four articles for a range of journals including the *Sewanee Review,* the *Journal of Philosophy, Commonweal,* and *Psychiatry.*[1] During this time he also wrote two novels which were not published. His first published novel, *The Moviegoer,* came out in 1961 without much fanfare and surprised many by winning the National Book Award. Alfred Kazin captures the moment and communicates much about Percy: "In 1962 the National Book Award for fiction was awarded to a first novel, *The Moviegoer,* by an unknown writer in Louisiana. . . . The astonished and grateful author . . . quietly accepted the award in New York . . . and returned to his house, wife and two daughters in Covington, in the parish of St. Tammany, a small town on the other side of Lake Ponchartrain from New Orleans, where he lived a most comfortable and studious existence and wrote in the bedroom. The ladies in their set—the best in Covington—often asked Mrs. Percy how she could bear having her husband around the house all day."[2] Since the award, the pattern of reading, writing articles, and working on novels has continued. *The Last Gentleman* (runner-up for the National Book Award) came out in 1966, followed in 1971 by *Love in the Ruins.* He continues to live quietly in Covington, writing on a range of topics, chief among them the philosophy of language, and is at work on another novel.

Percy's trilogy presents those common human predicaments which entrap and disable so many of us, maps the contours of the ailing American psyche, diagnoses the problem as essentially spiritual, and advances toward a Catholic resolution. His first novel, *The Moviegoer,* is about a young New Orleans stockbroker named Binx Bolling who acts out the role of successful businessman, Lothario, and son of the upper-middle-class South, while at the same time carrying on a private, metaphysical search. Binx quests after a way to live in the world yet be free from the despairing malaise of everydayness that stifles us and blinds us to the wonder and mystery of life. Percy's innocent-looking prose hypnotically draws the reader toward pangs of self-recognition. The novel can also be experienced as a purely abstract musical creation, mood filled, elegiac in style, lingeringly lovely and haunting. *The Last Gentleman* charts the psychic health and disease of a displaced Southerner named Bibb Barrett who has dropped out of Princeton to work nights as a humidification engineer at Macy's in New York. Until the plot gets underway, Barrett spends his days regretting his years in psychoanalysis and observing New York through his $1,900 telescope. Beset by amnesia, daydreams, and disorienting fits of *déjà vu*, Barrett struggles to discover how to live in the ordinary without succumbing either to it or to immuring eccentricity. Faint glimmers of grace and hope begin to lighten his way. Departing from his previous languid pace and elegant indirection, Percy's *Love in the Ruins* hits the reader full in the face with a rollicking, lusty satire set in Louisiana during the 1980s ("at a time near the end of the world"). Simultaneously frightening and outrageously funny, the novel describes a future America where our current problems—polarization, technological breakdown, psychic estrangement—have pushed us to the brink of apocalypse. The issues confronted and the solution suggested leave no doubt that Percy stands firmly, if humanly, in the orthodox Catholic tradition. Wilfrid Sheed remarks that "it is a risky thing for a satirist to blow his cover like this."[3] But Percy takes the risk and carries it off beautifully.

With three novels out, Percy is only in midcareer—despite his fifty-seven years. Yet the high critical praise and wide popular acclaim (one selection by the Literary Guild, another by the Book-of-the-Month Club) he has received mark him as undoubtedly one of America's most gifted writers. In a way, it is rather surprising. His first two novels give voice to intricate ideas which are elusive and only whisper to us from behind a gauze of mood. The third novel has been criticized for being so direct that readers miss the point. His prose is often mannered, almost courtly. His low-profile treatment of sex (fadeouts and sentences like, "He held her charms in his arms") annoys some reviewers. He is a Southerner but not really a "Southern writer." Wearing one's Catholic heart on one's sleeve while writing about the Fall and spiritual regeneration is not too fashionable. His removed way of life and relaxed personal style do not make exciting promotional copy.

(While appearing on William Buckley's "Firing Line" television program, Percy was his usual unruffled and civil self, despite the host's frenetic pace and jabbing comments.[4]) But he is hardly a prude or a Savonarola or a hermit. He sings the praises of all of nature (including the "fair sex"), wears his faith with "solemn levity,"[5] knows what is happening beyond the bayous. Clichés easily cluster around Percy: Southerner, Catholic, gentleman, moderate, etc. They seem to fit, and yet they do not. Percy draws on these traditions, but he reworks them slyly, wryly, takes the embarrassment out of them, gives them new life just when many thought they were going to expire. Perhaps part of Percy's depth and power derive from his ability to combine things which seem so permanently rent asunder these days—body and soul, hopes and fears, heaven and earth. He definitely seems to be onto something.

What is he onto? How did he get onto it? How has he moved from nontheistic humanism to Roman Catholicism? From pathologist of the body to diagnostician of the spirit? What are the religious and psychological wellsprings for this impressive literary achievement? How did Kierkegaard come to play so central a role in shaping his fiction? The interview which follows reveals Percy's own answers to these questions.

On the plane bound for New Orleans ("The City That Care Forgot," said the brochure), I had a few cares on my mind. The next day I was to interview American novelist Walker Percy at his Covington, Louisiana, home. I had never done anything like this before and was concerned about how the interview would go. Earlier I had written Percy to ask if I could talk to him about the influence of Søren Kierkegaard on his three novels. His acceptance had been most gracious and included an invitation to lunch for me and my wife, who now sat next to me in the plane thumbing a magazine. I was trying to concentrate on rereading Percy's latest novel, *Love in the Ruins,* but my mind kept straying to the upcoming interview. What will he be like? Will my questions lead anywhere worthwhile? Will his responses be open or guarded?

I had been reading Percy for several years and greatly admired his work, regularly including it in a course I teach on religion and literature. I had been reading Kierkegaard even longer, and kept finding

Kierkegaard's ideas—fragments of them, echoes, intimations—woven into the intricate design of Percy's prose. Or at least I thought I sensed them there. It was this elusive Kierkegaardian presence that I wanted to find out about. How much of it was really there and how much was I reading in? Had Percy read deeply in Kierkegaard, or had he skimmed off just enough for literary ornamentation? Had Kierkegaard really influenced Percy, or did they just sound alike? There were other questions, too. I had some guesses about the answers; tomorrow, I hoped, I would know.

The next morning my wife and I drove north from New Orleans toward Covington, the splendid causeway guiding the rental car straight as an arrow above the vast, sparkling waters of Lake Pontchartrain. We seemed to be leaving the busy mainland behind and sailing out toward some remote, unexplored island.

The Percys welcomed us most cordially, and, sherry glasses in hand, we strolled down to the bayou in front of their house and sat on the dock in the warm November sun and talked. After a delicious luncheon, the ladies went outside and I went to work. Only it did not seem like work. Percy's relaxed and unassuming manner had put me at ease, so that the next two hours of our "interview" became conversation.

I had been wondering for a long time just how Percy had gotten into Kierkegaard, how much he had read, and how developed his understanding was. Kierkegaard wrote numerous books, essays, and diaries. Much of his writing is devilishly hard to grasp, and the meaning of an individual book comes clearest only when it is seen in the interconnecting network of his entire voluminous literature. Many readers give up on Kierkegaard. Worse yet, others settle for a superficial or distortingly partial reading. How would it be for Percy? The flyleaf quotations of his first two novels are taken from Kierkegaard. Within the novels he refers to "the great Danish philosopher," locates the devil's homebase in Copenhagen, names a movie theater the Tivoli. Kierkegaardian concepts are openly named in the novels. These and other surface connections were obvious. But there were problems. Only half of Kierkegaard's concept of repetition (a variety of déjà vu with a theological dimension) was used. One flyleaf quotation seemed to be cited badly out of context. The darker aspects of Kierkegaard's writings—the suicide undertones in parts of *Either/Or,* the sufferings of religious martyrs, the anguish of doubt, dread, the absurd—did not seem present in the novels. But we began at the beginning.

Dewey: When did you first hear about Kierkegaard?

Percy: Reading the modern existentialists. You can't read much of Jaspers or Heidegger, or even Sartre or particularly Marcel, without coming across references to Kierkegaard. Of course I had heard of him before. But after I began reading the French existentialists I soon realized that Kierkegaard was the founding father of the movement. They all credit him with that, even the atheistic existentialists—Sartre, Heidegger.

Percy's opportunity for such wide reading came about in an unusual way. Born in Birmingham, Alabama, in 1916, he graduated as a chemistry major from the University of North Carolina in 1937 and received his M.D. from Columbia four years later. As a resident in pathology at New York's Bellevue Hospital, often performing autopsies on tubercular patients, he contracted pulmonary tuberculosis. After a year's convalescence he returned to teach pathology at Columbia Medical School, then suffered a relapse and spent several months in another tuberculosis sanitorium.

Dewey: Did you read any Kierkegaard in the sanitorium?

Percy: No. I was reading novels mostly, and linguistic philosophy, the philosophy of language. I was much more interest in Ernst Cassirer's philosophy of symbolic forms along with people like Susanne Langer and the logical positivists of the time. The existentialism came later. I guess it was a kind of reaction against the linguistic analytic philosophy of England and Austria. But that reaction came years later. Before that, I was much interested in Russian—European— novels, for example, Dostoevsky and Camus.

After working through some philosophers of language, European novelists, and existentialists, Percy came to Kierkegaard in the early 1950s. It was almost their first *and last* meeting.

Dewey: Do you remember the first book by Kierkegaard which you read?

Percy: Yes, it was his first one: *Either/Or.* I remember thinking that this was going to be an easy one because of the section on "The Diary of the Seducer" in there. I'd been reading that the existentialists claimed him as their intellectual progenitor, so I was expecting something as accessible as Sartre's plays and novels or Marcel's plays. It was very difficult to read. I thought it was a hopeless undertaking.

So after trying that I tried a couple of other things. *Sickness unto Death* is a great title but I found myself in difficulty all over again. It is very difficult to read. *Repetition* is difficult. But I had almost given up when I skipped to *Concluding Unscientific Postscript.* Either I had read somewhere or somebody had told me that that book had the most direct kind of communication. And fortunately, perhaps because I had had such trouble before, I had no difficulty. I could read that straight through. It was, to me, the real open door into Kierkegaard.

Of course, there is no trouble reading the *Edifying Discourses* since they are very homiletic in nature. But that wasn't what I was after, really.

Dewey: Kierkegaard's ideas on despair and the self from *Sickness unto Death*—how despair permeates society and how the individual struggles with this—seem to come through a lot in your novels.

Percy: I worked hard on *Sickness unto Death.* I knew he was getting at something very important, very important to me, and I finally got it. Strangely enough, the harder you work at it the more important it seems to be to you when you finally do understand what he is getting at.

The whole history of my reading Kierkegaard consists of repeated attempts of reading and then frustration, leaving it alone and then coming back to it and reading it again. I'd read *Postscript* then go back and try to read *Repetition,* because in *Postscript* he would sum up all the works and the different stages. I would read about the stages and then go back and try to read Kierkegaard's book, *Stages on Life's Way*—which I never did like as well as the description of the stages in *Postscript.* So really *Postscript* was a kind of oasis. I'd go back there to get straight on things, gather more energy, and get up nerve—then take out into the desert to try to figure out Kierkegaard's pseudonymous writings.

So reading Kierkegaard is like growing up; it takes a long time, many years, a lot of work. And I still can't say that I have read him thoroughly or even completely.

I empathized with Percy's pain, having experienced it myself. But my difficulties were eased by such helpful mentors as Paul Holmer and Gregor Malantschuk, along with the commentaries on Kierkegaard available by the 1960s. Percy had gone it alone, had persevered without benefit of graduate school seminars and interpretive guides.

Dewey: Did you talk to other people about Kierkegaard?
Percy: There was nobody to talk to.

Not only had he persevered, he had won. The more we talked, the clearer it became that Percy had read much of Kierkegaard and understood it deeply. I had been steeped in the academic side of Kierkegaard study for a dozen years—publishing a book and articles on him, teaching an annual Kierkegaard seminar—and my ears were tuned to the Kierkegaardian wavelength. Percy was definitely on it. As we talked, he moved progressively through the Kierkegaardian literature, using technical jargon (*sub specie aeterni*, teleological suspension of the ethical, Hegelian mediation, etc.) with ease and accuracy. He kept Kierkegaard's distinctions (immediate/mediate, Christianity/Christendom, etc.) clear, and deftly worked the Kierkegaardian dialectic which weaves fascinating relationships between the musical and the erotic, the comic and the religious. Before Percy the novelist emerged he had passed through the stages of Percy the ex-physician and intense reader of philosophy. Obviously he had read many of Kierkegaard's books, had worked for years to plumb their depths, and had acquired the kind of understanding which enabled him to apply Kierkegaard with accuracy and subtlety to today's issues.

Having learned that Percy had indeed read and understood much of Kierkegaard, I was eager to discover what personal impact, if any, Kierkegaard had made on him. Were there any lasting impressions, or had Kierkegaard been relegated to Percy's undifferentiated category of "interesting books once read"? We got onto that topic sooner than I expected.

Dewey: I am wondering about Kierkegaard's opposition to the idea of "going beyond" Christianity into some kind of vague, human-

istic mysticism. Hegel went beyond Christianity to a general humanism, blending all specific religions together into an absolute religion. It
seems that in all your novels there is someone who wants to go beyond Christianity.

Percy: Yes. But not just going beyond it. I would say that Christianity was absolutely the last solution they would have accepted.
They would begin by eliminating Christianity, and not even consider
it as a viable alternative. My own development, and it is also important in the novels, has been a relationship to humanism—humanism
understood as a non-Christian humanism, a secular, scientific
humanism. I suppose the great bombshell with me was the famous
passage of Kierkegaard's describing Hegel as the philosopher who
lived in a shanty outside the palace of his own system and saying that
Hegel knew everything and said everything, except what it is to be
born and to live and to die. He left out something! For me, the great
thing about Kierkegaard was that he expressed my own feelings
about the whole scientific synthesis. You see, my whole education
had been in science for twenty-five years, particularly at Columbia
University Medical School. You could describe that as almost the
quintessential institute of scientific humanism. And so I had my feelings that this was not enough, that there was something left over, that
after you say all this, after you learn everything that you can at Columbia about what it is to be a human being, there is something
awfully important left over. I was trying to systematize it, to see how
you could talk about it. And having been brought up scientifically, I
had a great respect for scientific rigor, rigor and precision of language.
I certainly didn't want to say, well, besides science we have emotion
and art—that's the alternative. Of course, that had been the standard
alternative, the American philosophical alternative starting with Dewey. On the one hand there was a science and on the other hand there
was art, or play, or emotion. I knew that wasn't right. There had to be
a more serious alternative than that. And so you can imagine what an
eye opener it was to stumble on a couple of passages by Kierkegard
who was saying (and the existentialists—like I said, I read the French
existentialists first—seemed to be saying the same thing) that something has been left out by any kind of synthesis, by a scientific synthesis or a philosophical synthesis. And that, namely, what is left out
is nothing less than the individual himself. This was a tremendous
breakthrough, very exciting—if this was true. Then of course what I

discovered was that this was Kierkegaard's main subject of interest. Number one, the fact that the individual—what it is to be a man, to live and to die, to be an individual—is left out of the Hegelian system. But then he goes on to define what it is to be an individual. This is the other great thing. Here he says something that is just as staggering as the first statement. Namely, that—did he say it in *Sickness unto Death?*—the only way to be yourself is to be yourself transparently before God. It was a most enigmatic statement, but very important.

So what was important about Kierkegaard to me was that he was a man who was trying to open up a whole new area of knowledge to me in the most serious way, in the most precise way—and quite as serious as any science, or more serious. And, of course, it is religious too. This was a far cry from the other alternative that I had always read about, that the alternative to science is art, play, emotion. I saw for the first time through Kierkegaard how to take the alternative system seriously, how to treat it as a serious thinker, as a serious writer. Before that I would have simply seen it as just religion or emotion. I hadn't seen any way to think about it. Kierkegaard gave me a way to think about it.

I was not really prepared for this disclosure that Kierkegaard had been an "eye-opener," a "great bombshell," who "staggered" Percy and provided him with a "tremendous breakthrough" in his own intellectual and personal development. I knew that sometime after his marriage in 1946 Percy had become a Roman Catholic. But it was quite a surprise to learn that it was Kierkegaard who had "opened up" the area of religion to Percy, who had previously been so steeped in the traditions of Southern Stoicism and scientific atheistic humanism. Later, as we discussed Kierkegaard's essay on "The Difference between a Genius and an Apostle," it was startling to hear Percy say, "If I had to single out one piece of writing which was more responsible than anything else for my becoming a Catholic, it would be that essay of Kierkegaard's." That revelation left no doubt in my mind that the Kierkegaardian impact on Percy's personal development had been powerful and pivotal.

Next I wanted to explore how much and what parts of Kierkegaard's personal impact on Percy carried over into the three novels. There were, of course, the two Kierkegaard flyleaf quotes and assorted Danish allusions. Kierkegaard had written a book called *Repetition* (about intentional *déjà vu* with a twist) and an essay titled "The Rotation Method" (a boredom avoidance scheme). Binx Bolling in *The Moviegoer* goes through what he specifically calls repetitions and rotations. Binx intentionally tries to repeat some of his previous experiences and muses about stimulating rotation experiments, real and imagined. In *Love in the Ruins,* when the devil tempts Dr. More with good bourbon, nubile women, and music, terms from Kierkegaard's essay on the musical-erotic occur in the text. The psychological malaise which pervades so much of *The Moviegoer* and *The Last Gentleman* is described in Kierkegaard's sociopsychological diagnoses, *The Present Age* and *Sickness unto Death.* And so forth. This was not all coincidence, obviously. But how conscious was the influence, how intentional the borrowing?

And how accurate? While *The Moviegoer*'s Kierkegaardian flyleaf quote fit that novel beautifully, the one selected for *The Last Gentleman* did not seem to fit at all. In fact it was quoted rather badly out of context. It raised some doubts in my mind about how Percy was using Kierkegaard. The flyleaf quote, "If a man cannot forget, he will never amount to much," is from *Either/Or* and is part of some rather cynical and demonic advice about how to maximize one's intake of egoistic, sensate pleasures without getting caught. In the novel, by contrast, it applies to a sometimes bewildered, mentally-ill amnesic who is not a would-be esthete at all—in fact quite the opposite. Slightly apprehensive, I asked Percy about how that quote fits into the novel.

Percy: The character Will Barrett had amnesia, and I interpreted the quote to mean simply that a man is better off being half-crazy. This young man Barrett was really sick, in the clinical sense of the word. Of course, the question is always posed there: Who is better off? This poor fellow who is desperately neurotic to the point of being amnesic, and wandering in and out of fugues, as bad off as he was? Or the so-called well-adjusted, productive businessman, and so forth, who is clinically sane by the same standards? Which one is better off? You can say that Barrett is better off. Sick as he is, he has got sense enough to know that it doesn't matter what has happened to him before; what matters is what he does, what he finds next. He

is a man in a desperate quest for his own soul, for his own identity.
I'm not sure he ever finds. In fact he may have failed at the end; he
may have wound up just like other salesmen of Confederate Chev-
rolets, or whatever it was, back in Birmingham. But at least he
doesn't have the despair—the Kierkegaardian quote from *The
Moviegoer*—of despair that does not know itself as despair. He
knows he is in trouble and he is willing to move, and he knows that
the important thing is what he finds. He is always searching—first
going back to find out what happened to his father and then looking
for Sutter. So the flyleaf quotation justified his amnesia, and it
doesn't matter whether he remembers or not. What counts is what
he does or what he finds. Now whether that is what Kierkegaard
meant, I don't know and don't even care. It doesn't matter.

So much for that. He had cited Kierkegaard's words out of context
but in the interest of making a larger, related Kierkegaardian point
about the quest for selfhood. Percy's answer had been forthright and I
felt a little like a pedant put in his place.

What about Kierkegaard's theory of the musical-erotic—the theory
of how and why music acts as erotic stimulus? Did Percy "not know
and not care" what Kierkegaard meant by that?

Percy: When I first read *Either/Or*, the only part that I liked was
the essay on Mozart and the musical-erotic. I was a great admirer of
Mozart and had never thought of him in connection with the erotic,
of all things. We tend to think of Mozart as so crystal-clear, eigh-
teenth-century, formal. So this was quite a shock.

In *Love in the Ruins*, the devil succeeds in tempting Dr. More with
Kierkegaard's musical-erotic. More knows exactly what he is doing.
He knows who Immelman is (the devil) and that the devil is tempting
him with the most beautiful of all things, namely, music and women.
More enjoyed women and music in the musical-erotic sense, as
beautiful objects of pleasure. I saw him really as a damned man—
Kierkegaard's esthetic damnation.

Right on target, I said to myself. He did know what Kierkegaard
meant, did care, and adapted it brilliantly to the special problems of
our own time and place.

My list of interview questions contained a whole series of questions about Kierkegaard-like portions of the novels. After a few acknowledgments that, yes, Kierkegaard was indeed the source for this and that fragment, the conversation took an unexpected turn, revealing a degree of indebtedness to Kierkegaard which I had not guessed.

Percy: The most important single piece that Kierkegaard wrote is something I seldom hear about and a lot of people don't know too well. It's his essay called "The Difference between a Genius and an Apostle." That was tremendously important to me. Kierkegaard says that a genius is a man who arrives at truth like a scientist or a philosopher or a thinker. Truth, as he calls it, *sub specie aeterni*. He can arrive at a truth anywhere, anytime, anyplace, whereas an apostle has heard the news of something that has happened, and he has the authority to tell somebody who hasn't heard the news what the news is. I made use of this essay throughout several of the books. The whole structure of Binx's search is based on it. He talks about the horizontal search and the vertical search. The vertical search consisted of the times when he would read books about the philosophy of life, or about Einstein's theory of the universe or Schrödinger's—the German physicist—*The World as I See It,* and a book called *The Chemistry of Life,* and he understood it all. But he finished the book by midnight, and then his problem was to draw one breath and then the next, which is like Kierkegaard. Kierkegaard had an example of a young man who was given a task of working all day long and he finished the job at noon. That was one of Kierkegaard's crazy allusions. So that's the vertical search, in other words, what Kierkegaard would call the work of a genius. The fellow who figures out all the systems and all the formulas—knowledge *sub specie aeterni*—which can be figured out anywhere, anytime, or any hour. But having done that, you see, he still has to draw one breath and then the next.

And then Binx goes to his horizontal search, which took the form in this case not of religion, but a kind of a debased religious fear of searching. He knew he had run out of the esthetic sphere—the women and music and science, and so forth. (And, incidentally, I place science in the esthetic sphere. I don't know whether Kierkegaard does that or not. I think that science and art are very closely allied there.) But he had run out of all this and had embarked on what he called a horizontal search. By this he certainly did not mean looking for God, although he talks about that. He rules out the search for God in the beginning, because he says that Americans already believe in God. Everybody believes in God, so how can you search for something everybody believes in? So he embarked on kind of an antic search which was still in the esthetic mode: going out, walking around, walking out to the lake at night, walking out to see the river, taking a ferry to Algiers, going to movies. So this is all still very much in the esthetic. But the two searches were certainly very much patterned after *The Difference between a Genius and an Apostle*—with that very much in mind.

I think Kierkegaard said if the hearer of the news asks the apostle, "On what grounds am I supposed to believe this news?" the apostle simply replies that "I have the authority to tell it to you, and if you don't believe me it is your fault. If I didn't have the authority, I wouldn't be telling you. You better believe it, and if you don't believe it it's on your own head." That was a tremendous distinction, a very clear distinction between the two. I used it very consciously at the end of *The Last Gentleman*. This priest who is a very ordinary, mediocre priest, has been dragged in by the scruff of the hair, so to speak, to baptize Jamie who was dying. Jamie can't talk to the priest; he is talking to Barrett. And Barrett is not aware of what is going on, exactly. All he has is a certain amount of equipment, a certain radar, a certain sensitivity. He knows that Jamie can understand him and he can understand Jamie. He can translate both to Sutter Vaught and to the priest. So the priest gives his spiel and says, "Do you believe in the Lord Jesus Christ?" He sets out the truths of the faith, like the Apostles' Creed. Jamie is supposed to say "Yes."

Jamie looks at Barrett and says, "What do you think? Am I supposed to believe this?" Barrett turns to the priest and says, "Is he supposed to believe this? How does he know it's true?" And the priest says, "If it wasn't true I wouldn't be here, that's why. I'm here. I'm telling you. If it weren't true I wouldn't be telling you." So that was a direct steal from Kierkegaard.

Dewey: Is there a parallel earlier in the novel when Val is in the library grinding out her doctoral thesis and a Catholic Sister proclaims the news to her and whisks her off to a nunnery?

Percy: Right. Of course Val was in a rather bad way and in a very receptive state. She had come to a kind of *cul de sac* in her life and was ready to hear the news. But she just happened to meet this Sister and the Sister says, "Well, look, here's the news. I'll tell you the news. Come with me." So off she goes. Yes, that was exactly the same thing.

By now it was obvious that Kierkegaard did not function for Percy as a mere supplier of phrases. Some phrases were there but, more significantly, Kierkegaard provided Percy with much of his underlying view of man, with much of the larger conceptual framework for the novels. Kierkegaard's ideas on the discovery and development of self-hood, on the stages along life's way, on the perplexities of the individual in mass culture—these turned out to be the fabric upon which Percy created his own unique designs. And, old Kierkegaard hand that I considered myself to be, I had missed it. I consoled myself, but only partly, by attributing this lapse to Percy's subtle adaptation of Kierkegaard's concepts and to the dazzling beauty of the Percyian prose.

I was not yet recovered from these disclosures about the Kierkegaardian bases of the first two novels when Percy volunteered that his last novel, *Love in the Ruins,* is in its entirety an intentional variation on a theme from Kierkegaard, a self-conscious novel-length experiment with the dialectic between the comic and the religious presented in *Concluding Unscientific Postscript.*

Percy: Kierkegaard has the strangest way of putting together categories you'd never thought of as associated before. Somewhere he has a section on the comic and the religious—on how close the comic is to the religious—which just bowled me over. I couldn't see any connection. But the more you think about it, the more you begin to see it. *Love in the Ruins* is an exercise in the comic and the religious. People are scandalized by this when I tell them you can have a book that is supposed to be comic and yet religious. But I don't see any contradiction. To me it is fitting. In this novel I was less interested in a search, in progressing from one category to the other, than I was in an exercise of the comic and the religious.

In *Love in the Ruins,* Percy's fine comic sense creates broad situation humor, insider jokes, social satire—playing delightfully over the entire comic range from knowing smile to belly laugh. Yet inextricably interwoven with the comic are the most sober, intense religious concerns about matters of faith and morals. With masterful control, and in Kierkegaardian fashion, Percy succeeds in the challenging task of blending together the comic and the religious.

By this point in the interview, Percy had acknowledged more indebtedness than even the most ardent Kierkegaard fanatic could hope for. But struck as I was by these disclosures, I was even more impressed by the style and grace with which Percy made them. There was no hesitancy, no holding back. He said more than he would have had to, and in fact called my attention to areas and degrees of indebtedness that I had not dreamed existed.

But Percy's praise and generosity toward Kierkegaard could not obscure his own independence and creativity. In several instances it turned out that Kierkegaard's influence, though significant, had been less that of tutor than of Socratic midwife. Frequently, Kierkegaard had not so much given ideas to Percy as he had contributed to the emergence of ideas already there. Although reading Kierkegaard had undoubtedly coalesced, clarified, and provided a context for Percy's developing ideas, those ideas were most often Percy's own.

Percy: The great thing about Kierkegaard was that he expressed my own feelings about the whole scientific synthesis. Also, his analysis of despair—the worst kind of despair as being unconscious of itself as despair—fitted exactly what I was trying to do. It was almost a coincidence that this insight came about the same time I was trying to do my first novel, *Moviegoer*. It was a happy coincidence of Kierkegaard's phenomenology of despair with what I wanted to do with Binx Bolling.

Dewey: Had you already been working on Binx before you read about despair in *Sickness unto Death?*

Percy: Yes, but it was a big help to have it. I guess the two went along together. I would have written *Moviegoer* without Kierkegaard but it was helpful, exciting, stimulating to have the categories there— to have them seen so clearly by Kierkegaard. It is a theoretical frame of reference.

Dewey: But the idea of being in some state of despair that you are not aware of, that had occurred to you and you had been working with that prior to reading *Sickness unto Death?*

Percy: Yes, although I guess I hadn't expressed it or made it as conscious as Kierkegaard had made it. So it was helpful to have him say it like that. Speaking in general, I guess my main debt to Kierkegaard is the use of his tremendous philosophical and theological insight as a basis to build on.

Although he probably would not have cracked a smile, Kierkegaard would no doubt have been pleased since he so self-consciously styled his indirect maieutic prose after that same "midwife" method used by one of his ideals, Socrates.

Much of Kierkegaard's writing appears anachronistic, locked back in the old philosophical debates of the last century. But if you have the key, those dated pages can lead right into the center of today's vexing issues. In order to tap the great Kierkegaardian resources, the reader must know how to separate the dated specifics in Kierkegaard's books from the timeless concepts which often underlie them. Once those universal concepts are isolated, their tremendous analytical and critical power can be applied to concrete situations in another time and place. Many readers get trapped in the footnotes and never get past the nineteenth century. Not so Percy.

Percy: One big difficulty for me in reading Kierkegaard was that I had no philosophical training at all, especially about Hegel or the German idealists. That was a great obstacle and stumbling block for years. Kierkegaard was attacking Hegel. For a long time I thought that was irrelevant. I said, well, what difference does it make whether he successfully demolished Hegel or not, until I realized that you could very successfully extrapolate his attack on Hegel against what we might call scientism. The same thing he said about the Hegelian system might be said about a purely scientific view of the world which leaves out the individual. So once I made that extrapolation from Hegel, whom I cared nothing about, to a whole, scientific, exclusive world view, it became very relevant.

One of Percy's more pungent "extrapolations" is seen in the distaste he and Kierkegaard share for liberal theology in its assorted guises. In Kierkegaard's day it took the form of Hegel's absolute religion and romantic religion which claimed to "go beyond" Christianity to an all-inclusive synthesis of man's common religious quest. In our day Percy sees liberal theology in the various syncretistic movements which appeal to free-floating feelings of vague religiosity, feed on theological permissiveness, and serve it all up with exotic aspects of the mystical, the Orient, the occult.

Dewey: The novels describe people who turn to "esoteric doctrines" for the answer. In *Moviegoer* it's Kerouac-esque Zen and Kahlil Gibran by candlelight. In *Love in the Ruins* Dr. More's wife falls in with an Englishman and is lured away by Eastern religion, ESP, theosophy. Would that fit into a kind of Hegelian system as a general, bland humanism?

Percy: Yes. I think that a lot of this esoteric philosophy and cults, Oriental cults, Satanism, and so forth, are the deliberate cultivation of experience—this savoring of experience for experiences' sake which is a pure Kierkegaardian esthetic. I think this is true of a lot of the kids—the commune experience, looking for something, group experience, the Oriental religions. I would sort that out very much in the esthetic sphere. I would imagine Kierkegaard would, too.

Strangely enough, *Love in the Ruins* got a rough press in England. I don't know why exactly, unless it was the repeated reference by Dr. More to what he called "goddamned, heathen, Oriental English."

Zealously looking for parallels, I pressed my luck too far and Percy called me back.

Dewey: Would your attack on liberal theology also be seen in *The Moviegoer* in Mercer's reading of Rosicrucianism?

Percy: Well, that's different. If you were from the South you would be familiar with this. It is a case of what Sartre would call lack of authenticity, namely, a black from black peasant origins who was trying to become middle class by reading things on how to improve yourself, how to develop your inner potential. That would be more a case of bourgois middle-class inauthenticity, falling prey to and being seduced by "information." Kierkegaard made a long attack on newspapers in *The Present Age* which I think is very close to this.

As our conversation progressed, further evidence of Percy's independence from Kierkegaard emerged. While reading the novels, I had sensed that even though some central characters were searching for the kind of individual selfhood which Kierkegaard endorsed, they also seemed to want more. The Kierkegaardian aura of enclosed, interiorized, radically idiosyncratic selfhood did not seem to fit Percy's goals. I asked him about it.

Percy: This has always been a stumbling block to me. I think that Kierkegaard was simply wrong or carried his opposition to Hegel's system—objectivity—too far. Kierkegaard seemed to set up subjectivity as the only alternative. That has always bothered me, because I think he is falling into the trap of emotion, inwardness. He talks about subjectivity, inwardness, and so forth, yet never makes any provisions, as far as I can tell, for understanding or an explanation of intersubjectivity—caring for the other person, or how to know other people.

Dewey: So much of it does take place just inside the person's head. It's very cerebral, which could account in part for his relative lack of interest in Christian communities, worshipping communities, communities of reconciliation. One is reconciled to God primarily, and one relates to God directly.

Percy: Maybe his extreme individualism, inwardness, subjectivity was justified by the blandness and overcorporate nature of Christendom at that time. Maybe it warranted such an attack.

About the time I was having trouble with Kierkegaard's subjectivity and inwardness, I got on to the Jewish writer-theologian, Martin Buber, who was strong on intersubjectivity. And about the same time I got interested in approaching it from the point of view of language, starting from behavior as the genesis of the spoken word. I thought I saw a way of developing a scientific view of intersubjectivity and wrote a couple of articles on the subject. I've been doing more work on language just recently.

Another stumbling block turned out to be the central Kierkegaardian idea of "radical doubt" which stresses that faith in God is not (by definition) a form of knowledge, that the truth of Christianity is not acquired as one acquires ordinary information. For Kierkegaard there can be no sufficiently persuasive rational arguments to move one from unfaith to faith. One simply gets clear on what the Christian life entails, then, if that be his choice, makes a "leap of faith," elects to believe despite the ineradicable doubt, opts to believe not in virtue of evidence but in virtue of the absurd. Percy does not like that. As he explains why, his Catholicism comes through clearly.

Percy: In a way I see what Kierkegaard is doing, but . . . in 1959 I wrote an article called "The Message in the Bottle." It starts out with two quotations. One was from Kierkegaard saying that faith is not a form of knowledge; faith is something of inwardness or of something absurd. The other was from Thomas Aquinas, saying that faith is a form of knowledge. It was a discussion, from my point of view, of the Gospel as a piece of news and how to place a piece of news in an information system, how to classify it as a serious statement. That was what interested me. And I was always put off by Kierkegaard's talk about inwardness, subjectivity, and the absurd, the leap into the absurd. I didn't think it was necessary to go that far. Of course, I understand he was always trying to divorce it from the objectivity of the Hegelian system. And he did make some memorable statements about absurdity. But for my purposes it was a trap and I wanted to avoid that.

Dewey: There is one of the darker sides of Kierkegaard where there can't be any certainty of any kind; where if you choose the Christian way you are leaping into the dark as it were, and you are acting only as if there were a God. The whole decision is made in anguish. Oftentimes there doesn't seem to be any peace or balance. It's as if one is always agonized, even after he has made the decision. I don't find that agony in the characters in your novels who move toward faith. There seems to be a kind of balance point that is reached, a kind of peace. That seems to be one place where you really diverge from Kierkegaard.

Percy: That's right. That's true both about Binx and Dr. More. That may be the Catholic milieu, New Orleans. That may be more of an Apollonian Catholic balance there, as against the Protestant anguish.

That same Catholic Apollonian balance reentered the conversation when we talked about the somber note of suffering which echoes through much of Kierkegaard's writing. Leaving aside the complex issue of Kierkegaard's own physical and psychic pain, his writings assert that the attempt to achieve developed selfhood, to speak the truth to mass culture, and to follow in Jesus' footsteps leads inevitably to suffering. There will be suffering caused by internal conflicts within the person's own mind, and external suffering at the hands of the opposition.

The inevitability of suffering, in its various forms ranging from mild anxiety to outright martyrdom, permeates several of Kierkegaard's central works. Having made his Kierkegaardian choice, one sets off toward his goal, thereby making himself vulnerable to the Dionysian forces of destruction which lie in wait for all such pilgrims. But for Percy, even suffering becomes a part of the Apollonian vision.

Dewey: Another thing that doesn't seem to be a part of the novels is the suffering of Jesus, the martyrdom of his followers who break themselves to pieces by attacking the corrupt culture and the corrupt church. Once again that Apollonian balance comes back in.

Percy: Yes. The thing to say there is that in the novels suffering is really used as a vehicle. In several places it is used as an asset, a cognitive avenue toward knowledge, or grace. I'm thinking of Binx Bolling's experience in Korea when he's wounded. That has another literary forebear, namely, Tolstoy's Prince Andrei being wounded in the battle of Borodino and having a spiritual awakening by simply looking up—wounded, sick unto death, as a matter of fact, he died—and seeing the clouds for the first time. This is a curious phenomenon, which is certainly not my discovery. Several writers have recorded what is discovered through ordeal. Suffering is an evil, yet at the same time through the ordeal of suffering one gets these strange benefits of lucidity, of seeing things afresh. In Binx Bolling's case his moment came by simply being wounded and lying under some bushes and seeing a beetle, a dung beetle of all things. That happens.

Dewey: How about when Kate experienced her moment of lucidity as a result of her fiancé's death in the car accident? Later, she said it was the happiest day of her life. Is that the same idea?

Percy: Yes. Although that was a much more suspect experience because she was benefiting from somebody else's dying. She was really glad to get out of that marriage.

In each of Percy's novels there is a child afflicted with a lingering,

fatal disease. Two of the children are believing Catholics and the third
is baptized on his deathbed by a priest. These children can be seen as
the theological foci of the novels, for in microcosm they represent the
paradox of unmerited suffering and a supposedly benevolent God.
Percy does not hide their pain; yet their hideous deaths are rendered
hauntingly beautiful through the ways that they, the afflicted, move
toward them. As their bodies are destroyed, somehow they become
whole, even victorious. They challenge the reader to see through their
eyes the vision of an Apollonian world full of God's grace where
sorrow and death do not have the last word. Of course, God is triumphant in Kierkegaard's theological works, but somehow that triumph
seems closer at hand, more intimate in Percy's novels.

Prior to the interview I had speculated that Percy's buoyancy and
balance would not be at all receptive to the depressing, dark mood of
the ninety gargoyle-like aphorisms which open *Either/Or.* I also could
not imagine his being enthusiastic about the suffering motifs in Kierkegaard's *Training in Christianity.* Since these writings are so central
to my interpretation of Kierkegaard, and seemed to be so absent
from the novels, I wondered if he had read them at all.

Dewey: Do you remember any reactions to reading the aphorisms
at the beginning of *Either/Or?*
Percy: None at all. I just blanked out, skipped them, couldn't
make head or tail out of them.
Dewey: Did you read *Training in Christianity?*
Percy: I don't know. I remember the title, but I don't recall.
Dewey: Kierkegaard talks a lot in that book about Jesus as a
model for the Christian life, Jesus as being contemporaneous with
the believer, about Jesus as a very concrete, real person rather than
an abstracted doctrinal construct.
Percy: I guess I didn't read it. I thought I had all the titles in the
Princeton series, but maybe I don't.

Kierkegaard and Percy also sharply diverge in the role they assign to
the physical world around us, whether it be the natural world of the
out-of-doors or man-made environments. Kierkegaard's more "literary" writings have characters and plots, but contain barely minimal
description of the locales in which the plots unfold. The idea content,

with lengthy theoretical asides, overpoweringly dominates. The few shreds of environmental description seem a begrudging concession to convention. Of course Kierkegaard was not a writer of fiction. But even in his philosophical and theological works, the physical world, natural or man-made, is markedly absent as a topic. Once again we find Kierkegaard's philosophical world to be exceedingly cerebral and interior. What goes on inside one's head is of prime importance: getting the categories straight, making the right mental moves. Theologically, God's presence on earth is certainly affirmed, but it occurred in one place for only thirty-odd years way back in the first century A.D. Aside from some references to an ever-contemporaneous "mystical" presence of Jesus, God is related to man, and vice versa, through that past event and its written witness in the New Testament. The Christian relates to Jesus via reading the New Testament and relates to God via Jesus. In Kierkegaard's view there seems to be a narrow vertical line straight up and down from God to man, not touching the believer's earthly surroundings at all.

How strikingly different it is with Percy. His novels are suffused with nature. No fewer than twelve species of birds appear in *The Moviegoer.* We are kept constantly, but gently, aware of the look of the sky, sounds, smells, the feel of things. At frequent intervals Percy locates us within the coordinates of his nature matrix, establishing the condition of the sky, the earth, the sense of the surroundings at that particular time and place. His characters feel their way around New Orleans, Chicago, New York, encountering the intangible "genie-soul" of each locale. His sense of place is magnificent. And within these broad descriptive sweeps he never loses sight of the rich possibilities of small details. Since we have become so unseeing, Percy's prose becomes a zoom lens magnifying what he calls "the wonder" of the world that surrounds us. As the lens zooms in on Binx's desirable secretary, one can feel himself engulfed in the whorl of down on her cheek. It is breathtaking to watch as "an amber droplet of Coca-Cola meanders along her thigh, touches a blond hair, distributes itself around the tiny fossa."

Dewey: I am struck by the pervasive presence of nature in the novels, in contrast to Kierkegaard's rather stark landscape. How did nature become such a part of the novels?

Percy: If you are talking about literary sources—and if you want a contrast with what the novels owe Kierkegaard—they owe something to an entirely different source: the English poet, Gerard Hopkins, who was a great nature poet and who wrote some beautiful nature diaries. And this is a much more, I guess, consciously Catholic attitude toward nature—nature, created nature, as a sacramental kind of existence. Hopkins made a great thing in poetry of being able to look at a cloud or a leaf or even a piece of rock and see in it what he called a certain "inscape," and thinking always that if your gaze was sufficiently fresh and if you could see it sufficiently clearly, you would see it as an act of existence, a gratuitous act of existence which was evidence of God's existence. He saw it in a very sacramental and religious way, which really owes a lot more to Aquinas than it does to the Kierkegaardian tradition.

Dewey: Coming down here on the plane, I was thinking about the birds in your novels. Maybe being up in the air had something to do with it. I don't want to play any cheap literary games, but the novels are full of birds; each novel has a key bird—an egret, a falcon, an ivorybill. I can still hear the gristle creak in the wing of the egret when Binx was on the dock. All those sensitivities to nature seemed so. . . . It's as if the whole universe is filled with grace. It's not just gracious Jesus, which is so Protestant. But the whole universe is suffused with grace.

Percy: That's right. I guess it's more or less consciously a combination of the Catholic sacramental view and the South—Louisiana, you know. People down here hunt and fish all the time.

As impressed as I had been by the parallels between Kierkegaard and Percy, as we talked I became equally impressed by how they differed. Nonetheless, while Percy's independent creativity often diverged from Kierkegaard in matters of content, they seemed quite agreed on matters of intent and form. Both Kierkegaard and Percy intentionally designed their works to attack the lack of individualism in mass culture, the errors of liberal theology. Percy is very sympathetic to Kierkegaard's polemical role, even excusing some of his "errors" on the grounds that he might have had to commit them in the interests of a more effective, corrective attack.

Kierkegaard's satirical jabs at comfortable bourgeois Christendom are deft and his frontal assaults punishing. Percy's genteel skewering is equally devastating. *Love in the Ruins* takes place at a future time when "our Catholic church here split into three pieces: (1) the American Catholic Church whose new Rome is Cicero, Illinois; (2) the Dutch schismatics who believe in relevance but not God; (3) the Roman Catholic remnant, a tiny scattered flock with no place to go. The American Catholic Church, which emphasizes property rights and the integrity of neighborhoods, retained the Latin mass and plays 'The Star Spangled Banner' at the elevation." Ouch!

Percy: Kierkegaard's whole polemical attitude is very valuable to me. The idea of being on the attack is very congenial to me because unless I can build up some steam, generate some polemical steam, I have difficulty writing. There has to be something under attack. In *The Moviegoer* it was scientific humanism on the one hand, and on the other hand was Southern Stoicism represented by Aunt Emily. Although it's admired, it's also attacked. Of course under attack in *The Last Gentleman* is what happened in the South in the 1950s and 1960s. The South was radicalized towards the right side by the whole race situation, the court decisions. It was a terrible thing, a terrible time to go through. A resurgence of Alabama racism, Mississippi racism, and all that. And then under attack in *Love in the Ruins* of course is polarization: white/black, young/old, liberal/conservative, North/South, psychiatrists.

The problem of which method of attack to use bothered both Kierkegaard and Percy for the same reason: The words they most needed to use were bankrupt, used up, co-opted by the opposition, or otherwise emptied of their power. To get around this, Kierkegaard had to invent a new set of philosophical and psychological terms and devise indirect tactics for reintroducing genuine Christianity into the established church. Percy learned from Sartre and adapted some devices from Kierkegaard's indirect method of sneaking up on his unsuspecting readers.

Percy: Sartre's first novel, *Nausea,* meant a great deal to me because of its success in translating a philosophy to art, to fiction. That was the first time I had ever seen it done. It's a peculiarly European

phenomenon, not to be found in this country much, where a
philosopher sets out to write a novel—and *Nausea* is a good novel.
We tend to think that when that happens it would be a disaster—that
a philosopher would simply load the novel with his ideas, that it
would be a didactic novel. But of course, this is a special case where
Sartre's version of existentialism was peculiarly suited to novel writing. So to me it was a very happy example of how a philosopher can
work successfully in fiction. . . . There is great difficulty for a novelist
trying to write in Kierkegaardian categories, using all manner of de-
ception, indirection.

According to one dominant school of Kierkegaard scholarship, Kierkegaard was using an indirect method of persuasion on his readers. He
was convinced that there were available to us only three basic "stages"
or "spheres" or types of life-styles: the esthetic (egoistic, immediately
pleasure oriented), the ethical (mainly secular, conventionally law
abiding), and the religious (committed to a complex theological ethic).
Speaking generally, the Kierkegaardian corpus is seen as a description
of these three life-styles which, presumably, could move the reader
from stage to stage until he chooses the highest religious stage. Kierkegaard's books can be placed along a kind of continuum which
ranges from the esthetic through the ethical to the Christian religious.
Certain readers may feel themselves moving voluntarily along the
continuum as the result of a series of complex interactions with the
literature.

Percy's novels are inhabited by paradigms of each Kierkegaardian
life-style as well as those en route from one stage to another. Binx in
The Moviegoer begins as an esthetic seducer of secretaries and moves
at the end of the book into the ethicality of marriage and medical
school. According to Percy, Dr. Vaught in *The Last Gentleman* "is a
conscious exercise in what Kierkegaard called graduation from the
esthetic to the religious sphere, skipping the ethical." When Kierkegaard's theory of the stages is applied to the novels, it fits like a
glove. Such an analysis leads to the conclusion that, for Percy, the
ultimate goal toward which his artistry moves is definitely religious,
specifically the preparation of his readers for and the presentation of
orthodox Catholic Christian truth.

During the interview Percy remarked that some "one-sided" commentary on his novels overlooked their religious dimension. Well aware that "religious" authors pay a price for their public commitment, he nonetheless hoped that if our interview got into print this point would be emphasized. He even joked about a publisher's sales department suggestion that the word "Catholic" in the subtitle of *Love in the Ruins* ("The Adventures of a Bad Catholic at a Time Near the End of the World") would hurt sales. It was suggested that he might "improve" the subtitle. He declined to do so. The subtitle for Kierkegaard's *Sickness unto Death* is "A Christian Psychological Exposition for Edification and Awakening." Given Percy's subject matter and his intent, that could fit his novels as well. During one long portion of the interview I had been focusing on the differences between Kierkegaard and Percy. He became uneasy about that emphasis and said, "Who was it said that what you do with a writer is to take what is useful to you about him and thank God for that. I don't worry about what Kierkegaard said that I couldn't use, that I didn't like." Toward the end of our conversation, he expressed his high appreciation of Kierkegaard in revealing superlatives: "Here I am a Catholic writer living in Louisiana, and yet the man to whom I owe the greatest debt is this great Protestant theologian."

As we said our good-byes and I walked back down the driveway, laden with my books and notes, I could not help but think about how Kierkegaard used to worry that some day he would become the exclusive property of footnoting professors. With Walker Percy around, he is safe for a while yet.

Notes

1. A chronological listing of Percy's writings is found in Scott Bird and John Zeugner, "Walker Percy: A Checklist," *Bulletin of Bibliography* 30, no. 1 (January–March 1973): 16–17, 44. See also the full bibliography of primary and secondary material in Martin Luschei, *The Sovereign Wayfarer: Walker Percy's Diagnosis of the Malaise* (Baton Rouge: Louisiana State University Press, 1972). A few items not listed in the above are found in *A Bibliographical Guide to the Study of Southern Literature,* ed. Louis D. Rubin, Jr. (Baton Rouge: Louisiana State University Press, 1969), pp. 257–58. A bibliography on William Alexander Percy is found in ibid., p. 258.

2. Alfred Kazin, "The Pilgrimage of Walker Percy," *Harper's Magazine* (June 1971), pp. 81–86. This is an insightful biographical and critical study. Percy has commented on his own life in his "From Facts to Fiction," *Book Week,* December 25, 1966, pp. 5, 9. Some insights into Percy's younger years can be gleaned from his foster father's autobiography: William Alexan-

der Percy, *Lanterns on the Levee* (New York: Alfred A. Knopf, 1941). An appreciative reappraisal of *Lanterns on the Levee* and its author, with interesting auotbiographical reflections, is found in Walker Percy, " 'Uncle Will' and His South," *Saturday Review/World,* November 6, 1973, pp. 22–25.

3. Wilfrid Sheed, "The Good Word: Walker Percy Redivivus," *New York Times,* July 4, 1971, Book Review section, p. 2.

4. "Firing Line," host William F. Buckley, Jr., originally telecast on PBS on December 24, 1972.

5. The phrase "solemn levity" was used to describe some of Percy's characters in a review of *The Last Gentleman* in *Virginia Quarterly Review* 42 (1966): cxxxvi.

Talking about Talking:
An Interview with Walker Percy
Marcus Smith/1976

From *New Orleans Review*, 5, No. 1 (1976), 13–18, and reprinted by permission.

NOR: Let's begin with *The Message in the Bottle*. One reviewer criticized you for "spiritualizing" or trying to spiritualize the theory of language. What's your reaction to that?

Walker Percy: I don't know what he meant really. It was precisely the "spiritualizing" of linguistic theory I was trying to avoid. It seems to me it is the new grammarians who "spiritualize" linguistic theory by dealing exclusively with formal entities, syntactic structures, "deep structures" which nobody has ever seen or proved. And of course at one point Chomsky even hauls in the mindstuff of Descartes which is about as spiritual as you can get. My approach is essentially behavioral, beginning with observable data, for example the actual words and combinations of words children have been observed to use in studies of the acquisition of language. On the other hand Chomsky's distaste for these behavioral studies is well known. I am mainly interested in a semiotic model. I claim along with Charles Peirce that you can't account for language without accounting for non-lexical items, such as looking at, pointing—everything that happens between two people when they speak. If that's what he means by spiritualizing, I guess I'm guilty, because I don't think you can account for sentential behavior without including semiotic elements.

NOR: Is your theory of language ultimately bound in with your religious perspective? Does it make any difference that you're a Catholic?

Walker Percy: I don't think so. I hope not.

NOR: Yet it seems that the theory of language you develop in the last chapter of *The Message in the Bottle* does establish a bedrock for metaphysical perspective. Or at least you attempt to reopen doors to

129

metaphysical questions that the behaviorists and others have implied
were permanently shut.

Walker Percy: In what sense?

NOR: Well, by emphasizing the mystery of man's predicament,
and language as a mediating instrument in that predicament.

Walker Percy: If by metaphysics you have in mind its traditional
meaning as the science of being or first principles, it was the farthest
thing from my mind. Of course modern man's predicament in the
world is something else again. Very few people are interested in
metaphysics but most people are aware of man's paradoxical plight:
of feeling homeless and dislocated in that very world which he has
most successfully transformed for his own use and comfort. This predicament of course is the main theme of many contemporary novelists and so-called existentialist philosophers. What I was interested in
doing was beginning with a behavioral approach, the phenomenon
of language which everyone accepts and about which there is no
dispute, and then seeing how far an analysis of language would take
us toward an understanding of these other equally unique human
traits.

There is one sense in which I plead guilty to the imputation of the
word "metaphysical" if it is used loosely, which it usually is. And that
is that the prime element of the theory of language which I propose
is, at least for me, a mystery. That is to say, in the explanatory model
for linguistic behavior, it is more or less obvious that there is such a
thing as a "coupler," an agent which couples, just as in Descartes'
Cogito, there is an "I" which thinks. If subject and predicate or name
and thing are coupled, there is a coupler. I do not presume to say
what it is. Helen Keller couples the liquid water with the word "water." Or the boy in Charles Peirce's example: his father points to the
balloon, and he couples the word with his perception of the object.
And I do leave the status of the coupler undefined. In fact the book
ends by saying, "I cannot speak about the behavioral or ontological
status of the coupler. I don't know whether it's mind, soul, I, self, or
some neurological corrolate thereof." I leave that completely
undefined. And in that sense I suppose you could say my theory is
consonant with Christian belief. There is the ultimate mystery of who
or what is the coupler. I think this is superior to Descartes' *Cogito
ergo sum* because you can't see Descartes thinking, and so you can't

prove his self. But I can see and hear you uttering a sentence. I say if there are elements of a sentence and if they are coupled, therefore there is a coupler. So I stop there. I say, "There is a coupler."

NOR: So it's almost as if you are transforming Descartes' *Cogito ergo sum* into *Nomino ergo sum:* I name therefore I am.

Walker Percy: Right, correct.

NOR: The importance you attach to the act of language seems to be sharply opposed to Faulkner, at least to the famous remark in the Nobel Prize address, where he speaks of man's "puny inexhaustible voice." You seem to be saying that man is extraordinary precisely because he does possess an inexhaustible voice.

Walker Percy: Right. In the first chapter of *The Message in the Bottle* I talk about the hypothetical Martian who's been reading books by physiologists and behaviorists and biologists explaining man. When he lands on earth he's astonished to find everybody's talking all the time, either talking or engaging in symbolic transactions. And he asks "How do you explain that?" The scientist and his companions give him the standard textbooks and keep reassuring him that man is not really qualitatively different from the animals, that both respond to stimuli. And the Martian keeps saying, "Yeah, but you're still talking!" To the Martian the scientist must seem like Kilroy—he is there, and he is always talking or writing, whether it is nonsense or whatever. He never quits. This is a peculiar phenomenon when you come to think of it. Any other creature would find it peculiar except man himself. He is too busy talking.

NOR: In *The Message in the Bottle* you put a great deal of emphasis, an almost crucial emphasis, upon the case of Helen Keller. It sent me back to her biography. I found there that she was nineteen months old before she lost her hearing and vision. You yourself state that it's the first two years of life that is crucial in language acquisition. Helen Keller had the bulk of those two years. Also, in the biography she describes that remarkable moment with Miss Sullivan, the water on one hand, the word on the other, as a recollection. Doesn't this reopen the behaviorism door?

Walker Percy: Yes, that's a very legitimate criticism, so much so as almost to disqualify that example, except for the fact that the same experience is reported in other cases, such as those of wild or feral boys. And more importantly, in the acquisition of speech by the normal child, you do have this extraordinary thing which Roger Brown and other psycholinguists talk about, of the child doing what Helen Keller does, not in the space of fifteen minutes, but stretched out over say three or four months. The child goes into the naming stage, and he seems to be interested in almost nothing else but going around naming everything, or asking its name, and being fascinated by this extraordinary connection between name and thing. So, if it all depended on the single case of Helen Keller, I think your criticism would be devastating. What was important to me was that the well-house episode distilled the essential elements of the normal naming experience.

NOR: Another related question, and one I'm sure you have thought a great deal about, is this: if neurophysiological research does indeed establish a coupler, and establishes it as some kind of a mechanistic thing, where does that leave us? Is that it? Still talking?

Walker Percy: That's the joker of the last chapter. When I talk about explanatory models, I'm very careful to talk about Charles Peirce's third theory of abduction. He talks about three kinds of abductions: one is statistical, one is mathematical, and the third, he says, its main virtue is its simplicity and workability. And that way it avoids what I call the extremes and pitfalls of ideology. You don't have to be committed to mechanism or to behaviorism or to formalism. So you see, the joker—it is an *explanatory* model. When you say explanatory model to a scientist you usually mean mechanism, you show how something works. When you show how something works, you're talking about secondary causes, and that usually means a mechanism. But notice that my theoretical model shows the elements of the auditory cortex, the visual cortex, and the coupler is a question mark.

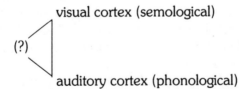

The coupler remains a mystery, and in my opinion it will never be accounted for mechanistically, or according to stimulus-response psychology, simply because the coupler has the freedom to couple any elements of the language. Of course, "freedom" must be qualified by all kinds of variables, all kinds of effects, influences and environments and so on. But the simple fact, the empirical fact of the infinite productivity of language, is all I'm talking about. Chomsky harps on this all the time. Any human child three or four years old, who is exposed to just a fragmentary input of the sentences that he hears around him, maybe with a little help from his mother, maybe not (even a street urchin who's bright and who hears a lot of language)—this child can understand and generate an *infinite* number of new sentences. *Infinite* is Chomsky's word, which he uses literally. He means it, he means that there's *always* another one, there's no end to it. So I think you just have to admit that no mechanistic model can *ever* account for that empirical fact. There has to be some element of the coupler, you have to have some component of originality. I didn't want to get into all that in the book, because as soon as you talk about that you get into what you call metaphysics. That was why I wanted to keep that last chapter as empirical and as linguistic as possible.

NOR: Are you taking a line of reasoning here that's basically established by Kant: you can talk all you want to about the phenomena, but finally there is a nouminal base, and this is really unapproachable by means of mechanistic or rationalistic procedures?

Walker Percy: I discuss that in the same chapter, when I talk about Charles Peirce's triadic theory of language, and the fact that he (and later Chomsky) are astounded by the fact that people can arrive at correct theories for things. Peirce is talking about scientists; Chomsky is talking about a child learning a language. I subscribe to Charles Peirce's realism, the fact that somehow or other a scientist who's faced with a mystery or phenomenon which he's trying to explain, and for which there can be a million or so hypotheses, only one correct, somehow can arrive at the correct hypothesis after three or four guesses. To Peirce this is a tremendous mystery, and so it is to Chomsky. Peirce explains it by saying that man is a product of the universe, that there's something in his mind that's a part of the universe, and therefore he can arrive at more or less correct interpretations. I would hope that I'm not Kantian, I do believe that scientific theory does gradually converge on a truth. Very few people would deny that Einsteinian theory is more correct than Newtonian theory.

NOR: But in that idea of Peirce's, that *we* are able to theorize correctly because we are part of the universe, and that we're more or less bound to operate as the universe operates, there is the element of reconciliation, which is one of the great things that you're trying to get at both in your novels and I think also in this book on language and which really gets you back into the world of Aquinas and Duns Scotus, where man is part of an order that he belongs to, and he's not . . .

Walker Percy: That's correct. However, the big question which the book addresses is this huge gap. You can say the same thing about a responding organism. Organisms are part of the universe too, maybe much more so than we are, because they coincide with themselves.

NOR: An anenome on a tidal flat is perfectly at home as far as I can tell.

Walker Percy: He's himself neither more nor less, whereas a man can either be himself or not himself—he doesn't necessarily coincide with himself. So you have this tremendous gap between accounting for animals and their behavior, which can be done by fairly adequate mechanistic models, and accounting for man, who can erect theories and utter sentences about these very creatures. Of course a major concern of my book is that scientists never even address themselves to the gap, let alone try to explain it.

NOR: Why do you think that's so? Why have they been so reluctant or hesitant?

Walker Percy: I think it's a kind of misplaced religion. The "biological continuum" is almost sacred dogma. You almost have to accept it as a presumption of science, that it is a burden of science to establish continuities, not discontinuities. And in fact it's worked marvelously well with all sciences, from subatomic physics all the way up to behavioral biology, approaching a continuum. And then for there to be a qualitative gap between non-speaking and the *speaking* animal is offensive to a person who posits continuity as the *sine qua non* of science. But suppose there is a qualitative gap—what are you going to do about it?

NOR: You either have to change man or change science . . . In other words, your theory of man (and you've spoken elsewhere of having become involved with the existentialists because they were searching for a radically new theory of man, a new anthropology) is

based on a perception that man is discontinuous. That seems to me
to throw you back into the Cartesian nightmare.

Walker Percy: That's what I was trying to get out of. To say man
is different is not to split him into mind and body.

NOR: For Aquinas and Duns Scotus, man is different from but
also he's a part of a continuous order, that goes all the way from the
stone or the toad up to God.

Walker Percy: That's true, but neither Aquinas nor Scotus are
acceptable to twentieth century scientists, because their realism depends on positing a psyche, an immaterial psyche or soul, so that in
order for you or me to know something, we know it by some opera-
tion in this immaterial substance. This may or may not be true, but
the twentieth century behavioral scientists just can't make head or tail
of it. It doesn't do any good to go back and talk about Aristotle's
immaterial way of knowing, even though for all I know it's probably
true. So it seemed to me that nobody ever tried to approach the
problem through language, which you can see and you can hear and
you can talk about. Once you open your mouth about Aquinas and
how you know things by their essences and by the unions of the
immaterial elements in the psyche, communication ceases for most
scientists.

NOR: Yet, I am not talking so much about the method of, or the
point of view of any of these people, but a certain payoff. You open
your book with a series of harrowing questions, these incredible
paradoxes having to do with the malaise; here we have every reason
for being absolutely secure and happy and yet our inner worlds are
confused and tormented.

Walker Percy: I think we're all children of our culture and our
times. I know that I start off with the dilemmas, predicaments, of the
late twentieth century. I think the reason this entire issue has chal-
lenged me over the last twenty-five years is the way I came on it. It
has to do with my whole education. I was brought up with a very
unbalanced scientific education. I took pre-med in college—in those
days the more science you took the better, and the less English, the
less history, the less humanities the better. At Chapel Hill I spent four
years in the laboratories, taking chemistry (I was a chemistry major, a
math minor), physics, biology—I took all the science I could, thinking
that would help me in medical school, and it did. Chapel Hill was

noted for its school of behaviorism, a very well-known school, one of the best in the country. Then I went to the College of Physicians and Surgeons at Columbia, which was noted for its emphasis on the mechanism of disease, which is a very beautiful and elegant idea, that disease can be explained as the response of the body to an invading organism. It's a beautiful concept—you can categorize a great deal of pathology as response to an invading body, a foreign element. I was going to go into pathology, and I loved the idea of looking at a microscope slide and seeing all those beautifully stained cells, the tubercle bacilli, the lung tissue responding to it, which you could draw a picture of and explain by chemistry, by transactions among the bacteria, the membranes and the lung cells. Then, while I was working in the TB division, where I did over one hundred TB autopsies, I contracted tuberculosis myself. So I was yanked out of this milieu of very rigorous, very satisfying and elegant scientific mechanism, a mechanical theory not only of electrons but of human tissue. All of a sudden I was completely transferred from this milieu into two years of enforced idleness, with nothing to do but read. It couldn't have been more different. I found myself reading what I should have read in college and didn't. I started with Dostoevsky.

NOR: This is probably well-known, but why is it that you read Dostoevsky and not trash? Lots of people get tuberculosis and lots of people have to go to a sanitarium but they sit and watch television or they read movie-romance magazines—they don't start reading Dostoevsky and Kierkegaard. Was it somebody who put you on to this?

Walker Percy: I guess it goes back to my uncle, a very literate man who had a great influence on me. I read *The Brothers Karamazov* in Greenville high school and was tremendously affected, but I abandoned it then for science (like Ivan in the book). So I took up where I left off, and that took me through two years of Dostoevsky, through Kierkegaard, into the French existentialist novelists and philosophers, Sartre and Marcel. I found myself in this very strange dilemma of still subscribing to the method of science, what science could explain, man and the world as explainable phenomena. On the other hand over one hundred years of novel-writing and philosophizing had to do with man as someone alienated. The whole modern novel is a novel of alienation, is about man as dislocated, disoriented, uprooted, homeless, not at home—which seemed absolutely the exact opposite of the thrust of the education that I had, where the whole burden of point-of-view was to fit man into a body of phenomena. So I was confronted with these two diametrically opposed views of man. To make a long story short, *The Message in the Bottle* is simply the outcome of a twenty-year struggle, mostly unsuccessful, to reconcile these two views from a scientific point of view. I approach it from a behavioral stance, I hope, though part of it is written from a phenomenological point of view, like a couple of chapters ("Loss of the Creature" and "The Man on the Train," for instance), but mostly it's from a behavioral point of view, beginning with words and sentences, and I have tried to bridge this huge gap between the scientist's view of man and the novelist-existentialist's view of man, both of which I thought were valid. And the only way to do it—it came over me as a kind of revelation—was through language. About the same time I was reading Ernst Cassirer and Susanne Langer, and it seemed to me that this was the great key, as Langer called it, only she picked it up and she dropped it, she didn't do anything with it, she didn't use the key to unlock anything. So in my naivete I said, "Well, the way to do this is to find out something about language and linguistics." I thought it was all there in the universities and libraries, so I spent the next few years trying to find out what linguistics was all about and what the philosophers of language had said. "My second great revelation was that either nobody knew much about it, or else were not interested—that in short there is no explanatory theory of language. To me this was really a stunner, to find out that man knew so damned little about the one thing that he does most. In fact, it seemed to me that ninety-nine percent of all theoretical effort went either into trying to account for language by animal responses, which can't be done, or else trying to abstract from the whole problem and erect formal systems, like Bloomfield, Harris and Chomsky, while maybe paying lip service to the behaviorists—and still leaving the gap between. So it struck me that the gap was still there.

NOR: Let's move from the problem of language theory to the language you use as a novelist. To me, this is an interesting question, because it's like a painter who painted canvases and also had done serious research into color theory. I don't know of any other novelists who have investigated the theoretical roots of language.

Walker Percy: It seems strange to me that they are not more curious.

NOR: Has your interest in language theory affected your practice as a novelist?

Walker Percy: I think they have very little to do with each other. Maybe it's just as well. God help us if a novelist was thinking in terms of theoretical linguistics when he was writing. It'd be pretty bad. Maybe there is a connection in my admiration of the precision of language and the possibilities of use and misuse. Maybe in that sense. And of course, there is my long-term interest in metaphor. I'm very much aware that any comprehensive theory of language has to account for metaphor, and current theories do not. I was and still am aware of the absolutely critical, central importance of the creative function of metaphor in language, both in the genesis of language in a child—when a child applies a sound to a thing he's making a very elaborate metaphor—and in the novelist's or poet's use or creation of metaphor for new meaning, being acutely aware of the central importance of metaphor and also acutely aware of the central importance of metaphor in writing.

NOR: You mentioned once that James Agee had brought back poetry into modern prose, and you acknowledged a very significant technical influence in the way in which he crafts a sentence.

Walker Percy: When I was talking about Agee I was talking about a certain kind of novelist who was very much aware of the poetic uses of language, which is almost the same as saying the metaphorical uses, the fact that you can create new language through metaphor. Being aware of this, I'm very much aware that not by conscious effort but occasionally by good luck, or something, Providence or whatever . . .

NOR: The coupler?

Walker Percy: Yes, somehow or other the coupler can put things together with happy results. Metaphors are very strange because when you put two things together it's a way of discovering meanings which haven't been discovered before. It's a very strange thing because you discover meanings which you know, and the reader knows, but neither one of you knew that you knew until you see it discovered by a new metaphor. This is a function of language not only from the beginning, with the child learning it or the Cro-Magnon Man discovering it, it's also the function of the novelist and the poet.

NOR: Are you able to re-examine what you've done as a novelist and look at your own work in terms of language theory?

Walker Percy: Sometimes it happens the first go-around, sometimes in revision.

NOR: You've also been involved with semiotics, and it seems your protagonists are semioticians in the sense that they are concerned with signs and indicators in their personal world. Their ability or their failure to register to signs very often accounts for their happiness or unhappiness, their well-being or ill-being. Has the whole idea or concept of semiotics been useful to you in your art?

Walker Percy: It depends on whether you use the term semiotics loosely or strictly. Semiotic theory to me is nothing more nor less than adequate linguistic theory. My quarrel with the bulk of psycholinguists, the transformational grammarians and behaviorists is that they are approaching one or another dimension of semiotic theory without putting the several dimensions together. What was attempted in the last chapter is a very simple-minded model, but it attempted to be a semiotic model and account for not only words and syntax but also for people, the coupler, the person who utters the sentence and the experience or object, and such things as looking, pointing at . . . behavior. So I would say in a larger sense that semiotics is nothing more nor less than an adequate behavioral theory of language. And I think Charles Peirce would probably agree with that. I hope so.

NOR: The reason I asked that last question is that I was looking again at *Love in the Ruins* and asked myself, "How would semiotics be useful in terms of reading the book?" At the beginning, Tom More is often in these terrifically powerful abstractions, and is missing all kinds of palpable signs—the hawk hovering over his head, which I guess is something magical and wonderful. Hopkins? But at the end his abstraction level is calmed down, he's able to pick up all sort of signs—the nyloned hip of Mrs. Prouty, and lots of other little indicators. So it's almost as if he moves from being semiotically obtuse to being semiotically sensitive.

Walker Percy: I was thinking not so much in terms of semiotics there as about a related thing, what More calls angelism/bestialism, where he sees himself as a split, sundered man, and most of his patients the same way—they're sundered between the angelic, abstract ego and the responding organism, the body.

NOR: Is your source for the angelism/bestialism scheme Pascal? There's a remark somewhere in Pascal that a man who tries to be an angel will turn into a beast.

Walker Percy: Yes, right. Arthur Koestler, too—Koestler's *The Ghost in the Machine.* So really what happens to Thomas More is a reconciliation and a convergence. He becomes a man rather than being a monster. To go back to something you asked about earlier, it's just occurred to me: there is a sense in which my interest in language does affect my novels. That is, I'm also interested in something that happens in the use of language, in the larger behavioral sense. There's nothing new about this, it's been noted before by people like Marcel—but language undergoes a period of degradation, words wear out. I think there's always an awareness in the novels, even going back to *The Moviegoer,* that people say words, and words have become as worn as poker chips, they don't mean anything. Particularly religious words: baptism, sin, God. These get worn out, and there's always a problem of rediscovering them. As the Psalmist says, you have to sing a new song: I think that's one of the functions of the novelist. Right now I'm trying to write a novel in which a man finds himself in some sort of a cell—it's not clear whether it's a prison cell or a sanitorium cell. He's there for several reasons—he's not quite sure, as a matter of fact he's amnesic. But he's very much aware that the language is worn out. And in the next room there's a woman who's in a state of catatonia; she's also mute, she's retreated from language. So he conceives the idea of trying to communicate with her by knocking on the wall. It doesn't matter, except that what I had in mind was the wearing out of language and the creation of new language.

NOR: So they're really involved in inventing a language?

Walker Percy: They're in adjoining cells, and their windows let on to the same scene, which is a very narrow slice of New Orleans, uptown New Orleans. It's a corner of the old Lafayette Cemetery, and a slice of the lévee, and a slice of a movie theatre—but you can see a lot, you know. It's a triad. The point also is, the idea of restriction being good. One review of Saul Bellow's latest novel. *Humboldt's Gift,* said that one of the arguments is that we're exposed to too much, there's too much stimulation. So this man is in this cell and he likes it there, because it's the purest kind of triadic situation—an "I" and a "thou," something to look at, and an opportunity to create a language, like Adam and Eve.

NOR: A number of women have objected to your fiction because it violates certain feminist canons; your women always end up in a position of dependence. Ellen at the end of *Love in the Ruins* is almost a caricature; she's barefoot and at the stove and the only thing we don't know is whether she's pregnant or not. So they dismiss you as another chauvinist. What is your response to this?

Walker Percy: Only that I don't know anything about women—that's more or less true. How many men do? Several women with whom I've discussed this new novel have said, "I had hoped you were going to get better and have a whole woman, a completely fleshed-out human person instead of these affected Southern types that you like. And now instead of gaining ground you're losing ground! You're starting out with a catatonic who can't talk, who can't eat!" So, it may be true.

NOR: Any idea when the new book will be . . .?

Walker Percy: Lord no, this is my fourth go-around at it. I've been at it for three years and I've torn up the last three versions. Who knows, if I'm lucky I'll get through it this time.

NOR: Let me return to the last chapter of *The Message in the Bottle* and ask you about some details. You're talking about language development in the child, the naming sentence, etc., and you say that as the child grows older and becomes more adept, the "context drops away." I'm not sure what you mean by context, because it would seem to me that if anything as the child grows older, the context becomes more enriched and more complicated. I'm thinking of the context of experience. You're obviously thinking of something else.

Walker Percy: I'm thinking of the very close contact between mother and child—mother and two-year-old, where the child is sitting on the mother's lap and they're both looking out the window and seeing a dog being run over by a car, and the child says, "Car, dog" and the mother knows exactly what he means. Of course the context is so explicit. Later if the child, ten or twelve years old, calls on the telephone and says, "The dog was run over by the car," he has to add all these functions and syntactical elements.

NOR: You say also in the same section, "Much of the linguistic activity of the first two years of life goes toward the building up of an inventory, or lexicon, of semantically contentive words through which the world of experience is segmented, perceived, abstracted from, and named." Through which? Why not "with which" or "by which"?

Walker Percy: "By which" might be better; "by means of which" . . .

NOR: And perhaps the most puzzling part for me is when you suggest that the contentive word in a sense contains the thing.

Walker Percy: This is not my discovery, this is dealt with by a pair of psycholinguists named Werner and Kaplan, who wrote a book called *Symbol Formation.* They used the word "chair." I use the word "yellow" or "glass." Do you find that hard to get hold of?

NOR: Well, this is really attached to another question. So much emphasis is placed in your discussion on the concept of "sentence." You're concerned with a theory of man, not just English-speaking man. I'd like to get a global linguist and ask, "Now look here, what is a sentence in Chinese? What is a sentence in Malaysian?" And the kind of thing that you define (using English) as a naming sentence, is that really a universal form?

Walker Percy: There's a book by Greenberg called *Language Universals.* He and the transformationalists agree that there are such things as linguistic universals, namely sentences, and that the sentence universally consists of noun phrase plus verb phrase, even agglutinative sentences, and that there are universal categories of experience, qualitative words, motion words, noun words, whether you call them nouns or not. And there is the universal fact of assertion. There is such a thing as a declarative sentence in every language.

NOR: And yet Whorf did so much to establish the idea about the controlling influence of language on the development of perception within a particular culture. The point is, if we sit here having had years and years of drenching in a particular verbal system, a particular syntax and laws and all sorts of temporal relationships established by the language that we use, of course we're going to find naming sentences. It's a hell of a problem.

Walker Percy: It sure is. I understand the Sapir-Whorf hypothesis is under attack by most linguists. That's not a critical issue as far as the thesis of the book goes, but the fact that a word can be transformed is. There is a curious psychological phenomenon, where you take a word like "glass," and I say to you, "It's very hard to hear the sounds of that word for themselves." When I hear the word, and maybe you, the word itself seems brittle and shiny and maybe even transparent. And then you say, "Well I don't believe that." And then I say to you, "Well if you don't think so, try saying it aloud fifty times or a hundred times." And sure enough something very peculiar happens.

NOR: But you'll merely create a kind of hypnotic state. It's like Lear in Act IV repeating "Kill, kill, kill, kill."

Walker Percy: Sure, but whatever it is, what happens is that the words sheds its transformation, and you can actually hear all the linguistic sounds. And yet it doesn't make any sense at all. Werner and Kaplan talk about this, they speculate on why this is, and it's a commonly recognized phenomenon.

NOR: One of the classic debates is the whole question of the onomatopoeiac origin of language, yet there are a number of beautiful counter-examples, terms which refer to exactly the same class of objects but which have phonemically opposite or counter forms. You say the word "glass" conjures up brittleness and shininess and so forth?

Walker Percy: Not originally, I say it's transformed.

NOR: Culturally?

Walker Percy: Sure. And that I think leads to something called false onomatopoeia, where you can ask certain people, "What do you think . . . is there any connection between the word 'square' and a square?" And somebody might say, "Well, 'square' sounds square, or 'yellow' sounds yellow—'eh' is yellower than 'blue'." But of course that's not true—the sound "eh" is not yellower than "oo." But yet, the transformation is so successful that you could swear that "yellow" sounds yellower than "blue."

NOR: Your concern with this is what it implies about the language capacity of man?

Walker Percy: Yes. One of the theses of the last chapter is that the child builds up an inventory of what I call "semophones," these very stable configurations where a word is informed by what it denotes. Nouns ("ball") or adjectives ("yellow") or qualities ("bad") or verbs ("broke")—these are what Brown called contentive words. And they all agree. Sure enough a child does form a lexicon, but I think it's these extremely stable interconnections in the cortex—nobody's ever given this a word, so I just made up a word, "semophone," a combination of meaning, semology, phonology and sound. You take two or three hundred semophones, words like ball, doll, cat, you begin pairing them, all of a sudden you've got fifteen or twenty thousand sentences.

NOR: One of the things that occurred to me when I was reading your discussion of the language acquisition device (LAD) and the first few years of human development is that we might have here a case of recapitulation. Is the development of language related to the evolutionary development of the larynx?

Walker Percy: Yes, it is often maintained that the reason a chimp cannot be taught speech is its lack of laryngeal development. Perhaps. Of course strenuous efforts have been made to teach chimps language by other means, for example, the international sign language. I can't say the results are very impressive. Trainers work for months, years, teaching a chimp like Washoe signs for "banana," "tickle," "hold me," and so forth. At the most the chimp may learn seventy-five such signs. Linguists don't seem much impressed.

NOR: It's very impressive in a chimp but not in a man.

Walker Percy: That's right. But it's still an open question, it remains to be seen. The question of course is whether the chimp has crossed the symbolic and syntactical threshold.

NOR: Yet there is a spreading body of data concerned with the communications systems of non-humans. Some of this is in the order of verbal communication—the study of mating songs of frogs. These creatures are obviously talking to each other.

Walker Percy: When you say "talking" I think you have to realize that you're using the word analogically. It's all right to do so, to say monkeys "talk" to monkeys. In the natural state the non-human primate may have a repertoire of twenty-five signals, sounds, signifying his emotional states—rage, fright, come here, and so on. It's all right to say that they're "talking" as long as you realize that the word is analogical, and it may apply to different things. I think it does. What you and I are doing is quite different.

NOR: We're talking about talking.

Walker Percy: Yes, that's right. We're using a metalanguage.

A Talk with Walker Percy

Herbert Mitgang/1977

From *The New York Times Book Review,* 20 February 1977, pp. 1, 20–21. Copyright © 1977 by The New York Times Company. Reprinted by permission.

"I lived a hundred miles from William Faulkner but he meant less to me than Albert Camus," said Walker Percy. "I may have been lucky that way."

Talking of his new novel, "Lancelot," the 61-year-old writer offered a few clues to his thought and work. None is more telling than his admiration for the French and Russian novelists—Camus and Sartre, Gogol, Tolstoy and Dostoyevsky. With a chivalric touch, he thought it best not to mention (and possibly offend by omission) his favorite American authors.

"The French have something that is rare for our fiction writers—a philosophical conviction with novelistic art," Percy said. "The combination is usually fatal, but the French seem to achieve it. Sartre solved the problem of joining art and philosophy in his best work, 'Nausea,' and Camus did so in several of his books.

"I worked on 'Lancelot' for three years, and I owe a debt to Camus. In his novel, 'The Fall,' one man talked to another man, and that's the way it goes in mine. It's an interesting form and a difficult one, something like a dramatic morality play.

"In constructing 'Lancelot,' I thought: Why not have the silence serve as a sort of dialogue? One of the ideas that I try to get across is the failure of communication between people. Lancelot is not altogether unhappy in his cell in the prison hospital. He feels better than his doctors in the so-called sane world on the outside. And the girl in the next cell is mute. Lancelot tries to reach out to her. Why not communicate by tapping on the wall? Words do get worn out. Maybe the purpose of language is to revive itself—including through the novel.

146

"In the novel I try to balance the hero between the normal and the pathological," Percy said. "Who is worse off, the patient or the doctor, the inmates or the outside world? The Lancelot character represents an honor code. If he had lived in the 12th century, he would have been a Crusader who believed in an idea, just as the Israelis in modern times have a noble idea. The only difference between the Crusaders and Israelis is that the Crusaders lost. Some time, I'd like to see Israel.

"The novel also aims to remind us about three revolutions—the first one in Virginia, when the British were kicked out by the framers of the Declaration and Constitution, the second one in the South, which was lost because of the wrongs of slavery, the final one entering the third century for the United States—where else, but in Virginia, where much of it all began?"

The idea for this novel took hold in Covington, the New Orleans suburban town of 10,000 where he lives with his wife Mary in a miniature French chateau. It is in bayou and pine-road country. Mrs. Percy and one of their two daughters started a bookstore-gift-antique shop called The Kumquat six months ago. With two grandsons in the vicinity, it is a comfortable and happy life for the Percys.

But New Orleans is not the South of the popular image, and Percy is far from being a lord of the manor. In the 1960's, he helped to form a biracial group, the Greater Covington Community Relations Council, which had its scrapes with the Ku Klux Klan. He voted for Jimmy Carter, "with fingers crossed," aware that the President is also an atypical Southerner.

It is the collision of cultures, the melting-pot of New Orleans, that keeps Percy there. The only other city he would live in, except that it's not in his native South (he was born in Birmingham, Ala.), is San Francisco, because of its many voices and races. What he deplores is the growth of the "Southern sunbelt" as a political idea, stretching from the Carolinas to Los Angeles, "dominated by such figures as Billy Graham and Oral Roberts, John Connally and Richard Nixon."

Behind the character of Lancelot, something of a failed N.A.A.C.P. lawyer, is what Percy calls "the Roman Stoic," and in the background of the novel is the changing face of the United States.

"One day my wife and I decided to see some of the old ante-

bellum mansions near Covington," Percy recalled. "Like New Yorkers who've never seen the Statue of Liberty we had never taken the
official tour. So we went down the River Road and made a discovery.
The young guides weren't much interested in General Beauregard
and the Confederacy. They only came alive when talking about the
last time a Hollywood company rented the homes for local color.
Where Olivia de Havilland stood in 'Hush . . . Hush, Sweet Charlotte' had become the new reality. That viewpoint became the
genesis for the novel, which shows the life of the River Road gentry
and Hollywood."

Hollywood holds a special fascination for Percy. Unlike Faulkner,
he never wrote for the screen and never intends to. But in his first
novel, "The Moviegoer," which received the National Book Award in
1962, the neighborhood movie houses became oases of reality in an
unreal world.

Here, Percy the New Yorker flicks across the magic lantern of his
life. His uncle, William Alexander Percy, author of "Lanterns on the
Levee," had sent him to Columbia University's College of Physicians
and Surgeons to become a doctor. He received his M.D. in 1941.

"I led a misspent youth while going to medical school," Percy said
laughing. "To get away from the grind, I'd go to the Loew's State on
181st Street and the R.K.O. Coliseum on 183rd Street. My uncle
would try to get me to come downtown to the opera house, but I
spent four years in the movies in Washington Heights. Did you know
that June Allyson is from Washington Heights?

"Then I interned at Bellevue Hospital. I performed autopsies on
more than 125 corpses, mostly alcoholics who had contracted tuberculosis. I got TB and was sent to Saranac Lake in the Adirondacks. It
took me two years to recuperate. I read the French and the Russian
storytellers. After that experience, I decided to do what I had always
wanted—write. If you want to be a novelist, I sometimes tell students
at Loyola or Louisiana State University, where I occasionally take a
class, work in the wards."

The author of "Lancelot" was in New York for a few days this
month before going up to Cornell to speak at a Chekhov festival.
"He was a doctor, like me, who also didn't particularly like
medicine," Percy said. The subject of his talk crossed both professions: "The Novelist, Diagnostician of the Contemporary Malaise."

But before doing so, he had a free evening while his wife was hunting down gifts and antiques for the bookstore. "If 'Dr. Strangelove' is playing somewhere, I'm going to see it again. It's the great American movie. I'd even go to a neighborhood movie in Brooklyn," Percy the moviegoer said.

A Southern Novelist Whose CB Crackles with Kierkegaard

William Delaney/1977

From *The Washington Star,* 20 March 1977, pp. C1, C4. By permission of *The Washington Star,* © 1977, and William Delaney. All rights reserved.

COVINGTON, La.—Here among the snug brick ramblers a mile from the St. Tammany Parish courthouse, in perpetual partial eclipse beneath the high canopies of pines, his neighbors call him "Doc," or "Dr. Percy."

Walker Percy doesn't like the constant reminders that he was once a physician, but he understands. The word doctor conjures up people we have all known and, usually, trusted.

"Man of letters" is quite another thing to bump into at the hardware store. But it is what Walker Percy is. And of that rare breed, he is one of our very best.

While his golf partners over at Tchefuncta Country Club may politely ask "Dr. Percy" about his grandsons or his daughter Ann's new gift shop, the sign hammered into a pine tree at a fork in the shell driveway leading into his property points to the right, and it says simply "Percy."

To the right, past a small pond and around a formal garden of camellias, looming amid the lush semi-tropical foliage is the two-story brick house, the upper floor concealed by a high-pitched roof modeled by the previous owner after a Loire Valley chateau, arched dormer windows poking out. Tradition. Elegance. A touch of Europe.

And coiling behind the house, intimately visible from the ceiling-fanned back porch, is the murky, tide-pulled Bogue Falaya, framed by moss-draped pines and cypress and magnolias reaching for the lowering sky.

On the pink-walled back porch this blustery gray afternoon Walker Percy and his "Bunt" (Bernice) and their daughter Ann and her hus-

150

band John are talking about a constant St. Tammany topic—the ar-
row-straight, 24-mile Lake Ponchartrain causeway that links them to
New Orleans, 50 minutes to the south.

Percy, who had earlier expressed pleasure in the utter serenity of
that commute, is now thinking aloud about the CB radio he is putting
into his truck, "to relieve the monotony" on the causeway.

No, he says, he hasn't decided on a "handle" with which to identify himself to other CBers.

"Lancelot," suggests a visitor, referring to the title of his new and
disturbing novel about a contemporary Louisiana aristocrat's violent
reaction to a society that no longer recognizes evil.

"That's not a bad idea," says Bunt. "Good publicity."

Percy groans.

Publicity.

Though he refuses to appear on television talk shows or at depart-
ment-store autograph parties, he has just returned from New York
and book-promotion press interviews there. Some things are necessary.

Yet without his seeking it, and largely because of New York City's
financial troubles, the mid-decade census report and the meteoric
ascent of Jimmy Carter, he has received increased publicity in the
past year since jittery New Yorkers discovered the prospering "Sun
Belt." That set journalists of all sorts to exploring the South anew,
explorations which often led them to the feet of its resident writers,
including Percy.

"People keep coming down here to ask me about the South," he
admits, "and my mind goes blank."

His Uncle Will, the Mississippi Delta lawyer-planter-poet William
Alexander Percy, wrote a brilliant autobiography from the Southern-
aristocratic viewpoint, "Lanterns on the Levee," which by coincidence ("same month, same publisher," marvels Walker Percy) came
out in 1941 with W. J. Cash's "The Mind of the South." Both authors
soon died, the ailing Cash hanging himself in Mexico City and Will
Percy suffering a stroke while discussing reaction to his book with
friends. Both books are still in print.

"It's funny," says the novelist, "because their books couldn't have
been more different. Cash writing about the poor whites in North

Carolina, the lintheads, and having not much use for what he called
the old captains. And Uncle Will of course representing that very
tradition."

Uncle Will, who adopted 14-year-old Walker and his two younger
brothers after their parents' deaths, is still a big influence in the mind
of his nephew at 60.

"He was," says Percy, "extraordinary."

To Will Percy, the problem of the South was not the blacks, whom
he admired in their white-prescribed place, but the ignorant, gullible
whites.

Will's father, LeRoy Percy, reluctantly got the Mississippi legislature
to elect him to the U.S. Senate to keep out the nigger-baiting
James K. Vardaman. But in 1912, when Senate elections were
opened to the masses, Percy "got his ass beat," recalls his great-
nephew. "Real bad. By Vardaman."

"In our brave new world a man of honor is rather like the Negro—
there's no place for him to go," wrote Will Percy. ". . . How breathe
the same air as the vicious who are strong?"

From the successive titles of his nephew's novels—"The
Moviegoer" (a 1962 prizewinner, dedicated in memoriam to Uncle
Will), "The Last Gentleman," "Love in the Ruins"—one might expect to find Walker Percy, like the non-Southerner Henry Adams,
preoccupied with alienation, with his family's sense of loss to the "vicious who are strong."

And to some extent he is.

"I hate to talk about having any one particular thesis," he says,
"but I guess I'm interested in decline and fall, and what are the options."

It is in the options that he splits with his uncle. Will Percy was a
lapsed Catholic who aesthetically admired the rich heritage of his
Creole mother, but remained fatalistic, adhering only to what he
called "the unassailable wintry kingdom of Marcus Aurelius."

Walker Percy, raised in religious skepticism and intrigued by H. G.
Wells' "The Science of Life," went from college at Chapel Hill to
Columbia University Medical School.

"I went there because I thought Uncle Will wanted me to, because
one was supposed to—either that or law school." One of his brothers

went into law and teaches it at Tulane; the other became a planter-businessman. "It never crossed my mind to become a writer, to have a vocation of letters."

His biography in "Who's Who" fastidiously lists the crucial, life-shaping event: "Intern, Bellevue Hospital, N.Y.C., 1942; writer, 1943–"

While examining the tissues of tuberculosis patients in Bellevue's pathology lab, while doing good for mankind, young Dr. Percy himself contracted TB.

Consigned to a sanitarium, facing what was to be two years of enforced inactivity in the midst of global warfare, he began reading. Dostoevksy. Kierkegaard. Thomas Aquinas ("the whole of the Summa Theologica"). The logician Charles Sanders Peirce. Sartre. Camus. Jacques Maritain.

"What began to interest me in this hiatus," he once wrote, "was not the physiological and pathological processes within man's body but the problem of man himself . . . specifically, the predicament of man in a modern technological society."

Strongly affected by the character of Ivan in Dostoevsky's "The Brothers Karamazov," and his entire diet of reading, Percy made a great leap.

He became a Catholic.

So did Bunt, whom he married 30 years ago (after a year in seductive but hectic New Orleans, they settled here, in a county named for a bogus saint invented by Revolution-era New Yorkers).

So, in turn, did their two Catholic-schooled daughters—Mary Pratt, a remedial reading teacher who lives two blocks from the Percys with her husband and two boys, and Ann, who has a cottage on the Percy property with her husband and is, to Percy's delight, expecting.

The whole tribe returning from mass together to his beloved Bogue Falaya . . . His new novel a Book-of-the-Month Club selection . . . The family involved in Ann's new gift-book-antiques shop, the Kumquat . . . Percy breaking his rule to appear at a "Lancelot" autograph party there. ("We sold TWO HUNDRED LANCELOTS in COVINGTON," anyone in the family will announce, as if expecting the listener to successfully refute the fact.)

"It's nice," says Percy.

Almost as nice have been the critical reactions to "Lancelot,"
which Percy variously describes as "an upside-down religious book"
and "a kind of cautionary tale."

But so different have been the reviews—some calling it good
fiction with a bad message, others convinced that it's bad fiction with
a good message—that Percy concludes:

"It's almost as if they were all reading different books. Which is
O.K. I don't mind that a all. I've only got two real bad reviews, both
of them in The New York Times."

While his first three novels dealt with "various aspects of Kierkegaardian philosophy, in this one I was more interested in the collision of traditions."

Personified by the driven-to-murder Lancelot is "what my Uncle
Will used to call the broad-sword tradition, that goes back to Ulysses
taking revenge on all the suitors who were hanging around his house
when he got back from his long voyage to Troy. He doesn't just
throw them out. He kills them all, you know. If somebody offends
you, you kill them."

This broad-sword tradition, symbolized by the dueling code and
remembered by Percy from Saturday-night parties in his Mississippi
youth, has always been strong in the South—maybe, he suggests,
even stronger than the Christian fundamentalism of Jimmy Carter.

Back in the 1920s, during the Klan revival, Uncle Will's father was
a target because of his wife's Catholicism. Will Percy, 5 feet 2 and
110 pounds, sought out a Klan leader, according to his tall and lean
nephew, and told him: "I'm holding you responsible. If anything happens to my father, I'm going to kill you."

That, says Percy, chuckling at the memory of his uncle's runty size,
is the broad-sword tradition.

The other tradition, the one that drives Percy's Lancelot to
madness and puritanical revolution, is the increasingly bland, permis-
sive, Christianity that regards sin as merely sickness, and asks a man
to forgive an unfaithful wife, to cheerfully accept the challenge to the
womb posed by women's lib.

In the book the Christian tradition—"in difficulty," Percy notes—is
personified by a physician-priest who silently listens to his friend Lancelot's rantings.

"I wrote the book in several versions, and none of them worked. I had two complete characters, long conversations between them. But as soon as the priest opened his mouth it was no damn good. Maybe it's because religious language is shot, just *defunct,* you know.

"The trick was to make the priest real without him saying anything, to make his silence operable.

"The clue to the whole book, which some people get and some people don't, is on the last page or two where Lancelot, who's been ranting and raving and trying to get this guy (priest) to say something, anything, finally says, 'Well, will you at least agree with me about this—it's either going to be your way or my way, it's not going to be their way.'

"The book, like most of my books, is an attack on the middle ground. It's saying the middle ground is not going to work, something's wrong with our democracy.

"It's really a kind of cautionary tale. Somebody like Lancelot, maybe not as crazy as Lancelot, but somebody can come along with sophistication and skill and rhetoric who could make George Wallace and Ronald Reagan look silly. Oh, he'd be a lot better than Hitler. Like Lancelot says, Hitler's mistake was picking on the Jews. It would be a strong man, an elite, some sort of aristocracy, a kind of fascism . . . ."

Percy is most comfortable talking of philosophy and of the uses and failures of language (a collection of his learned essays on both, "The Message in the Bottle," was published in 1975).

"I didn't name him Lancelot for nothing," he continues in his peppery drawl, peering out at the roiling storm clouds beyond the bayou. "He's fundamentally a religious man but can't make head or tail of the usual religious terminology, God and all that, so he turns the whole thing upside down, looking for the holy grail of evil.

"When he gets to the heart of evil, what he thinks is evil, he finds nothing—which is, incidentally, orthodox Thomist doctrine, you know. Thomas Aquinas defines evil as the absence of essence."

His visitor's ignorance of philosophy is painfully apparent.

"We're liable to have a real front coming through," he finally says, "a spring storm."

One of Percy's recurring fascinations is with the reaction of people to storms, how hurricanes can invigorate world-weary psyches, impart new purpose to bored suburbanites. Lancelot wreaks his vengeance during a hurricane.

But after three years of grappling with Lancelot, Percy is weary.

"To tell you the truth, I'm so fed up with that damned book. It's hard to think about it, get any perspective on it."

He isn't sure what he'll do next—maybe a novel on Lancelot's priest friend ("to give John Gardner an answer," he chuckles, referring to that novelist's critique of "Lancelot" in The New York Times Book Review), maybe some more essays on language (count on them to include that new CB radio).

"I don't know. I've always been interested in science-fiction . . ."

He no longer is the movie junkie he once was, and has trouble remembering the last film he saw. It must have been on television. Yes, it was Stanley Kubrick's "2001: A Space Odyssey." Seeing it for the second time, Percy loved it.

Bunt has just come in from the Kumquat, and is out on the porch, listening.

"You have always been interested in science-fiction," she says matter-of-factly. It sounds like a suggestion.

Son-in-law John, just out of college, comes in with Ann to report on his job-hunting efforts.

The Percys show their visitor around the yard, strolling to the flagstone area on the bluff above the bayou and their little dock, Bunt pointing out where a beaver has gnawed the trunk of one tree. Except for the live-oak pollen, which sometimes drives Percy off to Key West to sit it out, it is paradise.

Feliciana, the Spanish called this portion of their land before English-loyalist Americans like Charles Percy came here fleeing the Revolution (Louisianans still call this end of the state the Florida parishes, remembering its origins).

Percy loves the name Feliciana, offers it to readers of his books as if it were the rarest of wines.

"It was a happy land," he says, suggesting the early plantations, Charles Percy's Northumberland, "an extraordinary place."

But mention of a vote-fraud scandal currently embroiling this congressional district brings a sharp edge to his voice:

"Much as I love Louisiana and New Orleans, I finally get sick of this same old corruption. I don't know whether other states are this bad or not, probably not. The main sin in Louisiana is the sin of omission, nobody gives a damn."

Percy has given enough of a damn to have gotten involved in a biracial community group in the 1960s (as Lancelot did), and from time to time he will sound off in a letter to the New Orleans papers ("The States-Item is pretty good").

Unlike his Uncle Will, he does not regard lowly whites as a vicious class and in fact says he has a klan-type friend "who hates everything I stand for, yet if I got in a wreck or somebody got sick, he would do anything for me."

Asked why, if he gives a damn about clean politics, he stops short of standing for office, becoming another Sen. Percy like his great-uncle, he says, "That's a good question. Why don't I? My excuse is that I write books."

His visitor had begun with the question of what, if anything, is peculiarly Southern about Walker Percy's concerns as a writer. Percy had spoken of the broad-sword tradition, but traced it back to Homer, of the dueling code, of his interest in "decline and fall, and what are the options."

Perhaps that is it, the visitor suggests—a Southerner seeing decline and fall where a non-Southerner might see progress. But Percy isn't sure about that, suburban St. Tammany with its offshore geologists and airline pilots—and in fact most of the South—now see material progress while the Northeastern cities are in decline.

Compared to the fatalism of his aristocratic Uncle Will, and the messianic fury of Lancelot, Percy says he has much more hope.

"I'm a Catholic, and I believe that with all the difficulty it is having, the Judeo-Christian tradition is the last best hope of sustaining democracies. That sounds corny, and I hate speaking in ideological terms, which I avoid like the plague in novels.

"But," adds Walker Percy, gentleman to the last, "you asked me."

Questions They Never Asked Me
So He Asked Them Himself
Walker Percy/1977

From *Esquire*, 88 (December 1977), 170, 172, 184, 186, 188, 190, 193–94. Reprinted by permission of Walker Percy. All rights reserved.

Question: Will you consent to an interview?

Answer: No.

Q: Why not?

A: Interviewers always ask the same questions, such as: What time of day do you write? Do you type or write longhand? What do you think of the South? What do you think of the New South? What do you think of southern writers? Who are your favorite writers? What do you think of Jimmy Carter?

Q: You're not interested in the South?

A: I'm sick and tired of talking about the South and hearing about the South.

Q: Do you regard yourself as a southern writer?

A: That is a strange question, even a little mad. Sometimes I think that the South brings out the latent madness in people. It even makes me feel nutty to hear such a question.

Q: What's mad about such a question?

A: Would you ask John Cheever if he regarded himself as a northeastern writer?

Q: What do you think of southern writers?

A: I'm fed up with the subject of southern writing. Northern writing, too, for that matter. I'm also fed up with questions about the state of the novel, alienation, the place of the artist in American society, race relations, the Old South.

Q: What about the New South?

A: Of all the things I'm fed up with, I think I'm fed up most with hearing about the New South.

Q: Why is that?

A: One of the first things I can remember in my life was hearing about the New South. I was three years old, in Alabama. Not a year has passed since that I haven't heard about a new South. I would dearly love never to hear the New South mentioned again. In fact my definition of a new South would be a South in which it never occurred to anybody to mention the New South. One glimmer of hope is that this may be happening.

Q: But people have a great curiosity about the South now that Jimmy Carter is President.

A: I doubt that. If there is anything more boring than the questions asked about the South, it is the answers southerners give. If I hear one more northerner ask about good ol' boys and one more southerner give an answer, I'm moving to Manaus, Brazil, to join the South Carolinians who emigrated after Appomattox and whose descendants now speak no English and have such names as Senhor Carlos Calhoun. There are no good ol' boys in Manaus.

Q: In the past you have expressed admiration for such living writers as Bellow, Updike, Didion, Mailer, Cheever, Foote, Barthelme, Gass, Heller. Do you still subscribe to such a list?

A: No.

Q: Why not?

A: I can't stand lists of writers. Compiling such a list means leaving somebody out. When serious writers make a list, they're afraid of leaving somebody out. When critics and poor writers do it, they usually mean to leave somebody out. It seems a poor practice in either case.

Q: Do you have any favorite dead writers?

A: None that I care to talk about. Please don't ask me about Dostoevski and Kierkegaard.

Q: How about yourself? Would you comment on your own writing?

A: No.

Q: Why not?

A: I can't stand to think about it.

Q: Could you say something about the vocation of writing in general?

A: No.

Q: Nothing?

A: All I can think to say about it is that it is a very obscure activity in which there is usually a considerable element of malice. Like frogging.

Q: Frogging?

A: Yes. Frogging is raising a charley horse on somebody's arm by a skillful blow with a knuckle in exactly the right spot.

Q: What are your hobbies?

A: I don't have any.

Q: What magazines do you read?

A: None.

Q: What are your plans for summer reading?

A: I don't have any.

Q: Do you keep a journal?

A: No.

Q: But don't writers often keep journals?

A: So I understand. But I could never think what to put in a journal. I used to read writers' journals and was both astonished and depressed by the copiousness of a single day's entry: thoughts, observations, reflections, descriptions, snatches of plots, bits of poetry, sketches, aphorisms. The one time I kept a journal I made two short entries in three weeks. One entry went so: *Four p.m. Thursday afternoon—The only thing notable is that nothing is notable. I wonder if any writer has ever recorded the observation that most time passes and most events occur without notable significance. I am sitting here looking out the window at a tree and wondering why it is that though it is a splendid tree, it is of not much account. It is no good to me. Is it the nature of the human condition or the nature of the age that things of value are devalued?* I venture to say that most people most of the time experience the same four-o'clock-in-the-afternoon devaluation. But I have noticed an interesting thing. If such a person, a person like me feeling lapsed at four o'clock in the afternoon, should begin reading a novel about a person feeling lapsed at four o'clock in the afternoon, a strange thing happens. Things increase in value. Possibilities open. This may be the main function of art in this peculiar age: to reverse the devaluation. What the artist or writer does is not depict a beautiful tree—this only depresses you more than ever—no, he depicts the commonplaceness of an everyday tree. Depicting the commonplace allows the reader to penetrate the commonplace. The only other ways the husk of the commonplace can be penetrated is through the occurrence of natural disasters or the imminence of one's own death. These measures are not readily available on ordinary afternoons.

Q: How would you describe the place of the writer and artist in American life?

A: Strange.

Q: How do you perceive your place in society?

A: I'm not sure what that means.

Q: Well, in this small Louisiana town, for example.

A: I'm still not sure what you mean. I go to the barbershop to get a haircut and the barber says: "How you doing, Doc?" I say: "Okay." I go to the post office to get the mail and the clerk says: "What's up, Doc?" Or I go to a restaurant on Lake Pontchartrain and the waitress says: "What you want, honey?" I say: "Some cold beer and crawfish." She brings me an ice-cold beer and a platter of boiled crawfish that are very good, especially if you suck the heads. Is that what you mean?

Q: What about living in the South, with its strong sense of place, of tradition, of rootedness, of tragedy—the only part of America that has ever tasted defeat?

A: I've read about that. Actually I like to stay in motels in places like Lincoln, Nebraska, or San Luis Obispo.

Q: But what about these unique characteristics of the South? Don't they tend to make the South a more hospitable place for writers?

A: Well, I've heard about that, the storytelling tradition, sense of identity, tragic dimension, community, history and so forth. But I was never quite sure what it meant. In fact, I'm not sure that the opposite is not the case. People don't read much in the South and don't take writers very seriously, which is probably as it should be. I've managed to live here for thirty years and am less well-known than the Budweiser distributor. The only famous person in this town is Isiah Robertson, linebacker for the Rams, and that is probably as it should be, too. There are advantages to living an obscure life and being thought an idler. If one lived in a place like France where writers are honored, one might well end up like Sartre, a kind of literary-political pope, a savant, an academician, the very sort of person Sartre made fun of in *Nausea*. On the other hand, if one is thought an idler and a bum, one is free to do what one pleases. One day a fellow townsman asked me: "What do you do, Doc?" "Well, I write books." "I know that, Doc, but what do you really do?" "Nothing." He nodded. He was pleased and I was pleased.

I have a theory of why Faulkner became a great writer. It was not the presence of a tradition and all that, as one generally hears, but the absence. Everybody in Oxford, Mississippi, knew who Faulkner was, not because he was a great writer but because he was a local character, a little bitty fellow who put on airs, wore a handkerchief up his sleeve, a ne'er-do-well, Count No-count they called him. He was tagged like a specimen under a bell jar; no matter what he wrote thereafter, however great or wild or strange it was, it was all taken as part of the act. It was part of "what Bill Faulkner did." So I can imagine it became a kind of game with him, with him going to extraordinary lengths in his writing to see if he could shake them out of their mild, pleasant inattention. I don't mean he wanted his fellow southerners to pay him homage, that his life and happiness depended on what they thought of him. No, it was a kind of game. One can imagine Robinson Crusoe on his island doing amazing acrobatics for his herd of goats, who might look up, dreamily cud chewing for a moment, then go on with their grazing. "That one didn't grab you?" Crusoe might say, then come out with something even more stupendous. But even if he performed the ultimate stunt, the Indian rope trick, where he climbs up a stiff rope and disappears, the goats would see it as no more or less than what this character does under the circumstances. Come to think of it, who would want it otherwise? There is a good deal of talk about community and the lack of it, but one of the nice things about living an obscure life in the South is that people don't come up to you, press your hand and give you soulful looks. I would have hated to belong to the Algonquin round table, where people made witty remarks and discussed Ezra Pound. Most men in the South don't read and the women who do usually prefer Taylor Caldwell and Phyllis Whitney to Faulkner and O'Connor.

No, it is the very absence of a tradition that makes for great originals like Faulkner and O'Connor and Poe. The South is Crusoe's island for a writer and there's the good and bad of it. There is a literary community of sorts in the North. The best northern writers are accordingly the best of a kind. As different as Bellow, Cheever, Updike and Pynchon are, their differences are within a genus, like different kinds of fruit: apples, oranges, plums, pears. A critic or reviewer can compare and contrast them with one another. But Faulkner, O'Connor, Barthelme? They're moon berries, kiwi fruit, niggertoes.

Q: Niggertoes?

A: That's what we used to call Brazil nuts.

Q: How did you happen to become a writer? Didn't you start out as a doctor?

A: Yes, but I had no special talent for it. Others in my class were smarter. Two women, three Irish Catholics, four Jews and ten WASPs were better at it than I. What happened was that I discovered I had a little knack for writing. Or perhaps it is desire, a kind of underhanded desire.

Q: What do you mean by knack?

A: It is hard to say.

Q: Try.

A: I suspect it is something all writers have in greater or lesser degree. Maybe it's inherited, maybe it's the result of a rotten childhood—I don't know. But unless you have it, you'll never be a writer.

Q: Can you describe the knack?

A: No, except in negative terms. It is not what people think it is. Most people think it is the perfecting of the ordinary human skills of writing down words and sentences. Everybody writes words and sentences—for example, in a letter. A book is thought to be an expanded and improved letter, the way a pro ballplayer is thought to do things with a ball most men can do, only better. Not so. Or if you have an unusual experience, all you have to do is "write it up," the more unusual and extraordinary the experience the better, like My Most Extraordinary Experience in *Reader's Digest*. Not so. Psychologists know even less about writing than laymen. Show me a psychologist with a theory of creativity and I'll show you a bad writer.

Q: Can't you say what the knack is?

A: No, except to say that it is a peculiar activity, as little understood as chicken fighting or entrail reading, and that the use of words, sentences, paragraphs, plots, characters and so forth are the accidents, not the substance, of it.

Q: What is it if not the putting together of words and sentences?

A: I can't answer that except to say two things. One is that it is a little trick one gets onto, a very minor trick. One does it and discovers to one's surprise that most people can't do it. I used to know a fellow in high school who, due to an anomaly of his eustachian tubes, could blow smoke out of both ears. He enjoyed doing it and it was diverting to watch. Writing is something like that. Another fellow I knew in college, a fraternity brother and a trumpet player, could swell out his neck like a puff adder—the way the old horn player Clyde McCoy used to do when he played *Sugar Blues.*

The other thing about the knack is that it has theological, demonic and sexual components. One is aware on the one hand of a heightened capacity for both malice and joy and, occasionally and with luck, for being able to see things afresh and even to make things the way the Old Testament said that God made things and took a look at them and saw that they were good.

The best novels, and the best part of a novel, is a creatio ex nihilo. Unlike God, the novelist does not start with nothing and make something of it. He starts with himself as nothing and makes something of the nothing with things at hand. If the novelist has a secret it is not that he has a special something but that he has a special nothing. Camus said that all philosophy comes from the possibility of suicide. This is probably not true, one of those intellectual oversimplifications to which the French regularly fall prey. Suicide, the real possibility of self-nihilation, has more to do with writing poems and novels. A novelist these days has to be an ex-suicide. A good novel—and, I imagine, a good poem—is possible only after one has given up and let go. Then, once one realizes that all is lost, the jig is up, that after all nothing is dumber than a grown man sitting down and making up a story to entertain somebody or working in a "tradition" or "school" to maintain his reputation as a practitioner of the *nouveau roman* or whatever—once one sees that this is a dumb way to live, that all is vanity sure enough, there are two possibilities: either commit suicide or not commit suicide. If one opts for the former, that is that; it is a *letzte Lösung* and there is nothing more to write or say about it. But if one opts for the latter, one is in a sense dispensed and living on borrowed time. One is not dead! One is alive! One is free! I won't say that one is like God on the first day, with the chaos before him and a free hand. Rather one feels, What the hell, here I am washed up, it is true, but also cast up, cast up on the beach, alive and in one piece. I can move my toe up and then down and do anything else I choose. The possibilities open to one are infinite. So why not do something Shakespeare and Dostoevski and Faulkner didn't do, for after all they are nothing more than dead writers, members of this and that tradition, much-admired busts on a shelf. A dead writer may be famous but he is also dead as a duck, finished. And I, cast up here on this beach? I am a survivor! Alive! A free man! They're finished. Possibilities are closed. As for God? That's his affair. True, he made the beach, which, now that I look at it, is not all that great. As for me, I might try a little something here in the wet sand, a word, a form . . .

Q: What's this about a sexual component?

A: I'd rather not say.

Q: Why not?

A: Because no end of dreary bullshit has been written on the subject, so much as to befoul the waters for good. Starting with Freud's rather stupid hydraulic model of art as the sublimation of libidinal energies: libido suppressed in the boiler room squirts up in the attic. There followed half a century of dull jokes about x orgasms equals y novels down the drain, and so forth and so forth. Freud's disciples have been even more stupid about "creative writing." At least Freud had the good sense to know when to shut up, as he did in Dostoevski's case. But stupider still is the more recent Hemingway machismo number. The formula is: Big pencil equals big penis. My own hunch is that those fellows have their troubles, otherwise why make love with a pencil? Renoir may have started it with a smart-ass statement: "I paint with my penis." If I were a woman, I wouldn't stand for such crap. No wonder women get enraged these days. Some of the most feminine women writers have this same knack, or better, and can use it to a fare-thee-well—southern women like K.A. Porter, Welty, O'Connor—look out for them!

The twentieth century, noted for its stupidity in human matters, is even stupider than usual in this case. And in this case Muhammad Ali is smarter than either Freud or Hemingway. Float like a butterfly, sting

like a bee. Ali's exaltation and cunning and beauty and malice apply
even more to writing than to fighting. Freud made a mistake only a
twentieth-century professor would have been capable of: trying to
explain the human psyche by a mechanical-energy model. Take
away four hundred fifty psychic calories for love and that leaves you
four hundred fifty short for art. Actually it's the other way around.
The truth is paradoxical and can't be understood in terms of biological systems. Psychic energy is involved here, but it follows a different
set of laws. Like Einstein's theory, it at times defies Newton's law of
gravitation. Thus it is not the case that E minus one-half E equals
one-half E (Newton, Freud) but rather E minus one-half E equals six
E. Or simply, zero minus E equals E—which is more astounding than
Einstein's E equals MC squared.

I will give you a simple example. Let us say a writer finds himself at
0, naught, zero, at four p.m. of a Thursday afternoon. No energy,
depressed, strung out, impotent, constipated, a poet sitting on the
kitchen floor with the oven door open and the gas on, an incarnated
nothingness, an outer human husk encasing an inner cipher. The jig
is up. The poem or novel is no good. But since the jig is up, why not
have another look, or tear it up and start over? Then, if he is lucky—
or is it grace, God having mercy on the poor bastard?—something
opens. A miracle occurs. Somebody must have found the Grail. The
fisher king is healed, the desert turns green—or better still: the old
desert is still the old desert but the poet names it and makes it a new
desert. As for the poet himself: in a strange union of polarities—wick-
edness/good, malice/benevolence, hatred/love, butterfly/bee—he,
too, comes together, sticks his tongue in his cheek, sets pencil to
paper: What if I should try this? Uh-huh, maybe . . . He works. He
sweats. He stinks. He creates. He sweats and stinks and creates like a
woman conceiving. Then what? It varies. Perhaps he takes a shower,
changes clothes. Perhaps he takes a swim in the ocean. Perhaps he
takes a nap. Perhaps he takes a drink, flatfoots half a glass of bourbon. Then, if he is near someone he loves or wants to love or should
love or perhaps has loved all along but has not until this moment
known it, he looks at her. And by exactly the same measure by
which the novel has opened to him and he to it, he opens to her and
she to him. Well now, why don't you come here a minute? That's it.
Give me your hand. He looks at her hand. He is like the castaway on

the beach who opens his eyes and sees a sunrise coquina three
inches from his nose. Her hand is like the coquina. What an amazing
sight! Well now, why don't we just sit down here on this cypress log?
Imagine your being here at four-thirty in the afternoon. All this time I
thought I was alone on this island and here you are. A miracle! Imagine Crusoe on his island performing the ultimate stunt for his goats,
when he turns around and there *she* is. Who needs Friday? What he
needs now is her, or she him, as the case may be.

Such is the law of conservation of energy through its expenditure:
Zero minue E equals E.

Q: If writing is a knack, does the knack have anything to do with
being southern?

A: Sure. The knack has certain magic components that once came
in handy for southern writers. This is probably no longer the case.

Q: Why is that?

A: Well, as Einstein once said, ordinary life in an ordinary place on
an ordinary day in the modern world is a dreary business. I mean
dreary. People will do anything to escape this dreariness: booze up,
hit the road, gaze at fatal car wrecks, shoot up heroin, spend money
on gurus, watch pornographic movies, kill themselves, even watch
TV. Einstein said that was the reason he went into mathematical
physics. One of the few things that diverted me from the dreariness
of growing up in a country-club subdivision in Birmingham was sending off for things. For example, sending off for free samples, such as
Instant Postum. You'd fill in a coupon clipped from a magazine and
send it off to a magic faraway place (Battle Creek?) and sure enough,
one morning the mailman would hand you a *box*. Inside would be a
small jar. You'd make a cup and in the peculiar fragrance of Postum
you could imagine an equally fragrant and magical place where
clever Yankee experts ground up stuff in great brass mortars.

That was called "sending off for something."

It was even better with Sears and Roebuck: looking at the picture
in the catalog, savoring it, fondling it, sailing to Byzantium with it,
then—even better than poetry—actually getting it, sending off to
Chicago for it, saving up your allowance and mailing a postal money
order for twenty-three dollars and forty-seven cents and getting back
a gold-filled Elgin railroader's pocket watch with an elk engraved on
the back. With a strap and a fob.

Writing is also going into the magic business. It is a double transaction in magic. You have this little workaday thing you do that most people can't do. But in the South there were also certain magic and exotic ingredients, that is, magic and exotic to northerners and Europeans, which made the knack even more mysterious. As exotic to a New Yorker as an Elgin pocket watch to an Alabama boy. I've often suspected that Faulkner was very much onto this trick and overdid it a bit.

You write something, send it off to a *publisher* in *New York* and back it comes as a—book! Print! Pages! Cover! Binding! Scribble-scratch is turned into measured paragraphs, squared-off blocks of pretty print. And even more astounding: in the same mail that brought the Elgin pocket watch come *reviews,* the printed thoughts of people who have *read* the book!

The less the two parties know about each other, the farther apart they are, the stronger the magic. It must be very enervating to be a writer in New York, where you know all about editing and publishing and reviewing, to discover that editors and publishers and reviewers are as bad off as anyone else, maybe worse. Being a writer in the South has its special miseries, which include isolation, madness, tics, amnesia, alcoholism, lust and loss of ordinary powers of speech. One may go for days without saying a word. Then, faced with an interviewer, one may find oneself talking the way one fancies the interviewer expects one to talk, talking southern—for example, using such words as "Amon": "Amon git up and git myself a drink." Yet there are certain advantages to the isolation. At best one is encouraged to be original; at worst, bizarre; sometimes both, like Poe.

It was this distance and magic that once made for the peculiarities of southern writing. Now the distance and magic are gone, or going, and southern writers are no better off than anyone else, perhaps worse, because now that the tricks don't work and you can't write strange like Faulkner, what do you do? Write like Bellow? But before—and even now, to a degree—the magic worked. You were on your own and making up little packages to send to faraway folk. As marooned as Crusoe, one was apt to be eccentric. That's why Poe, Faulkner, O'Connor and Barthelme are more different from one another than Bellow, Updike and Cheever are.

The southern writer at his best was of value because he was some-

what extraterrestrial. (At his worst he was overwhelmed by Faulkner:
there is nothing more feckless than imitating an eccentric.) He was
different enough from the main body of writers to give the reader a
triangulation point for getting a fix on things. There are degrees of
difference. If the writer is altogether different from the genus *Writer,*
which is the only genus the reviewer knows, the reviewer is baffled—
as New York reviewers like Clifton Fadiman were baffled by Faulkner;
they were trying to compare him with such standard writers as
Thornton Wilder, and it can't be done. But if the critic recognizes the
value of difference, the possibility of an extraterrestrial point of view,
he will be excited. That's why the French went nuts over Poe and
Faulkner.

Meanwhile, Mississippians shrugged their shoulders.

Q: Would you care to say something about your own novels?
A: No.
Q: What about your last novel, *Lancelot?*
A: What about it?
Q: What do you have to say about it?
A: Nothing.
Q: How would you describe it?
A: As a small cautionary tale.
Q: That's all?
A: That's all.
Q: It has generally been well reviewed. What do you think of re-
views?

A: Very little. Reading reviews of your own book is a peculiar experience. It is a dubious enterprise, a no-win game. If the review is
flattering, one tends to feel vain and uneasy. If it is bad, one tends to
feel exposed, found out. Neither feeling does you any good. Besides
that, most reviews are of not much account. How could it be otherwise? I feel sorry for reviewers. I feel sorry for myself when I write a
review. Book reviewing is a difficult and unrewarding literary form
and right now no one is doing it. The reviewer's task is almost impossible. A writer may spend years doing his obscure thing, his little
involuted sexual-theological number, and there's the poor reviewer
with two or three days to figure out what he's up to. And even if the
review is good, you're in no mood to learn anything from it. The
timing is all bad. You're sick to death of the book and don't even

want to think about it. Then, just when you think you're rid of this baby, have kicked him and his droppings out of the nest forever, along come these folks who want to talk about him.

Q: Do you feel bad about a bad review?

A: Moderately bad. One likes to be liked. The curious thing is I always expect people to like me and my writing and am surprised when they don't. I suffer from the opposite of paranoia, a benign psychosis for which there is no word. I say "curious" because there is a good deal of malice in my writing—I have it in for this or that—but it is not personal malice and I'm taken aback when people take offense.

A rave review makes me feel even more uneasy. It's like being given an A plus by the teacher or a prize by the principal. All you want to do is grab your report card and run—before you're found out.

Q: Found out for what?

A: Found out for being what you are (and what in this day and age I think a serious writer has to be): an ex-suicide, a cipher, naught, zero—which is as it should be because being a naught is the very condition of making anything. This is a secret. People don't know this. Even distinguished critics are under the misapprehension that you are something, a substance, that you represent this or that tradition, a skill, a growing store of wisdom. Whereas in fact what you are doing is stripping yourself naked and putting yourself in the eye of the hurricane and leaving the rest to chance, luck or providence. Faulkner said it in fact: Writing a novel is like a one-armed man trying to nail together a chicken coop in a hurricane. I think of it as more like trying to pick up a four-hundred-pound fat lady: you need a lot of hands to hold up a lot of places at once.

There are four kinds of reviews, three of which are depressing and one of which is at best tolerable.

The first is the good good review. That is, a review that is not only laudatory but is also canny and on the mark. One is exhilarated for three seconds, then one becomes furtive and frightened. One puts it away quick, before it turns into a pumpkin.

The second is the bad good review. That is, it is the routine "favorable" review that doesn't understand the book. The only thing to say

about it is that it is better to get a bad good review than a bad bad
review.

The third is the bad bad review. It is a hateful review in which the
reviewer hates the book for reasons he is unwilling to disclose. He is
offended. But he must find other reasons for attacking the book than
the cause of the offense. I don't blame this reviewer. In fact he or she
is sharper than most. He or she is onto the secret that novel writing is
a serious business in which the novelist is out both to give joy and to
draw blood. The hateful review usually means that one has succeeded only in doing the latter. The name of this reviewer's game is:
"Okay, you want to play rough? Very well, here comes yours." A
hateful reviewer is like a street fighter: he doesn't let on where he's
been hit and he hits you with everything he's got—a bad tactic. Or
he lies low and waits for a chance to blindside you. A bad bad review
doesn't really hurt. Getting hit by an offended reviewer reminds me
of the old guy on *Laugh-In* who would make a pass at Ruth Buzzi on
the park bench and get slammed across the chops by a soft purse.
It's really a love tap. I can't speak for Ruth Buzzi but I can speak for
the old guy: all he wants to say is, "Come on, honey, give us a kiss."

The fourth is the good bad review, a rare bird. It would be the
most valuable if one were in any shape to learn, which one is not. It
is the critical review that accurately assesses both what the novelist
had in mind, was trying to do, and how and where he failed. It hurts
because the failure is always great, but the hurt is salutary, like pour-
ing iodine in an open wound. Here the transaction is between equals,
a fair fight, no blind-sliding. It makes me think of old-movie fistfights
between John Wayne and Ward Bond. Ward lets the Duke have
one, racks him up real good. The Duke shakes his head to clear it,
touches the corner of his mouth, looks at the blood, grins in appreciation. Nods. All right. That's a fair transaction, a frontal assault by an
equal. But what the hateful reviewer wants to do is blind-side you,
the way Chuck Bednarik blind-sided Frank Gifford and nearly killed
him. Unlike Chuck Bednarik, the hateful reviewer can't hurt you. He
gives away too much of himself. The only way he can hurt you is in
the pocketbook—the way a playwright can be knocked off by a
Times reviewer—but in the case of a book even that is doubtful.

Even so, one is still better off with hateful reviewers than with admiring reviewers. If I were a castaway on a desert island, I'd rather be marooned with six hateful reviewers than with six admiring reviewers. The hateful men would be better friends and the hateful women would be better lovers.

The truth is all reviewers and all your fellow novelists are your friends and lovers. All serious writers and readers constitute less than one percent of the population. The other ninety-nine percent don't give a damn. They watch *Wonder Woman*. We are a tiny shrinking minority and our worst assaults on each other are love taps compared with the massive indifference surrounding us. Gore Vidal and Bill Buckley are really two of a kind, though it will displease both to hear it. Both are serious moralists to whom I attach a high value.

Q: Do you see the Jimmy Carter phenomenon as a revival of Protestant Christianity or as a renascence of Jeffersonian populism or the southern political genius or all three, and if so, what is the impact on the southern literary imagination and race relations?

A: How's that again?

Q: Do you—

A: What was that about race relations?

Q: How do you assess the current state of race relations in the South?

A: Almost as bad as in the North.

Q: But hasn't there occurred a rather remarkable reconciliation of the races in the South as a consequence of its strong Christian tradition and its traditional talent for human relations?

A: I haven't noticed it. The truth is most blacks and whites don't like each other, North or South.

Q: But great changes have taken place, haven't they?

A: Yes, due mainly to court decisions and congressional acts and Lyndon Johnson. It was easier for the South to go along than to resist. After all, we tried that once. Anyhow, as Earl Long used to say, the feds have the bomb now.

Q: Can you say anything about the future of race relations?

A: No.

Q: Why not?

A: I'm white. It's up to the blacks. The government has done all it can do. The whites' course is predictable. Like anybody else, they will simply hold on to what they've got as long as they can. When did any other human beings behave differently? The blacks have a choice. They can either shoot up the place, pull the whole damn thing down around our ears—they can't win but they can ruin it for everybody—or they can join the great screwed-up American middle class. Of course what they're doing is both, mostly the latter. It is noteworthy that blacks, being smarter than whites about such things, have shown no interest in the Communist party. Blacks seem less prone than whites to fall prey to abstractions. Comradeship and brotherhood are all very well, but what I really want is out of this ghetto, and if I can make it and you can't, too bad about you, brother. But that's the American dream, isn't it? It will even make them happy like it did us—for a while. It will take them years to discover just how screwed up the American middle class is. I visualize a U.S. a few years from now in which blacks and whites have switched roles. The pissed-off white middle class will abandon suburbia just as they abandoned the cities, either for the countryside, where they will live in r.v.'s, mobile homes, converted farms, log cabins, antebellum outhouses, revolutionary stables, silos, sod huts, or to move back to the city, back to little ethnic cottages like Mayor Daley's, Victorian shotguns, stained-glass boardinghouses, converted slave quarters, abandoned streetcars—while the blacks move out to Levittown and the tracts, attend the churches of their choice, P.T.A.'s, Rotary, Great Books. In fact it's already happening. The only danger is that this happy little switch may not happen fast enough and the young blacks in the city who have little or nothing to lose may say the hell with it and shoot up everything in sight.

There is a slight chance, maybe one in a hundred, that blacks and whites may learn the best of each other rather than the worst.

Q: What is the worst?

A: Well, whites in the Western world don't know how to live and blacks don't know how to govern themselves. It would be nice if each could learn the gift of the other. But there are already signs in America that blacks are learning the white incapacity for life. For example, they've almost reached the white incidence of suicide and gastric ulcer and have surpassed them in hypertension. And some white politicians govern like Haitians and Ugandans. I've noticed that more and more blacks act like Robert Young as Dr. Marcus Welby, with that same tight-assed, suspect post-Protestant rectitude, while more and more white politicians act like Idi Amin.

Q: Can you describe the best thing that could happen?

A: No. All I can say is that it has something to do with southern good nature, good manners, kidding around, with music, with irony, with being able to be pissed off without killing other people or yourself, maybe with Jewish humor, with passing the time, with small unpretentious civic-minded meetings. Some whites and blacks are sitting around a table in Louisiana, eating crawfish and drinking beer at a P.T.A. fund raiser. The table is somewhat polarized, whites at one end, blacks at the other, segregated not ill-naturedly but from social unease, like men and women at a party. The talk is somewhat stiff and conversation making and highfaluting—about reincarnation in fact. Says a white to a white who has only had a beer or two: "I think I'd rather come back as an English gentleman in the eighteenth century rather than this miserable century of war, alienation and pollution." Says a black to a black who has had quite a few beers: "I'd rather come back as this damn crawfish than as a nigger in Louisiana." All four laugh and have another beer. I don't know why I'm telling you this. You wouldn't understand it. You wouldn't understand what is bad about it, what is good about it, what is unusual about it or what there is about it that might be the hundred-to-one shot that holds the solution.

Q: Why do you leave Christianity out as one of the ingredients of better race relations?

A: Because the Christians left it out. Maybe Jimmy Carter and Andrew Young and a few others mean what they say, I don't know, but look at the white churches. They generally practice the same brand of brotherhood as the local country club. If Jesus Christ showed up at the Baptist church in Plains, the deacons would call the cops. No, the law, government, business, sports, show business, have done more here than the churches. There seems to be an inverse relationship between God and brotherhood in the churches. In the Unitarian Church, it's all brotherhood and no God. Outside the churches the pocketbook has replaced the Holy Ghost as the source of brotherhood. Show me an A & P today that is losing money because it is not hiring blacks and I'll show you an A & P tomorrow that has hired blacks and, what is more, where blacks and whites get along fine.

Q: But aren't you a Catholic?

A: Yes.

Q: Do you regard yourself as a Catholic novelist?

A: Since I am a Catholic and a novelist, it would seem to follow that I am a Catholic novelist.

Q: What kind of Catholic are you?

A: Bad.

Q: No. I mean are you liberal or conservative?

A: I no longer know what those words mean.

Q: Are you a dogmatic Catholic or an open-minded Catholic?

A: I don't know what that means, either. Do you mean do I believe the dogma that the Catholic Church proposes for belief?

Q: Yes.

A: Yes.

Q: How is such a belief possible in this day and age?

A: What else is there?

Q: What do you mean, what else is there? There is humanism, atheism, agnosticism, Marxism, behaviorism, materialism, Buddhism, Muhammadanism, Sufism, astrology, occultism, theosophy.

A: That's what I mean.

Q: To say nothing of Judaism and Protestantism.

A: Well, I would include them along with the Catholic Church in the whole peculiar Jewish-Christian thing.

Q: I don't understand. Would you exclude, for example, scientific humanism as a rational and honorable alternative?

A: Yes.

Q: Why?

A: It's not good enough.

Q: Why not?

A: This life is much too much trouble, far too strange, to arrive at the end of it and then to be asked what you make of it and have to answer "Scientific humanism." That won't do. A poor show. Life is a mystery, love is a delight. Therefore I take it as axiomatic that one should settle for nothing less than the infinite mystery and the infinite delight, i.e., God. In fact I demand it. I refuse to settle for anything less. I don't see why anyone should settle for less than Jacob, who

actually grabbed aholt of God and wouldn't let go until God
identified himself and blessed him.

Q: Grabbed aholt?

A: A Louisiana expression.

Q: But isn't the Catholic Church in a mess these days, badly split,
its liturgy barbarized, vocations declining?

A: Sure. That's a sign of its divine origins, that it survives these
periodic disasters.

Q: You don't act or talk like a Christian. Aren't they supposed to
love one another and do good works?

A: Yes.

Q: You don't seem to have much use for your fellowman or do
many good works.

A: That's true. I haven't done a good work in years.

Q: In fact, if I may be frank, you strike me as being rather negative
in your attitude, cold-blooded, aloof, derisive, self-indulgent, more
fond of the beautiful things of this world than of God.

A: That's true.

Q: You even seem to take a certain satisfaction in the disasters of
the twentieth century and to savor the imminence of world catastrophe rather than world peace, which all religions seek.

A: That's true.

Q: You don't seem to have much use for your fellow Christians, to
say nothing of Ku Kluxers, A.C.L.U.'ers, northerners, southerners,
fem-libbers, anti-fem-libbers, homosexuals, anti-homosexuals, Re-
publicans, Democrats, hippies, anti-hippies, senior citzens.

A: That's true—though taken as individuals they turn out to be
more or less like oneself, i.e., sinners, and we get along fine.

Q: Even Ku Kluxers?

A: Sure.

Q: How do you account for your belief?

A: I can only account for it as a gift from God.

Q: Why would God make you such a gift when there are others
who seem more deserving, that is, serve their fellowman?

A: I don't know. God does strange things. For example, he picked
as one of his saints a fellow in northern Syria, a local nut, who stood
on top of a pole for thirty-seven years.

Q: We are not talking about saints.

A: That's true.

Q: We are talking about what you call a gift.

A: You want me to explain it? How would I know? The only answer I can give is that I asked for it, in fact demanded it. I took it as an intolerable state of affairs to have found myself in this life and in this age, which is a disaster by any calculation, without demanding a gift commensurate with the offense. So I demanded it. No doubt other people feel differently.

Q: But shouldn't faith bear some relation to the truth, facts?

A: Yes. That's what attracted me, Christianity's rather insolent claim to be true, with the implication that other religions are more or less false.

Q: You believe that?

A: Of course.

Q: I see. Moving right along now—

A: To what?

Q: To language. Haven't you done some writing about the nature of language?

A: Yes.

Q: Will you say something about your ideas about language?

A: No.

Q: Why not?

A: Because, for one thing, nobody is interested. The nature of language is such, I have discovered from experience, that even if anyone has the ultimate solution to the mystery of language, no one would pay the slightest attention. In fact most people don't even know there is a mystery. Here is an astounding fact, when you come to think of it. The use of symbols between creatures, the use of language in particular, appears to be the one unique phenomenon in the universe, is certainly the single behavior that most clearly sets man apart from the beasts, is also the one activity in which humans engage most of the time, even asleep and dreaming. Yet it is the least understood of all phenomena. We know less about it than about the back side of the moon or the most distant supernova—and are less interested.

Q: Why is that? Why aren't people interested?

A: Because there are two kinds of people, laymen and scientists. The layman doesn't see any mystery. Since he is a languaged crea-

ture and sees everything through the mirror of language, asking him
to consider the nature of language is like asking a fish to consider the
nature of water. He cannot imagine its absence, so he cannot consider its presence. To the layman, language is a transparent humdrum
affair. Where is the mystery? People see things, are given the names
of things when they are children, have thoughts, which they learn to
express in words and sentences, talk and listen, read and write. So
where is the mystery? That's the general lay attitude toward language. On the other hand there are the theorists of language, who
are very much aware of the mystery and who practice such esoteric
and abstruse disciplines as transformational generative grammar, formal semantics, semiotics, and who by and large have their heads up
their asses and can't even be understood by fellow specialists. They
remind me of nothing so much as the Scholastics of the fifteenth
century, who would argue about the number of angels that could
dance on the head of a pin.

Q: Haven't you written something about a theory of language?
A: Yes.
Q: Could you summarize your thoughts on the subject?
A: No.
Q: Why not?
A: It is not worth the trouble. What is involved in a theory of
language is a theory of man, and people are not interested. Despite
the catastrophes of this century and man's total failure to understand
himself and deal with himself, people still labor under the illusion that
a theory of man exists. It doesn't. As bad and confused as things are,
they have to get even worse before people realize they don't have
the faintest idea what sort of creature man is. Then they might want
to know. Until then, one is wasting one's time. I'm not interested in
butting my head against a stone wall. I've written something on the
subject. Maybe ten years from now, fifty years from now, some people will be interested. That's their affair. People are not really interested in science nowadays. They are interested in pseudoscientific
mysteries.

Q: Like what?
A: Laymen are more interested in such things as the Bermuda
Triangle, U.F.O.'s, hypnotic regression, Atlantis, astrology—
pseudomysteries. Scientists are more interested in teaching apes to

talk than in finding out why people talk. It is one of the peculiarities of the age that scientists are more interested in spending millions of dollars and man-hours trying to teach chimps to use language in order to prove that language is not a unique property of man than in studying the property itself. Scientists tend to be dogmatic about the nature of man. Again they remind me of the Scholastics battling with Galileo. Scholastics spent thousands of man-hours inside their heads trying to prove that Jupiter couldn't have moons and that the earth was at the center of the universe. To suggest otherwise offended their sense of the order of things. Galileo pointed to his telescope: Why don't you take a look?

Today we have plenty of scholastics of language. What we need is a Galileo who is willing to take a look at it.

Q: You still haven't said what you think of Jimmy Carter.

A: No.

Q: There is an extraordinary divergence of opinion. Some say he is the greatest of all southern con artists, that everything he says and does in the way of humility, sincerity, honesty, love, brotherhood and so forth is an act, a calculated living up to an image. Others say that these virtues are real. Which is it?

A: Is there a difference?

Q: Moving right along. . . . This is a pleasant room we're sitting in, overlooking a pleasant bayou.

A: Yes, it is. It is still a pretty country, despite the fact that the white man did his best to ruin it, ran the Indians off, cut down all the trees.

Q: Is that a portrait of you over the fireplace?

A: Yes. It was done by an artist friend of mine, Lyn Hill. I like it very much.

Q: I don't quite get it. What's going on there?

A: It shows me—well, not exactly me, a version of me—standing in front of what seems to be another framed painting. A picture within a picture, so to speak.

Q: What does it mean to you?

A: I can only say what I see. The artist may very well disagree, but after all the subject and viewer is entitled to his own ideas—like a book reviewer. I identify the subject of the portraits as a kind of composite of the protagonists of my novels, but most especially Lancelot. He is not too attractive a fellow and something of a nut besides. As we say in the South, he's mean as a yard dog. It is not a flattering portrait—he is not the sort of fellow you'd like to go fishing with. He is, as usual, somewhat out of it, out of the world that is framed off behind him. Where is he? It is an undisclosed place, a kind of limbo. It's a dark place—look at that background—if one believed in auras, his would be a foreboding one. It is a kind of desert, a bombed-out place, a place after the end of the world, a no-man's-land of blasted trees and barbed wire. As for him, he is neither admirable nor attractive. Rather, he is cold-eyed and sardonic. There is a gleam in his eyes, a muted and dubious satisfaction. He is looking straight at the viewer, soliciting him ironically: *You and I know something, don't we? Or do we?* Or rather: *The chances are ninety-nine in a hundred you don't know, but on the other hand you might be the one in a hundred who does—not that it makes much difference. True, this is a strange world I'm in, but what about the world you're in? Have you noticed it lately? Are we onto something, you and I? Probably not.*

But look at this apocalyptic world behind him. Something is going on. Is he aware of it? The dead blasted tree is undergoing a transformation. Into—? Into what? A bound figure? Figures? A woman? Lovers? The no-man's-land barbed wire is not really wire but a brier and it is blooming! A rose! Behind him there is a window of sorts, an opening out of his dark world onto a lovely seascape/skyscape. A new world! Yet he goes on looking straight at the viewer, challenging him: *Yes, I know about it, but do you? If you do, well and good. If you don't, there's no use in my telling you or turning around and pointing it out.* There's a limit to what writers can tell readers and artists can tell viewers. Perhaps he is Lancelot with the world and his life in ruins around him, but there is a prospect of a new world in the Shenandoah Valley. There was something wrong with the old world, the old things, the old flowers, the old skies, old clouds—or something wrong with his way of seeing them. They were used up. They have to be seen anew. Here is a new sky, a new sea, a new rose . . .

Q: Could you say something about your debt to Kierkegaard?

A: No.

Q: Could you at least explicate the painting in Kierkegaardian terms?

A: If I do, will you leave me alone?

Q: Yes.

A: Very well, I see the painting as depicting the very beginning of the Kierkegaardian stages of life—which can apply to an individual, a people, an age. It is the dawn of the aesthetic stage, the emergence of life from death, of light from darkness, the first utterance of words between people. The desert is just beginning to flower and there is the possibility that there may be survivors after the catastrophe. He, somewhat sardonic and smart-assed as usual, knows it but does not want to give away the secret too easily. So he keeps his own counsel, except for the faintest glimmer in his eye—of risibility, even hope?—which says to the viewer: *I doubt if you know what's going on, but then again you just might. Do you?*

Do you understand?

Q: No.

An Interview with Walker Percy

James Atlas/1980

From *The New York Times Book Review,* 29 June 1980, pp. 1, 30–31. Copyright © 1980 by the New York Times Company. Reprinted by permission.

It is a warm, sun-drenched afternoon in Manhattan, but the author of "The Moviegoer" is lying on his bed in a dark hotel room watching "Dial M for Murder." Like his character Binx Bolling, a troubled film enthusiast whose favorite moments happened in the movies rather than in his own life, Walker Percy seems happier in the realm of Hitchcock than of literary conversation. Rising reluctantly from his bed to discuss his latest novel, he displays the reserve, good manners and genial modesty one would expect from a white-haired Southern gentleman of 66, tempered by the shy, awkward uncertainty of a child eager for reassurance. He seems a composite portrait of the protagonists of his five novels: the brooding, disoriented Binx; Lancelot Andrewes Lamar, the zealous, faintly depressed prophet whose maniac soliloquy dominates "Lancelot"; Dr. Thomas More, the brilliant visionary in "Love in the Ruins"; and the sensitive Will Barrett, first encountered as a young man in "The Last Gentleman" and revived in "The Second Coming" as a middle-aged widower given to seizures and lapses of memory.

Like his bewildered, essentric personae, Percy has never quite had a profession; his biography reflects one of the more anomalous careers in contemporary American literature. The son of a Southern lawyer whose shade lurks in the background of all his novels, Percy was made an orphan at 15, when his mother died in a car accident two years after his father's suicide. He was raised by his father's cousin Will, a poet and the author of "Lanterns on the Levee," a collection of autobiographical essays about growing up in the South. After graduation from the University of North Carolina at Chapel Hill, the young Walker enrolled in Columbia University College of Physicians and Surgeons and in the winter of 1942 began a rigorous

internship at Bellevue. But within a few months he developed tuberculosis and had to be confined to a sanatorium. He never practiced
medicine. In the years that followed, Percy married, converted to
Catholicism, returned to the South and devoted himself to the
philosophical research reflected in "The Message in the Bottle," a
collection of essays—some of them quite technical—on philosophical
topics: existentialism, phenomenology, language theory. It wasn't until the late 1950's that he turned to fiction; "The Moviegoer" appeared in 1962.

What made him turn from philosophy to fiction? "It was reading
the French—writers like Sartre and Camus. The American novelist
tends to distinguish between reflections on our universal predicament
and what can be told in fiction, whereas the French see nothing
wrong with writing novels that address what they consider the deepest philosophical issues." ("Besides," he notes wryly, "I was tired of
getting paid in reprints.")

Those issues, so crucial in Percy's novels, declare themselves once
again on the very first page of "The Second Coming," in the peculiar
malaise of Will Barrett. "I didn't intend to write a sequel to 'The Last
Gentleman,' but after a hundred pages or so my character just sort of
became Will Barrett in middle age, still lost after 20 years of 'achieving his goals.' This book is about his belated crisis in coming to a
decision for the first time in his life." What brings on this crisis? "He's
facing death. It's only the prospect of death that enables him to act at
last."

The new novel represents a departure from its predecessors, Percy
claims, in that it ends happily. "It seems to me that these two characters achieve their lives in a way no other characters I've written about
have. I consider this my first unalienated novel. It's a very ordinary,
conventional story that could even be seen in Hollywood terms: Boy
meets girl, boy loses girl, and boy gets girl."

Yet in other respects "The Second Coming" echoes predicaments
and situations to be found in Percy's earlier novels: a cerebral main
character; an obsession with language; protracted meditations on the
nature of existence and polemics against the corruption of American
life. Does Percy worry about repeating himself? "It's been said that
all novelists write the same novel over and over again. And since the
kind of fiction I write is an exploration to begin with, all I can hope to

do is push the boundaries back. I'm convinced that in 'The Second Coming' there's a definite advance, a resolution of the ambiguity with which some of my other novels end: the victory, in Freudian terms, of eros over thanatos, life over death."

Percy himself radiates a sort of old-fashioned gentility, but a stubborn anger declares itself in his novels; "The Second Coming" is full of triades against this "Century of the Love of Death," this "age of madness." Will Barrett, he maintains, is "a voracious and enraged pilgrim" on a perilous journey-quest in search of reality. "Binx was trying to find someone to tell him the right psychology, or the right philosophy, or the right book—if he could only read the right book. But in the later books he reaches what Kierkegaard called the religious stage. I think of him as a Christian Jacob, the Jacob who actually wrestled with the angel of God and demanded God acknowledge him, and would settle for nothing less. Will Barrett is an absolute seeker—a seeker and a demander. He insists on finding what he calls the truth; and it's either that or death."

Apart from occasional remnisciences of a Southern childhood scattered through his work, Percy has written very little about his past; yet images of a remote, enigmatic father who dies a violent death figure in several of his novels. Is it possible that his impulse to question the evidence of his senses so tirelessly derives from his own early experience of the randomness of life and death? "Nothing like the father's suicide in this novel ever happened to me, but I did think Will's going back, after 40 or 50 years, and finally figuring out what happened was a means of recovery." But isn't this intense concentration on language simply another reflection of his wary attitude toward a world perceived since youth as treacherous? "I think the two are inseparable. What we're witnessing is a certain wearing out of the language, a certain exhaustion of the symbols of the culture—the linguistic, religious and esthetic symbols. And the only way to recover a new life is through a new language. Which is just what a good writer does."

Percy is fond of referring to himself as "an alien," "a stranger in a strange land"—cries of *anomie* more suitable to the writers of Eastern Europe in the era before World War I than to an affluent, well-groomed Southerner in 1980. But the novelist's sense of estrangement is genuine; his existentialist vocabulary is more than a pose. Like so many American novelists, he finds himself oppressed by his self-chosen isolation. "I've never been able to figure out where novelists were supposed to fit in, where they belong in American society, and I've never been able to figure out if novelists in other countries were as miserable as novelists in this country. Every novelist I know is miserable," he says in a plaintive voice. "It's a miserable, lonely life." Over dinner, he questions his guest intently. "Does Philip Roth visit William Styron? What do those writers do up there in Connecticut?"

Still, Percy has a way of turning his dilemmas to advantage. Recalling his years in New York during World War II, he declares: "I was the happiest man ever to contract tuberculosis, because it enabled me to get out of Bellevue and quit medicine." And when he was released from a sanatorium in 1946, the discovery that his past had vanished was "a great piece of good fortune. My uncle had died and I had no address. I had no place to live. But my feeling of dislocation happily coincided with what I discovered to be the state of man in the 20th century. So I've cultivated it with great enthusiasm ever since. It's a cultivated dislocation."

In a recent issue of Esquire, Percy reflected on why he chose to settle in Covington, a placid Southern town in "the green heart of green Louisiana, a green jungle of pines, azaleas, camellias, dogwood, grapevines and billions of blades of grass." What appealed to him about Covington was that it avoided "total placement"—a locale in which the writer is forced to compete with a too visible, dominating past—and "total misplacement"—living in some unfamiliar territory. For Percy the South offers both tradition and anonymity. "I'm aware of traditions here that I doubt I would have encountered in Ohio or Chicago or New York. My Uncle Will belonged to a very sturdy Greco-Roman stoic tradition; then there was the Catholic tradition in South Louisiana, and now the evangelical, born-again Christianity of the New South."

Yet his own allegiance to the South is tenuous: "The odd thing is that I don't fit in here. One would think my own sense of dislocation would coincide with the historical predicament of the South. Because we had lost the Civil War, Southerners were citizens of a defeated country—according to the common wisdom—and thus entitled to our own alienation. But I never fitted in with those fellows"—writers such as Allen Tate and John Crowe Ransom, who called themselves Fugitives and celebrated the traditional virtues of the South while denouncing the corrupt industrial North. "Faulkner and all the rest of them were always going on about this tragic sense of history, and we're supposed to sit on our porches talking about it all the time. I never did that. My South was always the New South. My first memories are of the country club, of people playing golf."

This geographical and spiritual perplexity appears to be widely shared, for Percy has acquired a devoted, even fanatical following that responds to his work in a very personal way; readers are forever writing and calling him up to discuss their problems. How does he account for this affinity? "The lucky moments in one's writing come when he's able to say something that everybody knows and yet doesn't know that he knows. The reader reads it and says, 'Why, that's me. I hadn't thought about it. I didn't know anybody else felt that way.' " What sort of people does he hear from? "A lot of younger folks write, and once in a while a contemporary of mine—a fraternity brother, say—might suddenly decide after a few drinks to call at three o'clock in the morning from a sales conference in San Francisco and tell me about his life." (Some of his supplicants are more general in their literary homage than others. When Percy asked a frantic woman who rang him up late one night why she had sought his advice, she replied: "Because I couldn't get Norman Mailer on the phone.")

Now that the fortunes of Will Barrett have been so happily resolved, what will Percy turn to next? "Well, I'm bloody sick of making up stories, I can tell you that! When you get through with a novel, you think, 'This is not a respectable occupation for a grown man.' " After spending a month in Toronto this summer attending a conference on semiotics—the theory of signs—he intends to start on a sequel to "The Message in the Bottle." "Perhaps I'll call it 'Son of Message in the Bottle' or 'Message in the Bottle Returns.' " And how will he deal with angst, alienation and other perils of the trade? "My solution is to work during the day, and drink and watch 'The Incredible Hulk' at night."

A Conversation with Novelist Walker Percy
Edmund Fuller/1980

From *The Wall Street Journal*, 16 July 1980, p. 24. Reprinted
by permission of *The Wall Street Journal.* © Dow Jones &
Company, Inc. 1980. All rights reserved.

"I have a very low threshold of taste. I will go to almost any movie
and watch almost any TV. I even watch 'The Incredible Hulk.' "

That is said with good-natured, characteristically self-deprecating
laughter by Walker Percy, whose fifth novel, "The Second Coming,"
reviewed here June 23, is receiving deserved acclaim. The confession
should not surprise us. His first novel, in 1961, was "The
Moviegoer," about an amiable young man of New Orleans, named
Binx Bolling, who is alienated from the real world and largely leads
his life vicariously through movies. Allusions to films and television
are prominent in the other novels, too. In his fourth, "Lancelot"
(1977), much of the action involves the making of a movie at an old
New Orleans mansion and those who make the product in this instance are seen to be as artificial as the product itself. Dr. Percy sees
movies and TV as the abstract and brief chronicles of the time. "They
say a good deal about the culture."

The state of the culture and the alienation of some people from it
are central concerns of his novels. I talked with him recently about
work new and old, not on his home terrain in Louisiana but reaching
him by telephone in Toronto where he was staying for a time, studying one of his many interests, semiotics, a branch of semantics concerned with the significance of signs, involving gesture and what is
now called popularly "body language" as well as words.

In spite of the long voice leap Dr. Percy was not remote. His affa-
bility, the easy warmth of his manner and speech, the tones unmis-
takably Southern but not broadly so, created a strong sense of
immediate presence, harmonious with what I know of his appear-
ance—a relaxed, lanky frame, strong interestingly seamed face, and
close-trimmed white hair. I felt I was meeting the man.

He is a physician who has never practiced except, as he says, that "I worked for a while as a pathologist at Bellevue." That was following medical studies at Columbia University where he had gone after graduation from the University of North Carolina at Chapel Hill. Tuberculosis interrupted the medical career and after his cure he did not resume it, turning to letters, at first as a writer of scholarly philosophical essays. Dissatisfied with these as a means of communicating his vision of life and character to a general audience, he turned to the novel, succeeding so strongly with his first effort, "The Moviegoer," as to win the National Book Award for fiction. From then until now, his reputation and his audience have grown steadily. Having recently turned 64, he is at the height of his powers with the best of his books and probably the bestselling, for "The Second Coming" is a Book-of-the-Month Club selection.

He is a writer capable of being surprised in the unfolding of his own work-in-progress—probably an attribute of every good novelist. The leading male character in "The Second Coming" is Will Barrett, now 55, who at 25 had been the protagonist of Dr. Percy's second novel, "The Last Gentleman" (1966). I ask if when he wrote that earlier book he had any intention of ever writing another about Will Barrett.

"No, nothing surprised me more. I was a good way into 'The Second Coming' when I began to realize that this middle-aged man, to whom I had given another name up till then, was Will Barrett twenty years later."

Having used Will Barrett in two books, and made him so appealing, does Dr. Percy identify with him more than with other characters?

"The things that happen to Will haven't happened to me, so in that sense, no, but I think I am fonder of Will than of any other of my characters."

Of equal charm is the young girl, Allie Huger, fighting her way back from mental illness, almost literally forming herself as she goes along, in whose recovery of speech we see reflected Dr. Percy's preoccupation with the nature of language. "I'm very happy about this girl, Allie. Women sometimes have charged me with not knowing anything about women, which may be true, but I like what I have done with Allie. I think she is my most successful woman character."

I inquire about a remarkable sequence in which Will attempts a perilous experiment to prove conclusively whether God exists. Dr. Percy responds: "In this I think of Will as a good Southern Episcopal Jacob—the Jacob who wanted to force God to show Himself, who wrestled with Him for an answer."

There are funny, but also harsh, thoughts in Will's mind about all the sorts of churches and styles of religion in the North Carolina mountain town that is the book's setting. Do these reflect Will Barrett or Walker Percy?

They're Will's views in a given time and circumstance. I'm a very ordinary Roman Catholic with no problems about the Church. But finally I think Will feels that he's gotten God's answer, though not in the way he had expected."

Walker Percy's previous novel, "Lancelot," in spite of its wit and strong plot, seems finally a negative book. Was he in a low mood when he wrote it?

"Not particularly. I live in a state of mild depression much of the time, which I'm used to. But Lancelot Lamar and Will Barrett represent opposite solutions to a similar predicament. Lancelot adopts a destructive one, the way of *Thanatos,* of death; Will adopts a constructive one, the way of *Eros,* affirming life. I was very conscious of the two men being much alike but taking different approaches to their problems." There has been a gestation period of five years or so between Dr. Percy's novels. Is a new one germinating?

His response is laughingly emphatic. "I feel like a woman who has just delivered a baby after a five-year pregnancy and I'm in the midst of full postpartum depression. The last thing I want to think about is writing another novel!" He laughs again, with an oblique promise: "I'll get over it, though."

Percy: He Can See Clearly Now

Marc Kirkeby/1980

From *Los Angeles Times Calendar* (3 August 1980), p. 52, and reprinted by permission.

New York City—With a hero and heroine who fall in love not entirely unconventionally, a few clearly dislikable villains and an ending that is happy, indeed joyous, Walker Percy's fifth novel, "The Second Coming" (Farrar, Straus & Giroux), marks a new turn of mind for the author who garnered wide acclaim and fame for his first novel, "The Moviegoer," surprise winner of 1962's National Book Award. This change, he admits, pleases him greatly.

"Most of my novels end up more or less inconclusively," he said in a recent interview here, "with the hero not having his problems resolved and being in a situation not greatly different from the beginning. This may be the first time where the ending is not ambiguous. Maybe for the first time I saw the possibility of a clear resolution, a classical, novelistic resolution, a victory of eros over thanatos and life over death. This man actually sees a possibility of achieving love, work that he likes, a sense of identity—as they say nowadays, that he's never had before, freedom to choose for himself, and he demands the presence of God on top of that. And I think it's clear that he gets it.

"I like to think, half-seriously, that this may be the first unalienated novel written since Tolstoy."

Alienation, and Percy's longstanding concern with the hazy line between sanity and insanity, haven't disappeared in "The Second Coming," but the violence and sense of foreboding that pervaded his last two novels, "Lancelot" and "Love in the Ruins," are gone.

Will Barrett, callow protagonist of "The Last Gentleman," Percy's second novel, returns here in prosperous but confused middle age, paired with the story's new element, Allison Huger, a young escaped mental patient who is Percy's first central female character. "I don't know where she came from," he said, "but I feel happier with her

190

than with any other female in my books. I receive complaints about
my books from women, who say to me I don't know anything about
women, which I'm the first person to admit. But Allison pleases me
very much."

She also gives Percy the chance to raise some questions from his
studies in semiotics, concerning "the peculiar phenomenon by which
language conceals, fails to communicate and becomes hardened and
opaque rather than transparent. I was very conscious of using her
language that way, almost as if she were aware ordinary speech had
somehow been worn out, that not only did it no longer convey what
it was supposed to convey, but sometimes it conveyed the opposite."

Percy, who trained as a physician but never practiced, discounts
the suggestion he practices a different sort of medicine through what
has been called "moral fiction." "If morality is defined as Aquinas
defines it, as entailing practical action that's not what a novelist is
about," he said. "A novelist, like any other artist,is trying to arrive at a
certain truth and I suppose immorality is a consequence of falling
short of that, or perverting it by pornography, simply catering to bad
taste or writing for other reasons than to convey what you consider
the truth of things."

Nevertheless, a novelist who has created a gallery of seekers after
truth, or God, or simply the proper way to live, must contend with
the apparently endless demands of real-life seekers. "I'll give you an
extreme case," Percy said. "The phone rings late at night. It's a lady
saying 'You don't know who I am, but I've just read your book "The
Moviegoer" and you know the answer. I'm contemplating suicide,
and unless you give me the answer in the next 30 minutes, I'm going
to do it."

"I tried to tell her that novelists are the last people in the world to
give anybody any answers, that the most the novelist can do is share
a certain truth about the way things are. As Kierkegaard would say,
it's not the novelist's business to be edifying, or 'bring the good
news.' I got her through the first half-hour, anyway. I hope she's still
around."

Sometimes the train of seekers to Percy's door brings more than
unanswerable questions. Perhaps the most singular instance occurred
last year when the novelist, teaching a creative writing course ("whatever that is") at Loyola University in New Orleans, began receiving

calls from an elderly woman who insisted he read her son's book, which she said was "perhaps *the* great novel."

"You can imagine how anxious I was to get hold of that," Percy recalled. "She simply showed up one day, with a black chauffeur, and white gloves, blue hat and a veil, a little, frail lady with a walker, and gave me this manuscript. I got irritated and forgot my Southern manners, and I said, 'If it's so damn good, why didn't your son bring it in himself?' She said he had committed suicide 10 years ago. That stopped me; I said I'd read a couple of pages; and it was just extraordinary, one of a kind."

Percy brought the novel, "A Confederacy of Dunces" by John Kennedy Toole, to the Louisiana State University Press, which published it without anticipating the stream of laudatory reviews and film offers that has followed. "They're in a state of disorientation," Percy said with a chuckle. "They've lost interest in scholarly books. They want to publish novels."

Percy worries, however; that first-novel success stories like Toole's may become rarer and rarer. "Maybe the novel will survive, maybe there's a reaction setting in against television. But I wonder if people will be buying novels 20 years from now, and if so, what kind of novels they'll be."

Neither these concerns nor his present work in semiotics will likely keep Percy from writing another novel, from "going through the misery of being locked up in a room for three years struggling with these people."

"Flannery O'Connor wrote me a letter in which she said 'The Moviegoer' is pretty good. Why don't you make up another one?' I'll probably end up making up another story."

Dr. Percy on Signs and Symbols

Henry Kisor/1980

From *Critic*, 39 (September 1980), 2–5. Reprinted by permission of Henry Kisor and of the *Chicago Sun-Times*, in which the interview first appeared.

TORONTO—Walker Percy isn't keen to be interviewed. He'll let in the *New York Times* and the *Wall Street Journal*, but that's usually that. You'd never guess how I got in the door.

As a child in the 1940s I was a pupil of the late Doris Mirrielees, a heroic and gifted teacher of the deaf. A decade and a half later, when she began working her miracles for the Percy's deaf daughter, Ann, she mentioned my name to them. When I called Percy a few weeks ago, it could still ring a bell after all these years.

"So when I found out who you were I wanted to meet you anyway," said Percy, every lean and weatherbeaten inch the Louisiana gentleman. At 64, with gulf-blue eyes, a tanned, furrowed face and white hair, he could be a Southern lawyer or doctor—which he once was. He greets the stranger at his door with grave courtesy, but a quick and generous laugh punctuates his conversation. His novels are packed with angst, but on this day at least, he sounds like a man who delights in life and the sharing of it.

He had taken a month away from his Covington, La., home, across Lake Pontchartrain from New Orleans, to be a visiting scholar at a conference here on semiotics—the study of signs and symbols.

"I became interested in man's use of the symbols of language when I discovered that my daughter was deaf," he said. "I'd been reading about Helen Keller's famous breakthrough in discovering that words stood for things: when Annie Sullivan poured water over her hand and spelled the word 'water' in her palm, and Helen made the connection."

Percy studies the subject "off and on; after I write a novel, I get sick and tired of it and never want to do it again. So, as a kind of vacation, I'll write about or study semiotics."

That interest led to his 1975 book *The Message in the Bottle,* a collection of scholarly essays about language, and it also figures in the person of Allison, the young woman in his new novel, *The Second Coming.* Her memory has been erased, zapped by shock treatments at the sanitarium she has just escaped, and she thinks and speaks in odd conundrums.

"There's such a thing as a schizophrenic language," Percy said, "that's very strange and peculiar, and can't ordinarily be understood. But schizophrenics are trying to say something which means a great deal to them. I like the idea of Allison starting a new life and, in a way, learning language from the beginning. She sees everything fresh and new and in her own way."

The notion, he said, gave him a character who was a total failure, starting a new life from scratch in a greenhouse in the woods, without the slightest idea how to get along with people. But she's full of hope compared with the man she meets at the greenhouse, Will Barrett, an aging lawyer whom we first encountered as a young, bemused Candide in Percy's 1966 novel, *The Last Gentleman.* Barrett is successful, wealthy and respected, educated and traveled, but full of despair and depression—"death in life." Thus two slates: one blank, one crammed. A useful paradox upon which to build a novel.

The older Barrett seems slightly changed from the young protagonist of *The Last Gentleman.* Not just in age and weariness, but in odd mechanics, such as a trick knee that had plagued him throughout the earlier novel but which has disappeared. This leads me to ask whether *The Second Coming* was conceived as a true sequel, or as a self-contained novel.

Though both can be read as a single entity, Percy replies, he hopes *The Second Coming* won't be received as a sequel. "People who haven't read *The Last Gentleman* might be put off by that. But *The Second Coming* stands by itself."

"I'd forgotten about the trick knee," he added with a chuckle. "To tell you the truth, when I was 100 pages into the writing of *The Second Coming* this man had a different name. I wasn't thinking of *The Last Gentleman,* of Will Barrett. Suddenly it occurred to me that my character *was* Will Barrett, 20 years later."

Speaking of medical symptoms: Percy is an M.D. who quit practicing after he contracted tuberculosis as a young doctor. Thus his character's anguish is manifested in clinical symptoms that in many ways can be taken as ironic comments on American life. Will Barrett, for one, suffers "strange spells," as he calls them. He falls down for no visible reason. Quirks of memory and swings in mood bedevil him.

"It's one of my concocted diseases," Percy said. "I made it all up and called it 'Hausmann's syndrome,' but there's no such thing. Actually, a neurologist read the manuscript and said, 'Well, this is what's called temporal-lobe epilepsy.' I was glad it coincided with a real disease."

The inevitable question. How much of Will Barrett is Walker Percy?

"Not that much. You know, I think there's a fashion in American novels for the novelist actually to write a straight *roman a clef*, to write about his adventures in life for the previous two years. Mailer does that. I suspect Malamud does that.

"Of course, all your characters are projections of yourself. Will Barrett is like me, but also so is Binx Bolling in *The Moviegoer* (Percy's National Book Award-winning first novel of 1961), and so is Thomas More in *Love in the Ruins* (Percy's 1971 novel). And Will Barrett is not like me. What happened to him did not happen to me.

"Barrett is a frantic searcher after the truth, seeking God, demanding God, and reacting violently against the churches, against Christendom, against unbelievers; he's always been on a pilgrimage. Well, that's not like me. I'm a Catholic and have been for years. I don't have these violent perturbations of feeling."

Percy has long been labeled a Catholic novelist, and has produced some sharp and even startling satires about religion in his novels. *The Second Coming* tosses a wicked dagger at the recent resurgence of piety in America.

"It's precisely Will Barrett's difficulty," Percy said. "He lives in the most Christian county of the most Christian state of the most Christian nation—a part of the country where there's a tremendous return to religion, the return of the militant, evangelical Christians. Far from being attracted, he's repelled by them. Yet he's essentially a pilgrim, ever searching.

"What does a man do who has an insatiable desire for ultimate answers, who's equally repelled by Christianity and by unbelief? He says—and you can't quote this in the newspapers [but I'll try]—"If belief is s----y and unbelief is s----y, what does that leave?"

Percy satirized his own Catholicism in *Love in the Ruins*. In *The Second Coming* he parodies the Roman Church's theological country cousins, the Episcopalians, in the person of Jack Curl, a priest to whom trendiness is next to godliness. Percy's choice of target is deliberate.

"The South is mostly Protestant and Episcopalian," he said. "If you write a 'Catholic' novel about the South, maybe anywhere in the country, it has ethnic overtones. You're either writing about French Catholics in New Orleans or Irish Catholics in New England. I didn't want an ethnic background. I wanted something laid in the heartland of the South."

In that respect, Percy added, he felt considerable kinship with Flannery O'Connor. "She was a strong Catholic, but her books are about fundamentalist Georgia Protestants. 'That's my metier,' she said, 'that's my region. These are the people I know.' So I'm really writing about the people I know best where I come from—Alabama, Georgia, North Carolina."

That's a good opening for a question I've wanted to put to Percy for a long time. He also knows the deaf very well, having a deaf daughter and a grandson who is partially deaf. There's a dearth of good fiction about deafness; only Joanne Greenberg's novel *In This Sign* comes to mind. Has Percy even considered writing a novel in which the central character is deaf? Surely he must have, for the notions of language and its learning are central to the subject.

His reply is blunt and honest. "Do you think that anybody who's not deaf could write such a novel? Do you think a hearing person could ever really know what it means to be deaf? My daughter says it's impossible."

Well, yes, I think, but perhaps a writer with Percy's gifts of intellect and curiosity, not to mention imagination, could take a flier.

"My daughter's been quite severe with me about that. She says, 'Why don't you write about the cause of the deaf, the predicament of the deaf?' She's very militant about discrimination against the deaf. I don't know what exactly she wants me to do, but. . . ."

What Percy has chosen to write about is considerable enough, and it has taken an interesting new tack in *The Second Coming*. At the end of that novel Will Barrett is reborn; he has found himself, Allison, and his people. He has a new life, a new mission. It's that rare literary event, a happy ending.

"I feel that I made a breakthrough in this book," Percy declared. "It has a feeling of affirmation, of celebration. I've never done this before. I feel better about it. We live in the age of alienation, and novels about alienation are the sort one almost naturally writes. And I think this is the first time I've actually seen a way out of this predicament."

If there's anything Percy is pessimistic about, it's the future of the novel. "I'm not sure that in the year 2000 anybody will be reading novels. In fact, if I was starting over, I think I might like to make films."

The filmmaker, he added, shares something with the novelist: plenty of room, the freedom to swing an intellectual cat. "I've never written a short story for that reason; it's too constricting. In a novel you can go where you want to. In a film, too, you're free to do anything you like.

"Yes, making a film is a huge undertaking that requires a lot of people and a lot of money. But it's almost as difficult to get a first novel published today, what with publishers being taken over by conglomerates."

To Percy, being even a renowned novelist isn't particularly agreeable. "It's a very lonely, isolated life, and you don't see many people," he said. He gives university seminars occasionally to break the monotony, "but I wouldn't like to be in an academic atmosphere all the time. Come to think of it, it's remarkable how few first-class novels come out of acadame.

"I don't think the novelist in America has ever figured out where he's supposed to be, what his place is—whether in the university or a small town or community of other writers. Faulkner lived in a small town in the South. I live in a smallish town. I think I like it better than I would living in New York, even though I would see more writers there. There would be a danger being around too many writers. Instead of writing you might spend most of your time talking about books, agents, contracts and advances."

But Percy has firm ideas on the role of the American novelist: To question the values of society. "Somebody—I've forgotten who it was—compared the serious writer to the canary miners used to take down into the shaft to test the air." If the air was bad the canary would swoon; it'd sense that something was wrong before the miners could.

"It may seem to most other people that their lives are normal and that they have everything they want, and here are these writers giving off symptoms and signs. Writers and artists and poets are like that. When something goes wrong with society, they're the first to know."

And, as *The Second Coming* affirms, if it can be put right (call it redemption, if you like, or something as simple and seemingly banal as keeping the faith), writers and artists and poets—Walker Percy, for one—can light the way.

Walker Percy Tells How
to Write a Good Sentence

Dannye Romine/1980

From *New Orleans Times-Picayune/States-Item,* 4 September
1980, p. 4. Reprinted by permission of Dannye Romine and
Knight-Ridder Newspapers.

HIGHLANDS, N.C.—"I'll walk out to the highway and meet you
down at the bottom of the driveway," says Walker Percy, in a last-
gentlemanly voice. "I'm a guy who's wearing yellow pants, and there
ain't many other guys up here wearing yellow pants."

Ain't many other guys up here in these North Carolina mountains
as extraordinarily concerned with the ordinary as Percy, either.

From the time he contracted tuberculosis in a medical school and
lay upon his sickbed reading the existentialists—e.g. Gabriel Marcel—Percy began developing a zealot's passion for examining the
human soul.

A passion both lofty and lowly. Sublime and ridiculous.

A lust for the extraordinariness of human beings that arises from
the ordinariness of human beings.

Winner of the 1962 National Book Award for "The Moviegoer,"
his first published novel, and author of "The Last Gentleman,"
"Love in the Ruins," "The Message in the Bottle" (essays), "Lancelot" and recently, "The Second Coming," Percy, 63, is gazing out
upon glinting Mirror Lake from the honeysuckle-wrapped front porch
of a summer house he's renting in Highlands, a place he chose to
"flop, fish, read," after finishing this novel.

His visor-like forehead hoods pale blue eyes, and he's slim as a
reed—although he has a sweet tooth and says he's rather eat in a
Waffle House than anywhere else.

"Walker says I'll spend $100 on groceries and not buy one bag of
sugar," says Mary "Bunt" Percy, fishing in her purse for hotel sugar
packets she's saved to sweeten her husband's iced tea.

"Bunt"—a nickname from her Doddsville, Miss., childhood—and Percy's brother LeRoy (Emphasis on the Roy) and wife Sarah of Greenville, Miss., are off for the one-mile trip to Highlands for lettuce, tomatoes, cucumbers, sugar.

Percy's writing before he entered the University of North Carolina at Chapel Hill as a freshman in 1933 consisted of a gossip column for the Greenville (Miss.) High School newspaper.

But a Greenville cousin—"Uncle Will"—early imbued Percy with a love for reading. "He knew how to communicate the excitement of good literature," Percy says. "Uncle Will" (William Alexander Percy), a poet-planter-lawyer best-known for his "Laterns on the Levee," adopted the three Percy brothers—Walker, LeRoy and Phinizy—when they were orphaned. Percy's father committed suicide in Birmingham, Ala., in 1929 when Percy was 13, and his mother died in a car wreck two years later.

"Uncle Will had gone to Harvard, but he thought Chapel Hill was the best state university in the South," said Percy. "It was, and, as far as I know, still is. LeRoy and I both went. Tuition was $100, and there was no entrance requirement."

There was, however, a placement test in English, with classes divided, as Percy says, into "advanced, average and retarded." Percy had just finished reading William Faulkner's "The Sound and the Fury," and when he wrote his placement theme, he chose a Faulknerian style: no capitalization, no punctuation. "They put me in the retarded English class," he says, "and the professor really thought I was hot stuff. Compared to the rest of the dummies, I guess I was."

Percy majored in chemistry and minored in math and German, but one of his most vivid memories of Chapel Hill is sitting on the porch of the SAE fraternity house reading Douglas Southall Freeman's four-volume work, "Robert E. Lee, A Biography" (Scribner's, $90).

"It was natural to read things I really wanted to read," he says. "I can't imagine anyone wanting to become a writer without some other writer getting him excited."

As for becoming a writer himself, Percy says it never crossed his mind. At the College of Physicians and Surgeons at Columbia University—from which he graduated with honors in 1941—he vascillated between psychiatry and pathology. "I think I would've ended up in psychiatry," he says. "Pathology is the most elegant of the medical fields, and psychiatry is the most interesting. I felt more at home on the psychiatric ward than anywhere else," he says. "Maybe it takes one to know one."

Percy believes there's a very close relationship between pathology and novel writing. "You might say I'm a pathological novelist," he says, chuckling. "Or a pathologist novelist. Novels are really exercises in pathology. The natural set of pathology is of someone trying to discover the lesion. The novelist says, 'What's wrong with this person? What's wrong with the best of all possible lives? What's gone wrong in the best of all possible environments?'" The Pathologist says, 'What'd he die of?' "

Investigation is only one aspect of writing, however. There's also craft, which, says Percy, "Gets more difficult the longer you do it. It's not like bricklaying, which must get easier."

In his new book, there's a particularly fine sentence among many fine sentences: "The darkness sprang back like an animal." Did he "make it up" or did it "just happen?"

"It's a small thing," he says. "But a small, good thing. I don't know how that happens. A little figure like that makes you feel good. Every now and then, things break right.

"It's a matter of letting go," Percy says. "You have to work hard, you have to punch a clock, you have to put in your time. But somehow there's a trick of letting go to let the best writing take place.

"Maybe it's a day you wake up and you've had good dreams, and the day before you've left off at a good place. Hemingway always said, 'Quit while you still have juice, and the next day the juice will still be there.

"Well, that ain't true. When everything's going right, you can sit for three hours and stare at a blank piece of paper.

"But say everything's going wrong. It's a Monday morning, and you've had bad dreams, and you know nothing good is going to happen. But you go anyway. You go into your little office, and you look at a blank wall. And you give up. It's a matter of giving up, of surrendering, of letting go. You say, 'All is lost. The jig is up. I surrender. I'll never write another word again. I admit total defeat. I'm washed up.'

"And you stay there, and after an hour, you say, 'Oh, well. I've been cast up on an island. I'm a wreck. But here I am. Still Alive.

Here's a pencil. Here's the paper. Here's the three-ring binder and
the Blue Horse paper. And you say 'Since I'm here, why don't I write
something. Life is finished. Western civilization is destroyed. I'm sitting in the rubble of Manhattan—everything's gone, everybody
dead—except a girl. There's always a girl. Me and this girl. We'll just
see what happens.'

"What I'm telling you is, that's when things happen.

"What I'm telling you is, I don't know anything. It's a question of
being so pitiful God takes pity on you, looks down and says, 'He's
done for. Let's let him have a couple of good sentences.'

"It's a strange, abject little-understood profession," Percy says.
"Saul Bellow said being a writer reminds him of the mating of dogs."

Percy practices this strange, abject profession in a rented attic room
over his daughter's bookstore in Covington, La. He's lived in
Covington since 1950, raised two daughters there, become a grandfather four times over, watched the population double to 10,000. He
describes Covington, 40 miles north of New Orleans, as "neither
here nor there."

"It's just an ordinary place in the pine trees, and we live in an
ordinary house by a bayou."

He practices there what he preaches in his novels: The art of staying put, sticking with it. "The trick is doing what you're doing without
getting the itch," he says. "The itch usually doesn't work. You move
on, and it's the same thing. Repetition is one of the six great themes
in literature," he says. "Figuring out how you can live in the same
place without being miserable."

"It takes," he says, "a conscious cultivation of the ordinary."

Laying the Ghost of Marcus Aurelius?

Jan Nordby Gretlund/1981

From *South Carolina Review,* 13 (Spring 1981), 3–12. Permission to reprint by *South Carolina Review* and Jan Nordby Gretlund.

I KIERKEGAARD'S STAGES

Gretlund: To what extent do you consider your first three novels "a gloss on Kierkegaard"?

Percy: That's my own expression. It is an exaggeration, but I wanted to pay due homage to Kierkegaard. Insofar as one thinks in a philosophical frame of reference, when I was writing *The Moviegoer,* also *The Last Gentleman,* and maybe also *Love in the Ruins,* I was thinking in terms of the three spheres of existence. It is a very convenient frame of reference, particularly when you are writing a novel of quest, pilgrimage, or search about a young man "on life's way," as Kierkegaard would say, to think of him going through the aesthetic stage, the ethical stage, and then the religious. Although most of the novels are about the aesthetic stage.

Gretlund: Isn't there something to be said for living on the aesthetic stage? As Binx Bolling does initially.

Percy: Of course. Kierkegaard would certainly agree. His hero of the aesthetic was Mozart and his Don Giovanni. He loved Mozart more than any other composer. The aesthetic stage is the stage of the highest enjoyment—of artistic enjoyment. You don't have to leave it. Kierkegaard never said we exist in one stage altogether. All people are probably a combination of the three stages. The three generally overlap, though there are "pure" cases, mostly literary, like Don Giovanni.

Gretlund: When the English edition of *The Moviegoer* appeared in 1963, one Danish reviewer commented: ". . . Bolling seems to have given up his strange search, he has groped around until his thirtieth year, and perhaps that is just as well, for how much can Kierkegaard . . . and religion really help us?" (My translation)

Percy: The reviewer should have gotten the overt reference to

Kierkegaard in the "Epilogue." Binx had gone through a stage, the aesthetic stage, he stopped going to movies, he stopped playing those games about neighborhoods, movie houses, past experience, repetition, rotation. And he finally decided he wanted to do something, he takes Kate by the hand. He tells her it is all right for her to ride the streetcar alone. He takes responsibility. Binx's attitude to the stoic Aunt Emily is somewhat ambiguous. That's what I like about *The Second Coming,* it is not ambiguous. It is absolutely clear what Will Barrett is going to do.

Gretlund: Is Sutter Vaught in *The Last Gentleman* a stoic?

Percy: No, Sutter is desperate. He has exhausted the aesthetic sphere. I would go further than Kierkegaard, I would combine the aesthetic with the scientific. I think the two are parallel. I think Mozart and Einstein are on the same plane. They are both writing about how the world is. Music is cognitive and science is cognitive. And you have the observer writing about it, communicating with the fellow-scientists and communicating with fellow music-lovers. Sutter is in that tradition. He was a scientist, but he was also in despair. He understood the good news, the Gospel, he knew exactly what was going on in that baptism when the priest baptised Jamie. But Sutter was an unbeliever, he didn't accept it. With him it was an either/or, either belief or unbelief, and he was an unbeliever. His sister Val was a believer. Sutter was in despair.

Gretlund: You seem to take issue with Kierkegaard on the function of knowledge in attaining faith.

Percy: Well, it is a classical dispute between Catholics and Protestants whether faith is a form of knowledge. I thought it was a very nice opposition to have Kierkegaard making a clear statement that faith *is* not a form of knowledge, it is a leap onto the absurd. St. Thomas Aquinas saying in his classical thirteenth-century way that faith *is* a form of knowledge. It is different from scientific knowing, but it is a form of knowledge. I tend to agree with Aquinas there, even though I am more sympathetic with Kierkegaard. I am on his wavelength, I understand his phenomenology, his analysis of the existential predicament of modern man. Aquinas did not have that, but I think Aquinas was right about faith. It is not a leap into the absurd, it is an act of faith, which is a form of knowledge.

Gretlund: Kierkegaard might well ask "what kind of knowledge?"

Percy: A knowledge that God exists and that man is created in His image.

Gretlund: But isn't that simply faith?

Percy: Well, I don't think so. In fact, the burden of my non-fiction is a demonstration that man is different from other creatures. That he has this extraordinary capacity to know things, a certain freedom, and he can find himself in a predicament. You can't explain these things by deterministic biology. Ordinary epistemology does not take account of news as a form of knowing. I addressed that in *Message in a Bottle.*

Gretlund: Does religion offer Will Barrett a solution to his existential problems at the ending of *The Last Gentleman?*

Percy: *The Last Gentleman* ends ambiguously, too. I had a priest tell me it was clear to him what happened at the end of *The Last Gentleman,* that when Will Barrett stops Sutter in the Edsel and goes off with him, he said, obviously what they both do is they go to Sutter's place and they both commit suicide.

What was intended was, Will Barrett knew Sutter was onto something. Will Barrett had good antennae, good radar, and he knew when people know something or don't know something. Even at the end of *The Second Coming,* he knew this senile priest knew something he didn't know. He knew that Sutter knew what was going on, so he asks him. But Sutter is not going to tell him anything. He knows what it is Will wants from him, and that if he told him something, he would accept it in a psychological mode. It would be something like "How to Improve Your Life"—so Sutter is not going to tell him anything. In other words he is leaving it to him to live his own life. The implication was that Will Barrett was going to go back to the South, probably marry Kitty, and probably go into business with the Vaughts and their Conferate Chevrolet agency. That was the implication.—But he didn't. [See *The Second Coming.*]

II SCANDINAVIAN COPY

Gretlund: At one point in *The Last Gentleman,* Sutter Vaught formulates man's choice as he sees it: ". . . to live like a Swede . . . Or: to live as a Christian among Christians in Alabama? Or to die like an honest man?"[1] Would you explain this passage to me?

Percy: I have forgotten I said that. If Sutter said that, he is rejecting both. When he says "Swede" he is talking about a purely materialistic society. When he is talking about Val, his sister, he is talking about an incarnate Christian society. She has this Christian community in South Alabama. And for Sutter "to live like a man" is simply to be oneself, to choose despair or whatever he chooses.

Gretlund: In your essay "The Man on the Train" you mention that these materialistic Swedes will not use the resort areas the Swedish government set aside for recreational purposes.

Percy: A Swede told me that. His favorite place was up north. But to get away from the government reservations, to find a place which had not been set aside for recreation, he had to go to English villages. This again goes back to Kierkegaard, he was the first one that gave it a name, he called it "a rotation." He says one becomes *Europa-müde,* and if you live in Austria you'll go to the south of France. Or, if you live in Paris you'll go to outside of München, and if you're German you'll go to the coast of Spain. And it is certainly true of this country, too. People are always looking. . . . It is the favorite American pastime to go to Mexico to find an unspoiled village. [See the essay "The Loss of the Creature."]

Gretlund: One of your characters in *Love in the Ruins* seems to have made it into a career to bring others to his home-base in Copenhagen.

Percy: If Art Immelmann was living in Denmark, he was an immigrant from Germany. For after all, the original Immelmann was a German WW I ace, and he invented the Immelmann turn. My father was a WW I flyer, and I remember him describing to me the Immelmann turn. It was a combat tactic, he would loop and at the top of the loop would do a barrel roll to escape. So I heard about him from my father, and he *was* a German ace. I don't know why I made him the Devil, but it seemed to be a good idea.

Gretlund: Art Immelmann promises Dr. Thomas More a job as a brain specialist at the University of Copenhagen.

Percy: [amused] I combined the best of both worlds: German genius and Danish spirituality.

Gretlund: There isn't much Christianity in Scandinavian spirituality nowadays.

Percy: That's why the next saint is going to come from Sweden,

because you have to go all the way to the bottom to come back up.
He is not going to come from Christian Carolina, I can promise you.

III LANCELOT OR PERCIVAL

Gretlund: Lancelot's plans for a new start in Virginia with Anna
are by some Scandinavian critics seen as the preparation for a leap
onto a religious stage.

Percy: It would be a sort of inverted religious stage, a caricature of
the religious stage. After all, Lancelot was not in quest of the holy
grail. He was in quest of the unholy grail. So, it was the religious
stage turned inside out.

Gretlund: But at that time Lancelot had realized that there wasn't
any holy or unholy grail.

Percy: True. But when he was headed for the Shenandoah Valley
and Virginia to meet Anna, he was still planning what he called "a
third revolution," a very violent, almost fascist revolution.

Gretlund: So Cleanth Brooks is right in lining up Lancelot with
Adolf Hitler and Idi Amin?

Percy: If you subtract the Holocaust, the persecution of the Jews,
he'd probably be more right than wrong. Lancelot liked to say the
Nazis were stupid, that they could have accomplished the same thing
without killing the Jews.

Gretlund: What about Lancelot's desire for a distinction between
good and evil, his ability to act, and his readiness to accept a responsibility. Aren't these positive features?

Percy: Sure. He was in many ways like Aunt Emily in *The
Moviegoer*. In one way he was worse, in another way he was better.
He was worse because he didn't have the ethical values of Aunt
Emily; she would not have been in favor of killing the enemies of
society. He would have. After all, he did kill three or four people
when he blew up the plantation house. But he was "better" in the
Kierkegaardian sense of being aware of a progression toward the religious sphere in his own way. He was "better" in realizing that the old
methods of communication, the old cultural values were dead, and
there had to be a new world and a new life—some sort of rebirth.
And he envisioned a rebirth and a new communication by tapping
on the wall, and through the wall with the girl next door: Anna. And

he saw the possibility of a new life with Anna, and the possibility of a third revolution, as he thought of it, in Virginia, which had its positive elements.

Gretlund: Would they, among others, be to get rid of the pornography and swinishness he had been fighting?

Percy: Yes. But also to get rid of Aunt Emily's values. To begin a completely new life, Aunt Emily would have gone back to the Greco-Roman Stoicism.

Gretlund: I had the impression that Lancelot's new life would be based on Aunt Emily's old values.

Percy: No, he was going to make it up from scratch and find his own way. He thought of himself . . . there is a scene where he sees a young man standing in one of the passes in the mountains of the Shenandoah Valley. I had several things in mind. One was a Confederate soldier, one of Stonewall Jackson's men crossing Massanutten Mountain about to defeat the Northern army. The other was Robert Jordan, the hero of Hemingway's *For Whom the Bell Tolls,* who is fighting in the Spanish Civil War. Remember the scene where he is lying with his gun waiting among the pine-needles. . . . And the third is a young Nazi storm-trooper. I spent a summer in Germany in 1934, and I lived with a family in Bonn. The father was a member of the S.A., *Schutz Abwehr,* and the son was a member of *Hitlerjugend.* There was a tremendous excitement at the "rejuvenation" of Germany, and the creation of new values in the Nietzschean sense: the death of God, the death of old values, and the creation of new values. I remember this young *Hitlerjugend* was very excited about the possibilities of the future. There was nothing about the Jews at the beginning. I had all this in mind when I thought of a young man standing in a pass of Massanutten Mountain. Lancelot is a conscious combination of something quite positive and quite evil.

Maybe I was also thinking of Gabriel Marcel, he is French, a Jew, a Catholic convert, who had the nerve to say: we tend to overlook something positive about the mass movements. It is easy to say how wrong they were. It is easy to overlook the positive things: the great sense of verve and vitality. This I was very much aware of in Germany in 1934. It made it even more seductive. Just as in the movie *Cabaret,* when that young German stands up in a beer garden and sings.

Gretlund: I thought Lancelot Lamar was so deeply rooted in the values of the Old South that it would be impossible for him to escape his heritage and start from scratch.

Percy: That's true. What I was doing was to try to destroy the middle ground. I tried to see what would happen if he *lived up to* his tradition. And his tradition is similar to Aunt Emily's tradition. He was not a Christian; as a matter of fact I had less in mind Sir Lancelot than Ulysses. In the old Greco-Roman tradition, if you had been mortally offended, if suitors had moved into your house and had taken advantage of your *wife*, what you did was go kill them. So in my own sneaky way—that's the only thing a novelist can do now is to be deceptive and sneaky—I try to raise questions which slip up on the reader. The question is: why shouldn't Lancelot do this? Instead of dealing overtly with Christianity, I deal with the old Roman ethic: what's wrong with him taking revenge in the way he did? Would Aunt Emily object to that? What he is doing is carrying Aunt Emily's ethic to its logical conclusion. If he has been cuckolded by somebody, a Hollywood producer, then what he does is *kill* him. That's what Ulysses did, and we look on Ulysses as one of the great heroes of Western Culture. Ulysses and Telemachus kill everybody! Lancelot only kills three people, I think, I've lost count, but Ulysses and Tele-machus kill all the suitors. And we applaud Ulysses.

Gretlund: How does the murderer compare morally with his victims?

Percy: In the end I regarded Lancelot as demented, as a man who has gone into the religious stage in a demented way. He has got hold of it in a sense; and he is a man of action, he is a man who believes in putting his beliefs into action. Do you remember he said at one point—I don't know whether I got this from Kierkegaard or Nietzsche—he said: if one man comes along who believes something sufficiently, just one man, who is willing to act on his belief, then everybody will follow him. Because nobody else believes in anything, and nobody else knows what to do. Lancelot did this, it was partly admirable, partly crazy. But the novel, like most of my novels, is also an attack on the 20th century, on the whole culture. It is a rotten century, we are in terrible trouble.

Gretlund: Scandinavian critics tend to make Lancelot more of a true hero than you have intended.

Percy: But they leave out the other pole. The other pole is Percival. The critics are right in that the point of satire was to destroy mushy American liberalism. The mushy way of approving everything which is "life-enhancing," or "self-improving," or "how to cultivate personality." To cut it down to an either/or—I'm always trying to cut it down to an either/or—it has either got to be one way or the other. That's what Lancelot says to Percival: would you agree it has either got to be my way or your way—it is not going to be their way. That's the last question, and Percival says "yes." These reviewers are partly right, but they leave out Percival. Isn't that a sign of the times?

Gretlund: Is Percival the real hero of your *Lancelot?*

Percy: I was trying to do something there, I'm not sure it worked. It worked for some people. Percival, the priest, is never described. He was never in the story. Yet he was supposed to be present. He was listening, he was the one who is hearing all this. He only says about two words at the very end. It was my intention that his character should be known indirectly through what Lancelot said about him.

Gretlund: Virginia Woolf did something similar in *The Waves.* She also used the name Percival.

Percy: I didn't know that. When I first began to write that novel, I was going to write it about two men. As a third-person narrative. And the part about Percival did not work. So I wrote out Percival, and I wrote it as a dramatic monlogue with Lancelot, which was the way it should be. But it confused a lot of people. They didn't realize who Lancelot was addressing at the beginning—whether this person was real or not. A dramatic monologue apparently puts people off.

Gretlund: What is Percival's role at the ending? Is he a personification of the Church?

Percy: What does that mean? He went back to be an ordinary priest in a parish in Alabama.

Gretlund: Is that, as Lancelot said, copping out?

Percy: That's for you to decide. (Come to think of it, it's exactly what Kierkegaard wanted to do.) The issue is there. Percival agrees with Lancelot about the way the world is: the world is a rotten place. They agree that there's a lot wrong with the world, and that they ought to condemn what is rotten. But they don't agree what should

be done about it. They have different ways. It is supposed to be a
very conventional, classical statement of two different traditions. One
is, well, Cleanth Brooks would call it gnostic, I hadn't thought of
gnosticism, but I was thinking of good pagan Greco-Roman Nazi and
so forth tradition: Aunt Emily on one side and orthodox Christianity
on the other. At the end of *Lancelot* I was trying to present two
radical points of view, neither of which is accepted by most people,
most Americans. One is: Lancelot goes to Virginia for the third revolution, he rejects the world. The other is: Percival goes to a parish in
Alabama, and he hears the confessions of Buick-dealers. They
couldn't be more different, and yet they have something in common:
they both know there is something radically wrong with the world.

IV. WOMEN AND INSANITY

Gretlund: Why is it that women reviewers are not satisfied with
your women characters? Are there any "normal" women in your
novels?

Percy: What about Allie in *The Second Coming?* She is crazy, but
she is pretty normal. And what about Aunt Emily in *The Moviegoer?*
She is not only normal, but normative. As normative as Marcus Aurelius.

Gretlund: Why are the girls we like in your fiction at least mentally unstable?

Percy: Well, that goes back to a device I use consciously, namely,
to arrange the placement of the hero and the heroine so that it is
always a question: who is crazy? Whether he is crazy and the rest of
the world is sane—or, he is sane and the rest of the world crazy.

It is supposed to be a delicately balanced issue, so that many people can read it and say: well, I am also crazy. Allison is a crazy woman
living in a sane world, or maybe she seems crazy because she is
reacting sanely to an insane world. Someone like Allison, who is beginning a new life, starting afresh, even creating a new language—
maybe she is on the track of sanity. It is not difficult to make out a
case that the world is mad.

Gretlund: Is it a trend in modern American fiction that the heroes
are considered insane by society?

Percy: Right. This is, of course, the thesis of R. D. Laing, the psychiatrist, that schizophrenics in their own way are sane. I think that most psychiatrists disagree, and they may be right in that Laing takes it to an extreme, but for literary purposes it is a convenient thesis. A schizophrenic may be on the track of sanity; he finds the world unbearable, and maybe the function of the novelist is to show that the world is, indeed, unbearable. And that there are certain strategies you have to take to live in it, and there are persons who are entitled to have a psychotic reaction. At any rate, it is a delicately balanced issue; the reader can read it either way.

Gretlund: The women in *The Last Gentleman* get a particularly harsh treatment.

Percy: Yes, and those in *The Moviegoer,* too. I don't know whether that is anti-feminism on my part, or the difficulty for a male novelist to create a woman. Good women writers have an easy time creating men. But, how many women did Hemingway create?

Gertlund: It seems they were all either whores or motherfigures.

Percy: True, or in my case, neurotic or psychotic. Maybe it is because men do not understand women. I didn't have any sisters, and maybe if I'd had sisters I'd do a better job. But to me "a normal" woman is an absolute mystery. I can only understand her if she is as neurotic as I am.

Gretlund: You did create some wonderful women for *Love in the Ruins.* They all seem, however, to be seen at a distance.

Percy: But the last one, Ellen Oglethorpe, I think is a . . . she is drawn from my Georgia background. Part of my family comes from Georgia. My mother's family were Georgia Presbyterians. So I thought it would be nice to have a voluptuous Georgia Presbyterian girl. And she is not neurotic, she knows exactly what she wants. She may not be very deep; I wasn't too interested in her, I just wanted to have her there.—I plead ignorance, I don't know enough about women.

V. WRITER AND SOCIETY

Gretlund: Do you think many readers cherish your novels for your satiric portrait of contemporary America?

Percy: Oh sure.

Gretlund: In *The Second Coming* there are a love story *and* the continued satire of society. Do you fall between two stools?

Percy: It may be o.k. because that may be what saves me from being a very bad novelist. It would be a bad thing to write simply a novelistic explication of Kierkegaard, or Marcel, or whoever. But since I'm a Southerner and an American, and since I get angry about a great many things that happen in this country—I am by nature a satirical novelist, and a humorist. I'm always pleased when people find the novels funny, because so many take them so seriously.

Gretlund: One of the features of your American society is that new Christian movements multiply. What do you think of them?

Percy: I have mixed feelings about them. I am a Catholic, and I have re-born Christians come and say to me: "Why don't you become a re-born Christian?" I would think that by definition a Christian *is* somebody who's re-born. So is it a question of being born a third time—or how many times?

Gretlund: What do you think of the support Ronald Reagan has received from these movements?

Percy: I think he is a little worried about it, a little uneasy about it. I think he is backing off from the embrace of Jerry Falwell. I think there are some good things in the new movements. They are reacting against some obviously evil forces in society: pornography in the movies and films, the decay of the American family. . . . So I sympathize with their concern about that. But two things worry me about them: their wanting to get into politics, which goes against the American grain, and the other is the commercialism of it. There's a great deal of money involved: heavy media involvement with tremendous appeals for money. And it is not clear where the money goes, or how sincere the ministers are. So I have mixed feelings about it.

Gretlund: The modern trends the new Christians seems to be fighting are the very same Lancelot rebelled against.

Percy: True. Except Lancelot wouldn't have much use for Christians of any kind, at all. And, of course, Will Barrett in *The Second Coming* finds himself in the strange position of disagreeing with both nonbelievers and believers. He doesn't like either one. So he is looking for a *tertium quid.*

Gretlund: Does he find one?

Percy: Well, that's a good question. That's for me to ask you.

Gretlund: Will Barrett is also concerned that one place is much like any other place. Is the South much like any other place nowadays?

Percy: The South has a greater sense of place than other parts of the country; but the South is changing. The South is more like the rest of the country now. I regret it in some ways, not in other ways. I saw a map of what's happening to the demography of the country, and what's happening is that the population and the wealth are moving south. The sunbelt is gaining, that's good in a sense, because there have been so many poor people, who have been in a wretched situation ever since the Civil War. That's good. But it is a terrible price we have to pay. All you got to do is to drive through the suburbs of New Orleans and of Baton Rouge, and it looks like Los Angeles. There is a word for it. It is called: losangelization. The South is going through the process of losangelization. That's not good. The trick is, given the New South, which is not the South of Faulkner, not the South of Eudora, it is not the South of Flannery, it is the South of Interstate 12 and Highway 190. It is the South of Los Angeles. How to humanize that! How do you live with that? What I am trying to do is to figure out how a man can come to himself, living in a place like that. So at the end of *The Second Coming*, very deliberately, I've Allie and Will leave the greenhouse, go to a motel, the first coming together takes place in a Holiday Inn. Which incidentally is a good Holiday Inn, I've been to one like that, where they have turnip greens, cornbread, and grits.—And from there . . . You know where he proposes to live with Allie, while they are going to build log-cabins for old people; he proposes to move into a G.E. Gold Medallion home, a mass-produced home. And they could be happy there.

. . . .

Gretlund: Are you writing any philosophical essays now?

Percy: That's what I am working on. I am working on a semiotic approach to consciousness. Consciousness itself, which American psychology, behaviorism, can't handle. It has no way of getting hold of it. So I am trying to get a hold of it by a science; and it is not going to be a conventional science of secondary causes.

Gretlund: Is the philosophy something you write to charge the batteries before returning to fiction. Or do you write fiction to relax between philosophical essays?

Percy: I don't know. When I finished this last novel it was as if I had been a woman who had been pregnant four years. And you know, women go into what you call a postpartum depression. I went into a terrible depression, and all I knew was that I would never write another novel again as long as I lived. What I can do is to write dry stuff like these semiotic essays.

Notes

1. *The Last Gentleman* (New York: Farrar, Straus and Giroux, 1966), p. 379.

The Study of Consciousness:
An Interview with Walker Percy

Linda Whitney Hobson/1981

From *The Georgia Review*, 35 (Spring 1981), 51–60, © by the University of Georgia. Reprinted by permission of *The Georgia Review* and Linda Whitney Hobson.

Walker Percy's fifth novel, *The Second Coming,* was published in July 1980, and although he says he "is not interested in it any-more"—he has put it away from him and is onto other things—one afternoon recently he talked with me about that novel, as well as his plans for a collection of essays on language, mass communication, and psychiatry. In his new book, to be called *Novum Organum,* he intends to set forth the model for what he calls "a radical science," which will provide a way of describing and talking about, rationally, what human consciousness is and how it is different from the other data scientists study.

As usual, Percy is honest and straightforward about his present work and what he hopes to accomplish in the future. He says that if he had it all to do over again, he would study semiotics because he believes that study has the best chance of defining just exactly what it means to be human and to find oneself in predicaments so complex that theology, sociology, and psychiatry have provided, at best, only partial answers to the malaise which besets all of us, and which he has tried, for the last twenty years, to dramatize in his fiction.

In pursuance of his study of semiotics, he attended a conference on primatology in New York in May 1980 and spent the following month in Toronto at a seminar on language and semiotics. His research continues, and one senses that Percy believes *Novum Organum* will be the most important book he has written. "Man is in trouble," Percy says. One cannot help but agree and hope that his new study of the breadths and depths of that trouble will serve to explain and possibly even to minimize its pernicious effects.

216

Q: What is it about writing that fascinates you?

A: That goes way back to high school, when I discovered I had a knack for writing—not to write well, but to write. The pleasure of writing was the contrast between writing as a way of ordering a life and the disorder of life itself. As Johnny Carson says, what he likes about being shy at parties and not shy on the stage is that on the stage he is in control.

Q: So writing is a way for you to control the chaos of existence?

A: Actually, living is often absurd, preposterous, painful, and out of control. Writing allows you to establish some sort of control, even if you're writing about chaos. The very fact of writing about it establishes a certain kind of authority over it. And it's impossible to write about chaos without establishing some sort of order over it.

Q: Is that similar to your illustration of alienation? That the man on the train who is alienated, and who then reads a book about a man who is alienated, is no longer alienated?

A: That's the aesthetic reversal, which I noticed way back. It's a curious thing. I don't think enough attention is paid by psychologists or by semioticists to the curious fact that situations which are experienced directly can be painful (or of not much account, or even of not much meaning), but when they are read about or written about, a kind of reversal takes place—and the reader or the writer takes pleasure in it. The pleasure is a fundamental thing, going back to the origins of speech or consciousness, either in the phylogenesis or in the way a child does it at the age of one or two in the pleasure that a child takes when some segment of his environment is named. And it has a very strong social dimension, also. Someone gives a thing a name for the child, and the delight occurs in the transaction between the person who gives it and the person who hears it. This inconsequential object, or even this object which is unpleasant, once it is seen in common and the name-teller tells the name and the child or the reader hears the name and recognizes it, then something extraordinary happens. I think that is not only the beginning of consciousness of language and speech, but it also goes to the heart of good fiction, of good poetry.

Q: In what way?

A: The times when you're best or when you're luckiest—you know it, incidentally, when you're doing it—are the times when you

hit on something which comes almost subliminally out of your unconscious. It was there all the time, but you're naming it for yourself
for the first time. And then the reader will tell you, and now and then
write you, and say: "That's the way it is, and nobody has ever said
that before." And what I "name" is the Judeo-Christian view of man
in trouble, as the sparks fly up, which is the way man is. The other
thing I am concerned with is the peculiar predicament of late twentieth-century man, and especially in the American South.

Q: Why especially in the South?

A: Well, in writing *The Second Coming,* I found the South, and
particularly North Carolina, a valuable setting because of the peculiar
confluence of two things that have happened in the South in the past
ten or twenty years: number one, what's been called the power
shift—the shift of power and money to the South. For the first time
since the Civil War, the South is getting rich. And the other thing is
the tremendous re-Christianization of the South—high-powered
evangelical Christianity. Thus, it's of value to me to take a man like
Will Barrett and set him down in the South: he finds himself in what
the psychiatrists call a "double bind"—a no-win situation. From the
beginning, and all through his life he has experienced a loss of sovereignty which has occurred in the lives of most of us as well, even
though we appear to be freer, to have more, to be more individualistic, to have access to more than any people on earth. Despite this, a
loss of sovereignty has occurred so that we are more subject to invisible authority—scientists and so forth. We now think of what one
should do in a certain situation, not what I should do. Will Barrett is a
man who, whatever his faults, has reclaimed sovereignty; he demands to know what it's all about—and he always has.

Q: Your reference to North Carolina as the most valuable dramatic
setting for *The Second Coming* recalls the ending of *Lancelot,* as
Lance hopes to begin life again in the Shenandoah Valley with Anna,
and it's not at all certain that he will. Is there some sense in which
Will's and Allie's new life in the Blue Ridge is a working out for you
of that same plot idea, with characters who could have a better
chance of making it work?

A: I hadn't thought of that, but there's certainly some truth in that.
I chose North Carolina because it's kind of a no man's land between
Virginia—which is a country all to itself, drenched in all sorts of blood

and history—and the deep South, where one is apt to be overtaken by all the literary clichés which are hard to get rid of, and because it's away from New Orleans. North Carolina is a neutral sort of place; it has the best and maybe the worst of both North and South.

Q: Despite your own background as a Southerner from the deep South, there has been a good deal of critical argument about whether you are writing strictly from the tradition of Southern writing—believing strongly in the importance of place, as Eudora Welty does and as Faulkner did—or whether you are an American novelist whose substance just happens to be the South. What do you think about that controversy?

A: Well, it would be impossible for me to write as I do unless I were a Southerner. One is simply stuck with one's place, and God help you if you're not. But I'm not a Southern writer in the same way as Faulkner and Welty and maybe even Flannery O'Connor. I'm not interested in the particular mythos and mystique of the South. I have other concerns. I simply use the Southern experience to serve my novelistic concerns. For instance, in *The Moviegoer*, I was not interested in New Orleans particularly. What I was interested in was having a conflict, a confrontation of two cultures—the Greco-Roman Stoicism of Binx's father's family and the Roman Catholicism of Binx's mother's family—and seeing what happened when these two met.

Q: So that dramatic conflict is really what you're interested in, and if there is the right kind of conflict in the South then you will use it?

A: Right. It's extremely valuable for me to live in the South. I don't know what I'd be writing if I had been born and raised in Idaho. Maybe it's lucky for me, because the South has a unique tradition.

Q: And it's not leveled out yet to the point at which conflict is minimal?

A: No, not quite yet.

Q: As long as we're discussing dramatic conflict, let's discuss the conflict between you and classical psychiatry. The relationship between Will and Allie in *The Second Coming* seems to belie what psychologists and psychiatrists counsel people to do these days. They tell people to sit down and come to know and approve of themselves by themselves, and there's a fallacy in that kind of solitary pep talk.

A: Yes. You have to define that self through ordeal, which the psy-

chologists don't tell people. And God knows, it takes an awful lot of
ordeal—Will has to almost shoot himself and Allie has to go crazy—
and what I'm saying is that it takes an awful lot these days to come to
a sense of self. It doesn't do any good to be told how to live, and it
doesn't do any good to tell yourself how to live. You have to learn it
yourself, through ordeal. And the language fails, unless you do it by
ordeal.

Q: Speaking of language, what sorts of things are you thinking
about in that field right now?

A: As you know, I'm interested in semiotics, and, since I watch a
lot of television—I like the Shakespeare series on the Public Broad-
casting Service but also *The Incredible Hulk*—it would be interesting
to figure out the nature of the effect television has had on people's
consciousnesses. You know, when you think about it, people watching television is the biggest cultural revolution that I can think of.
Much bigger than the invention of the printing press, which was, after
all, up until the nineteenth century, enjoyed only by the upperclasses.

But when you consider the fact that the average American spends
five or six hours a day watching television, you must realize that television has an enormous effect, input, on the mind. And no one
knows that happens. They have some vague ideas of the correlation
between watching violent programs and then being violent. But those
are very gross correlations.

In fact, watching five or six hours of television means that people
do more television watching than anything else except working and
sleeping. A lot of television is bad, because it's passive. And one
thing that happens, I'm sure, is that when you see serials, sitcoms,
you have a predicament and resolution within a half-hour. Now, if
one sees maybe six such resolutions per night and thirty or forty a
week, surely the concept must be formed in the viewer's mind that
this is the way life is supposed to be. So what happens when kids
grow up with the idea that life is supposed to have this form?

Of course, this has happened for the last three or four hundred
years, when people read plays or went to the theater, and later, to
films, but that happened only occasionally, and the action or predicament and resolution were prolonged over the course of the story or
the two or three hours in the theater; but when this massive repetition of easy solutions to problems happens on television, right in your

house, I wonder whether there isn't a perceived contrast between the order on television and the manifest, preposterous disorder of life.

And wouldn't this also make for a certain revulsion from life and a turning to television for order? I must say that in a certain sense I'm hooked; I watch more than I should, but often I will turn the sound off and leave the picture on, and I often wonder why that is. People kid me about it and say that I do that so that if the end of the world occurs, I will know it instantly. You know, there's liable to be something horrible happen in the Middle East any minute, and if the picture's there, there will be a bulletin flash across the screen.

Q: I can see that you're serious about this study of the effects of television on human consciousness, but I'm also interested in your own life. How would you characterize your life? John Cheever, for instance, has characterized his life as "a droll adventure" during which he has had "no memory for pain."

A: Well, my life has alternated between successive periods of mild disorientation, depression, punctuated by occasional periods of happiness and productivity in writing.

Q: You appear to have had a very full life, but despite your productivity, is there anything you regret not having done and what do you look forward to doing?

A: I think if I were doing it all over again, I would study linguistics, because it is going to be the new science. Incidentally, I am presently writing a book called *Novum Organum*, which is based on the belief I have that we are increasingly unable to understand ourselves based on our magnificent, triumphant science. What we have is a nonradical science, a technology which understands the interaction between things and things, and between things and organisms, but which has nothing whatever to say about what it is to be a human being, to find oneself in human predicaments. And the question is whether science can address itself to these things at all; most people say no. They say that maybe a novelist can talk about it, and maybe a phenomenologist can talk about it, but science cannot. But I think there may be such a thing as what I call a "radical science."

We now call it semiotics, which has to do with the interaction between people, and people and things, and people and symbols. I'm sure that the human experience cannot be reduced to any science, but you need a way of thinking about all these situations I write about and other novelists write about—upside-down situations like enjoying a hurricane. Like any other animal, we should be getting the hell out of there. And by the same token we should be happy when we have achieved our "goals," as they say, and are living well in East Orange, New Jersey. Things should be fine when you come home from work on a Wednesday afternoon, yet they're not fine. So there should be a way of thinking about these things rationally.

I write about these things, Cheever writes about them, Updike writes about them, Bellow writes about them. But are we saying that we're going to leave it to the novelists, that nobody but novelists or maybe theologians can write about these things? Or is there a way of thinking about it rationally? Getting some ordered discipline? I would like to think that, sure enough, you can make a model or develop a theory (which has already been done—it's been started by people like Charles Peirce) of what it is to be the organism which uses language. It means that instead of having an environment, instead of having interaction of energy exchange, you have other variables, other parameters, and you have a world. An animal responds to the world according to its genes and according to a good or bad environment, whereas a person is always in the world in certain ways. For instance, a scientist is in the world in a very particular way: he is outside the world, he's looking at the world as data. He likes to look at the world and get an idea of it, from certain formulas and equations which explain what it's doing. But I like to think of what scientists are doing when they are doing this, you know. Scientists are strange people, as are artists. What are artists up to? And what does it mean to be a scientist, being out of the world, playing God and arranging order in the world, and then, as Kierkegaard would say—or as Binx said as he was lying in a hotel room in Birmingham—what do you do when you develop a theory? Then how do you live the rest of the day?

Q: That problem reminds me of the painting of Will Barrett over your mantel. In the painting, he stands between the second painting behind him and the viewer he's looking toward, as an interpreter of art to the world, in the similar, but substantially different way a scientist interprets the world to the layman. Is that what you're looking for in this radical science you speak of—a way to correlate the problems of living which the artist can only dramatize and the scientist can only analyze? Do you see yourself as this kind of interpreter?

A: Yes, and I'm trying to figure out what it means to live in a world where science is triumphant, where we all recognize that there are "experts" for all of our problems.

Q: And we feel placed in the corner, dispensed with, and even put down by them, too.

A: Yes, we are all lay people regarding ourselves. If I suffer anxiety and depression, my natural inclination is to go to an expert on anxiety and depression, you see. He treats it like a case of appendicitis, and treats it with drugs. I was thinking at this conference on primatology about whether or not chimps can use language, to figure out the passions involved. I mean, the people who have spent years of their lives trying to prove the thesis that chimps can use language—why this great passion? What are they trying to prove? It has to do with Darwin, but even before that, for the last three hundred or four hundred years, it has to do with the displacement of man from the center of the universe, the way he was in Christian theology. He was dethroned first by Copernicus, who said that the earth was no longer the center; and then by Darwin, who said that man was no longer the unique species; and then by Freud, who said that we were no longer sovereigns of our own consciousness.

But the interesting question is what about the scientist who was saying these things? What is he saying? We demand a continuum, we are all a part of the same continuum, but where is the scientist standing as he is saying this? So, *Novum Organum* will deal with the question of where the scientist is as he pronounces his theories. I think there is a theology involved. The scientist is trying to get rid of God; he's trying to get rid of the uniqueness of man. He does not like a break in the continuum, the proposition that man may be qualitatively different from the other species. That's part of the scientific effort of the last four hundred years. Where does the scientist stand *vis à vis* this continuum? He wants to stand outside of it.

Q: He wants to be Prometheus.

A: Yes. He's not part of it. His consciousness of it does not fit into the continuum. Thus, I'm interested in him. The artist does something similar, but it's different, too. He also stands to the side and talks about the way things are, you know. And he also has trouble getting back into the world. But the way scientists live is different. They split the world into a continuum of physical processes, yet here you have a consciousness and you then have a problem of reentry. How do you get back into this world? So I'm looking for a way of thinking about people and things and symbols. The scientist thinks about interaction, energy exchanges, but the scientist who writes a paper can't explain what he's doing when he actually writes that paper. He's writing a paper for somebody else to read, yet we literally don't know what happens when two people are talking about something—we don't know what language is. That's why I like to start with chimps; I like to start with chimps who do hand signals and designate balls, and then think about what happens when human beings suddenly put two words together and make a sentence—something very strange happens. Bam! That's a world out there.

Q: That's connected to the importance you attach to naming?

A: Yes. And what I would really like to get onto is the study of consciousness. Believe it or not consciousness has just now become a respectable subject in the scientific world. Until a few years ago, the behaviorists had their way of ignoring consciousness or even denying it existed. So, what sort of scientific discipline do we have for thinking about the fact that I am a conscious person—that I am aware of you, for instance, and everything around you. I don't know who I am, though. It's very strange, because even though you are closer to yourself all your life than anyone else, a stranger seeing you on the street can see more about you, can see something about you that you in your entire life will never see. He can observe you in the way you take in a plant or a flower or the fan on that ceiling, and he can see you. But yourself is forever beyond conception in the ordinary scheme of how you take in the world. As Sartre would say, you, yourself, are the great vacuum, the great nothingness.

The trouble is, right now there are eighteen or so different theories of psychotherapy—Freudian, transactional analysis, Jungian, cognitive—they all have different models, but I think *Novum Organum* is going to deal with the psychotherapists. It's going to say where the psychotherapists stand with regard to the patient. This is a strange little world in the psychotherapist's office, where one person talks to another person, and they're out of the world in a sense, and each of the two is in the world in a different way. Now if I come to you for therapy, I am applying to you as an expert for what ails me, and you are there as someone who knows; but outside, there's the world, you see. And we're talking in symbols, transacting in symbols; I'm talking, you're listening.

This new thing called semiotics, started by Charles Peirce and Saussure, has a future in it. With a good theory of semiotics, we could get at what I was talking about before—what happens when people watch so much television. We don't have a conceptual means of getting at it right now. All we know is that if kids watch violent programs, they go out and act violently, but that's behavioristic. We don't have any way of thinking about what happens to their consciousness in the process. Maybe it can't be done; I don't know. Of course, if I watch enough of *The Incredible Hulk,* either I'll get anesthetized or I'll have an idea.

Q: Despite the possible danger of anesthetization and more probable danger of boredom from *The Incredible Hulk,* it sounds like a valuable study.

A: Well, I've been interested in the past in examining the human predicament novelistically, and now I think I want to see if it can be done semiotically. Nobody's ever done it. The semiotics of the self.

Q: So your *Novum Organum* will take up the semiotics of the self? You've spent some time in your fiction dealing with the evocation of your characters' memories. Will the book deal with that, too, as a phenomenon of human consciousness?

A: Yes, probably. I think that I've failed in these five novels and in *The Message in the Bottle,* but I've got a good idea for the next one. You know, I'll tell you a secret: I think the only thing that keeps the novelist going (and I'm not sure that any other novelist would admit this) is that you are going to do the really big one.

It's like the story Tolstoy used to tell. When he was a little boy, his brother told him while they were walking in the woods that there was a green stick buried on the estate, and if he found it he would have the key to immortal life. So whenever he went out walking, he always searched for the green stick. And so, all I'm saying is that the novelist is like the fisherman—always after the big one—the really big one. Otherwise he wouldn't bother, because it's a pain in the ass to write.

Q: You're still after the big one, then?

A: Oh sure, sure. Aren't you?

An Interview with Walker Percy

Ben Forkner and J. Gerald Kennedy/1981

From *Delta* [Montpellier, Université Paul Valery], 13 (Novembre 1981), 1–20. Reprinted by permission of *Delta* and of Ben Forkner and J. Gerald Kennedy.

(This interview is a much shortened version of a long conversation held on August 5, 1980, at the Percy home in Covington, Louisiana. We would like to thank Walker Percy and his wife for their hospitality, for a delicious, relaxed lunch, and for his patience in answering our questions late into the afternoon. The interview begins with a discussion of some of the ideas on language, metaphor, and naming that Percy explores in his collection of essays, *The Message in the Bottle.* The first question refers to the following passage from the beginning of the essay, "Metaphor as Mistake": "I remember hunting as a boy in South Alabama with my father and brother and a Negro guide. At the edge of some woods we saw a wonderful bird. He flew as swift and straight as an arrow, then all of a sudden folded his wings and dropped like a stone into the woods. I asked what the bird was. The guide said it was a blue-dollar hawk. Later my father told me the Negroes had got it wrong: It was really a blue darter hawk. I can still remember my disappointment at the correction.")

Ben Forkner
J. Gerald Kennedy

BF: When you first heard it, was "blue dollar" a name for the bird, or was it also a description of it? Were there associations that you made between dollar and bird?

WP: Well how do you feel about it? Wouldn't you prefer blue dollar as a name to blue darter?

BF: Well I do, but not because there's any particular meaning to it, but because it makes your imagination strain.

WP: It had to do with a theory of metaphor. Actually, of course, in *The Message in the Bottle* I traced it back to Helen Keller with the word "water;" it's a symbol for the thing, water, and she understood water through this symbol. But the two couldn't be more different; I mean the symbol water couldn't be more different—whether spoken or spelled into her hand—than the liquid flowing over her other hand. So you can hear her saying it, but there has to be a space, separation, or difference between the symbol and the thing in order for the thing to be grasped. Like Dr. Itard said once about the wild boy of Aveyron; he said he could not get the boy to understand that a perfect drawing of a cup was the symbol for a cup. They were too much alike. But the word cup, maybe because of its very difference, can be understood. And yet somehow or other, the thing has to be conceived through a symbol, which is very different, rather than through something very much like it. There has to be a space or difference in order for a thing to be conceived as a thing.

BF: But when we hear the words blue dollar hawk it's not as if we're naming something for the first time; we know what "blue" means, we know what "dollar" means, we know what "hawk" means. We wonder about the associations, about how these words apply.

WP: We wonder how it means what it means.

BF: So metaphor is not the same thing as naming something.

WP: Well yes, I think it's probably a lot closer than we ordinarily think. You talk about the acquisition of language, and children go through a stage when they're around two or a little after when they begin to associate names with things. They start making a connection between the word "ball" and the thing, ball. And I feel certain that something has to happen in the child's mind. How does this word *mean?* How does this word mean "ball"? Actually, some psychologists have done some work—Werner and Kaplan—on symbol formation. How does the word "brittle" mean brittle? Actually the word gets transformed, because it actually sounds brittle; the word "brittle" sounds brittle. That's called false onomatopoeia. Of course the word "brittle" is not brittle; it doesn't sound brittle to a Frenchman who doesn't know English. Why does it sound brittle?

BF: You could try to explain it by saying that "t" is a kind of consonant which easily gives way. . .

WP: I don't know how you do it, but it's also a two-syllable word which breaks in the middle, breaks around the "t".

JK: Doesn't it also demonstrate what Susanne Langer talks about, the natural tendency toward a convergence of the symbol and the thing, until we can't tell them apart anymore?

WP: Right.

JK: So that the word brittle becomes the experience of brittleness.

WP: Absolutely. And to get back to the blue dollar; the boy is intrigued by this, but he sees this hawk and he's trying to fit the word to the extraordinary thing that he sees. The guide says, "It's a blue dollar hawk." He's trying to connect it up. How is it a blue dollar hawk? So he asks the guide; the guide says, "Well, 'cuz he balls hisself up an' rolls," you know, when he dives in the woods. The space allows the boy to conceive the hawk; whereas blue darter gives a name to the hawk as "blue" and a "darter."

BF: Would another name be equally as good? What I'm trying to get at: how is a metaphor different from just a name? For example, my own name is Ben. I could think of it as a metaphor for myself, but I'm not sure. That's a different kind of problem, but it seems to me a metaphor must evoke associations.

WP: There has to be a similarity, an association.

BF: But names don't always do that.

WP: True. I don't know why that works, although the answer would be some kind of analogy, but there's got to be a space too—they can't be too close. But what's interesting about your raising the subject is that I was very much interested in just that linguistic issue in this book, *The Second Coming,* because I was thinking about the language of these two characters, the two main characters, Will Barrett and Allie—Will, of course, speaking the ordinary language of the day. The inference is that something has gone wrong with the ordinary, normal language of the day. It gets overused, worn out; it's lost its symbolic mystery and has become a kind of a sign, a low-grade sign. Allie notices this; she says things like, "How are you supposed to understand words?" When somebody says to you, "I know how you feel. I know everything is OK." But actually they don't mean that at all; they don't mean "I know everything is OK." It's a sign that things are not OK. But I wanted Allie to start off afresh with language. It was an experiment; I wanted to see what could be done working on Will Barrett with a used-up language—and he was very much aware it was used up—and Allie, using schizophrenic language, which incidentally I took many liberties with. I knew a little about

schizophrenic speech, but a psychiatrist could very well complain that
it wasn't truly accurate.

JK: You'll get some letters.

BF: Do they really rhyme words?

WP: Yes, they do rhyme words. But I left myself a good loophole,
because it's not clear she's schizophrenic, and she's probably not, but
some psychiatrist could say that I had romanticized schizophrenics
and gone down the R. D. Laing Garden Path, where you insist
schizophrenics are the only ones that know what's going on and normal; the crazy people are normal and normal people are crazy. I
wasn't really trying to do that, but I was interested in the linguistics of
it, so that I was trying to get her to use schizophrenic speech in the
same discovering way of metaphor as a two-year-old child, so that
she actually rediscovers language all over again. In a way she does
that. I wanted to see what could be done by using pathological
speech to recover a certain freshness, vividness, a way of looking at
things. And I'm happy about Allie. She's one of the few women
characters I've been pleased with.

JK: When did you get the idea of shifting the narrative point of
view back and forth? That's the first time you've done anything like
that.

WP: Yes. I guess . . . I don't know. I started out with these two
people; I didn't know exactly what was going to happen between
them. In fact, I didn't know until I was into it a couple hundred pages
that the man was Barrett. I was writing about this guy and I suddenly
realized that he was Will Barrett, which made it awkward, because
then I had to go back and get the chronology right, connect up the
fact that he had been in New York, Princeton, had been at Macy's,
and that he was I think thirty years old in a place like Birmingham.
He was thirty years old when he went back to the South with the
Vaughts. So that presents all kinds of time problems. I had to figure
out how old he had to be for his girlfriend Kitty to have a grown
daughter and for him to have a grown daughter. I fudged it a little bit,
I left it a little open. I left the date a little open, because when Allie
finds that Gulf calendar in the restroom of the Gulf station at the very
beginning—and this is how a good copy reader works—at first it was
definitely a 1980 calendar. So the copy reader reads it and she says,
"That can't be, because Wednesday does not fall on October the

31st." So I backed up. I made her find a smudged 1979 calendar; so
it might be 1979 or a few years later. Also the matter of Will's playing
in the Seniors': he had to be old enough to play. Does that mean he
was fifty, fifty-five? I think it's fifty-five, isn't it.

JK: Fifty now.

WP: Fifty? Well, that fits in. Because that shows there was a rules
change.

JK: He's just on the edge.

WP: Yeah. So he could have played. That meant he had to leave
Birmingham at age thirty; he went out to Santa Fe, came back, did
not marry Kitty, went to law school. That meant he had to meet this
girl Marion Peabody in New York and marry her in law school in
order to have a child old enough to get married. So there was a bit of
a time problem.

JK: Did you go back and reread parts of *The Last Gentleman* to
make sure? Because I was checking details and I thought, "It's all
there."

WP: Well, I hate to go back and reread, but I forced myself to
reread the chronology enough to try and get it right.

BF: Just to return to metaphor and language for a moment. Like
Joyce, you do treat the roles of perception and language as central
problems in your characters' lives, and somehow too you relate this
to the condition of alienation. Is there any similarity or sympathy with
Joyce in the book?

WP: I hadn't thought of it . . . didn't think of Joyce. I'm just aware
of what I can't help but think of as the pathology of the modern
writer, the pathology of the century. I don't know whether that comes
from being trained as an M.D., a physician, and specifically a
pathologist, trained to notice when something is wrong, something
has gone wrong. And of course something has gone wrong, and it
has to do with the paradox between the good life, the affluent life, a
wealth of perception on the one hand, and yet a sense of poverty at
the very base of this wealth. Something has gone wrong with perception itself. Now what's going on? Is it something that has to do with
language? That's what I don't know; that's what I'm exploring.

BF: I wonder if you would say as categorically as Joyce would that
it's a problem of language? In all his novels people speak in out-

moded language and clichés, and then there are these sudden flashes of brilliantly-rendered perception . . .

WP: To answer your question, I hadn't thought of it, but now that I think of it I do remember reading *Portrait of the Artist* where he first starts doing that, using ordinary, common, everyday used-up speech, and yet he, that is Joyce, or what's his name, Stephen Dedalus, would come out with this absolutely magnificent prose. He had one paragraph—I think I've quoted it—about the clouds from Europe, the nomadic races of Europe, and all of a sudden this magnificent, fresh discovery of language. But I think he was much more obsessed with language than I am. I think I'm more interested in what's happened.

BF: Joyce definitely saw language as one means of salvation. Stephen sees his salvation in becoming an artist but Joyce would probably include anyone conscious of the way language works. Would you agree with him?

WP: No, unfortunately I'm much more pessimistic; I would see Kierkegaard as a good corrective of that. I could imagine Kierkegaard seeing—had he lived after Joyce—seeing Joyce as what he would call a hero of the aesthetic, seeing salvation through art and language. What is that great phrase that Stephen Dedalus uses in one place: "forge in the smithy of my soul the uncreated conscience of my race." Kierkegaard would say that's the aesthetic sphere.

BF: That leads me to a question about the novel as an extended version of language as redemption and salvation; because the novel is a literary form that can incorporate everything, the aesthetic, the ethical, and the religious.

WP: That it does, and I'm glad to hear someone say something good about the novel for a change. You're exactly right. And I can imagine what Flannery O'Connor would say if she were around. She wouldn't think much of what you said about salvation through language; she would say that the great virtue of the novel is that it describes man in transit, what Marcel called *homo viator.* She would look on the novel as the Judeo-Christian form par excellence. I think she would say that's why the best novels have been written in the Judeo-Christian tradition, why very few have been written in Eastern cultures.

BF: Why is that?

WP: Well, because in the Judeo-Christian tradition man is seen in the first place as a pilgrim, in transit, in a predicament, in a fix, fallen. And this suits the novelist to a T; this is exactly where the novelist wants him. Whereas if you're a good Buddhist, and you see reality as an illusion, as *maya*, you can't get too much material from that. Man is in a real predicament.

JK: Could I follow up on your comment about Flannery O'Connor? Could you say something about her encouragement at the beginning of your career? And which of her works do you like most?

WP: That's a good question, but I like all of them very much. . . . I was trying to remember the connection; the connection happened by way of Caroline Gordon. Flannery sent Caroline *Wise Blood,* and about the same time I sent Caroline a novel—a novel I wrote that's never been published.

JK: Was this *Charterhouse?*

WP: Yes. How the hell did you know that?

JK: I keep up on that stuff.

WP: He's got ESP. It's true. And Caroline was very kind, and she said it was good to get two novels from two Southerners at the same time. *Charterhouse* was a very bad novel, and *Wise Blood* was a very good one. I never really saw Flannery. She wrote me afterwards one of her laconic letters saying, "That was a good story. I hope you make up another one." But to answer your question, I guess you'd have to say that what means most to me are maybe a dozen or so of the short stories, the classic short stories, like "A Good Man is Hard to Find" or what is the name of the. . .

JK: "The Displaced Person"?

WP: Of course that's a great one. But the only one she ever wrote about the quote "race problem."

JK: "Everything that Rises Must Converge."

BF: "The Artificial Nigger"?

WP: It wasn't "The Artificial Nigger." About the angry young liberal guy who has . . .

JK: "Everything that Rises."

WP: Who has a frump of a mother who gets socked in the head with a purse. It's witty; really it's almost a masterpiece, I think, because you know Flannery lived through the whole period of all the troubles, when all Southern writers were exercised in writing about the race, and these were disastrous times. And she always stayed clear of emotion, nearly all the time. And this was the nearest that she came to making a statement, and it is a remarkable statement, which embraces all of the complexities of the situation. Instead of there being two classes of people—the bad racists, and the good liberals and the good blacks—it's all mixed up. The liberals are bad, and the racists are pretty good, and the blacks are just mad as hell, properly so. Her sufferings were extremely powerful. Her Catholicism was never far from her mind, I think; she was very polemical in her writings. And that's a question I've never been quite clear about, to tell you the truth. She would tell you, and has said, that she was very much aware of certain periods in her short stories where she means that the reader is supposed to understand that an action of grace occurred, a supervention of grace, especially in "A Good Man is Hard to Find," when the old lady embraces the Misfit. We're supposed to understand that she has seen the light, that the act shows grace. Well I'm not sure you really see that.

JK: Or in "The Artificial Nigger" where the little boy forgives his grandfather.

WP: Right, that's what I mean. She sees her fiction in much more univocal, theological terms than I would see it. I think it works without that rather simple theological reading, and I think it had *better* work without that, or otherwise, if you have to share that feeling of grace with her to understand her fiction, I think she's in trouble

JK: A lot of people have spent a lot of time arguing that very question.

WP: Yeah. All I know is, they work for me, even though I'm not sure I always understand that the Holy Spirit is operating in the denouement of the story.

JK: Have you seen Huston's *Wise Blood?*

WP: I have not; I've been tracking it down but I haven't caught up with it.

JK: Well, it's in Baton Rouge.

WP: It's good?

JK: Yeah, it is good. It made me think about the problem of O'Connor's satire and how it works. Ben and I were talking about this yesterday, trying to figure out what your satire is finally about, how it works. In traditional satire, there's usually a norm, but that's hard to find in your work and it's hard to find in O'Connor's. That is, you both seem to operate in terms of presenting a world where everyone is crazy or mean or something like that, and the thing that the satirist cares about is affirmed only by its absence. Does that make any sense in terms of your work? Because you have Will Barrett saying "There are two classes I hate, believers and unbelievers."

WP: You're quite right, Jerry, Barrett disposes of the human race by saying "There are two kinds of people I can't stand—there are two types of assholes, the unbelievers and the believers." I've been taken to task for that. Well, after all, don't forget what happens at the end. I really surprised myself because I'd never done it before. This man actually figured out what to do with his life. He figured out a way to live, to love, and to work. My novels have been criticized— maybe justifiably—by saying that they nearly all end ambiguously: you never know what happened to Binx Bolling; it's sort of up in the air. He makes a separate peace and not a very good peace; it's compromised. Will Barrett in *The Last Gentleman;* Thomas More [in *Love in the Ruins*] is just sitting there on the bayou. Fishing, not even talking. But in this case I surprised myself and I was pleased that this man actually figured out that he could work with people, actually within the system. I mean, it was a business proposition; he was going to practice law; he was going to live in what they call a garden home, all-GE Electric Medallion home for awhile. He was going to put these old people to work, get them out of the rest home and put them to work.

JK: He was going to search titles, or something like that.

WP: Yes, he was going to use Allie's property, divide it up, and it wasn't a harebrained scheme either. Ten acre parcels of land and get the old man to build log cabins, sell the whole thing for $25,000 and make money. So that's not so destructive and satirical. And of course he says he wants the best of both worlds; he wants Allie and he wants Jesus Christ. Not only wants; will have.

JK: But don't your novels have to end at that point? In other words, essentially what you're interested in is in the wandering and the searching and being in doubt, but once the character makes his commitment, that's the time when you've got to hit the road and end the book.

WP: You've got to get out, you have to get out. But what was different about this novel was I could actually see how he could join the human race. Your question was the function of satire. Satire implies a norm, implies something to be gained. This morning I've been reading *Candide* and I was wondering about Voltaire, because his satire is so skillful and so destructive that you don't know really what he wants. He seems not to imply a norm. He's got the theme of, what, working in the garden? But I think at the end of this [*The Second Coming*]—, he actually sees a way to live and to work, and she does too. I mean, I do believe that I actually came on a happy ending.

JK: This book strikes me as one in which you take more risks than you have in any other novel. I mean, the narrative point of view, and the time sequence, which is quite complicated. I started charting Will's movement from present to past and to intermediate points in his life. And then the business of the affirmative ending, which is a kind of risky thing to do.

WP: It really is. I make only one small, single modest claim for this book; it's the first unalienated novel since *War and Peace,* that's all. (laughs) Name another one! Thanks to the French, it's been downhill ever since.

JK: It seemed to me that in this book too, that it implied taking risks in the sense of working more closely with what seem to be actual experiences of yours.

WP: Well, none of those things happened to me, except my father committed suicide, that's all. He did shoot himself. But I never went through any of these cataclysms, cycles of belief and unbelief. And I don't have a girlfriend out of bounds over at the Covington Country Club. But she's a nice girl.

JK: Yeah, she is.

BF: Is there a greenhouse like that somewhere?

WP: No (laughs).

BF: But the air through the window; it's a perfect idea. It would work.

WP: Yes, it works. I moved that cave from Tennessee to North Carolina; there's such a cave in Tennessee called Lost Cove Cave. But you're right. The main risk was—and it was interesting, it was what made the novel fun to write—was to start with these two people: Will Barrett, who had won, who had achieved all his goals, as they say, by American standards, by businessmen's standards; he'd done everything right. And some of the reviewers were unfair, I thought, by saying all my characters are loafers, they don't do anything. Why, he had worked very hard and had done exactly what he was supposed to do: he'd gone to college, to law school, he worked for a firm, made a lot of money, married a rich girl. I mean, it's the American success story. But more than that—I mean it wasn't just material things—he had cultivated himself; he was well-read, loved music, and achieved everything he had set out to do. And yet his life had fallen apart. I've met more than one person that that actually happened to.

JK: But it's interesting that it happens to fall apart at the moment it does, and it's that sound of the wire fence that dislodges him in a sense and opens a door to his past. Is that consciously Proustian?

WP: I don't know whether it is or not. Like the taste of the cake at the beginning of *A La Recherche?* I don't know. I've forgotten. But I was more interested in what was the matter with him, and what was peculiar was that I had given him a syndrome which involved the opposite of amnesia. He was remembering everything; he was time-tripping, you know, in the past, and remembering everything. He also had a kind of sexual disfunction, suffering from wahnsinnige Sehnsucht—I thought that was a nice German term. And also falling down in the sand trap. Incidentally, there is such a syndrome, called temporal-lobe epilepsy. A doctor friend sent me an article which described the temporal-lobe epilepsy, comprised of all these signs and symptoms.

BF: He had auras too?

WP: Auras? Well, not always. But he has a kind of aura; he would be overtaken by memory; he thought about this girl he knew in high school just before he fell down. I made up a name for it—Haussmann's syndrome.

JK: Oh, you made it up?

WP: Did you think there was such a thing?

BP: I did.

WP: And I made up a treatment for it, and it might work—with hydrogen ions. But to answer your question, the risk and the fun was to get him, who was a total success and yet had collapsed into a

depression, and her, who was a total failure, failed at everything . . .
And I'm sure you've known even more girls than I have, being a
professor, that this has happened to—awfully bright girls who just
don't know how to live; she flunks ordinary living. She doesn't do
anything right; she doesn't go out with anybody, doesn't join a soror-
ity, doesn't have a vocation, doesn't go to law school, doesn't do
anything. She ends up back at home, utterly disgraced, for an American girl. So she flunks ordinary living and collapses into schizophrenia, or something like that. And yet she's the one who has the
new life; she starts out with a new life, with hope, with a kind of
joyous expectation of things, that she can hoist things, that she can
name things. She talks about naming the things in a hardware store.
So that was the risk—he starts from up going down, she starts at the
bottom going up—to make them cross. Linguistically and psychiatrically and philosophically.

JK: It works.

BF: Allie also reminded me of Binx Bolling. At the end of *The
Moviegoer* he says, this is my document. She keeps a journal that
saves her. It's only by reading what she's written in the past that she's
able to recover herself.

WP: That was tricky too. I didn't know whether that was going to
work. I had to start out in that first chapter, if I remember, with her
reading a note from herself to herself. You know that's very tricky to
do in a novel, but nobody seemed to mind. It seems to have worked
OK. The thing that maybe did not work, that has been more
criticized, has been the long letter from Will Barrett to Sutter, in which
he vents his spleen against the human race, believers and unbelievers, and develops a harebrained scheme for Sutter to leave for Israel
and watch for the Second Coming. That was a big risk that maybe
didn't pay off.

JK: But I noticed something interesting that happens at that point.
All of the "Will" chapters, up to that point, are narrated from a point
of view that is virtually indistinguishable from Will's. And yet at that
point, there's this sudden split, and the narrator is calling Will a crazy
man, stepping back from him and in effect disowning him.

WP: That's true. But that happens in the first chapter too. I say,
"What to make of this man?"

JK: Yes, that's right.

WP: That was a risk that maybe didn't work.

JK: No, I wasn't put off by it. I was trying to answer the question, "Why does the split take place here?" Does this represent a kind of schizophrenia, or . . .

WP: See the trouble is, I would like to have written it again. I sent it to the publisher and was just so damned tired. I was sick and tired when I sent it to the publisher, and of course as soon as he gets it, he wants to put it in the hopper and get it published. So if I'd written it again, I think I would have had less about his interior suffering, flashbacks. But on the other hand, I'm not sure, because for the story to work, for this unlikely romance to work, he has to be as odd as she is. He can't be just an ordinary, disenchanted, bored businessman, who develops a bad slice. His displacement had to be given sufficient weight to make it work, and yet I was never very happy with his long interior monologues. I'm much happier when something's happening.

JK: I liked the memory flashbacks.

BF: Won't he keep on having these; the flashbacks weren't caused *only* by the epilepsy? Even though he's cured in a medical sense, or brought back to some sort of balance, he's going to be the same Will Barrett, reacting to the past—maybe not falling down, but . . .

WP: Is he better off cured or not? When he's cured, when he's taking his acid and his pH is normal, he's convinced that the Jews have not left North Carolina, and nothing's wrong with the world, and everything's fine, and he forgets about Allie. It's only when he forgets to take his acid that his pH rises—it gets up to 7.6, normally it's about 7.2—it gets up in the alkaline side. Then, as I say, he gets haunted by great heavy molecules; when the hydrogen ions leave so do the Jews. But he also thinks about Allie, he wants to see Allie; so that's the question: is he better off with his high pH, abnormally high pH, or is he better off on the treatment? You know the case the Duke doctor describes, of the man who's been cured of the syndrome? He wanted to sit among the sand dunes in the middle of the night, and now he's a hard-working math professor who never looks back. That question is open, see?

JK: I think the scene where Will takes the guns out of the trunk and pitches them over the cliff really confirms the importance of the memory sequence and posits a definite solution.

WP: Well I'm glad you thought so, because a lot of people, a lot of Northeastern reviewers, thought that was a little Faulknerian, that the business with the father and the quail hunting was too Faulknerian. But it was absolutely necessary.

JK: I thought that worked beautifully.

WP: I got several letters that mentioned that same scene and one reader had such anxiety that he was going to commit suicide. And the guy said that if he had, if Will had taken the gun and committed suicide, he, the reader, would never have forgiven me.

JK: One question that I've always wanted to ask you: in the books that are out now, there are a few biographical details that are pretty well known, but your biography is still kind of mysterious. I was fascinated by your story [told during lunch before the recorded interview had begun] about being in Nazi Germany in 1934. And I was thinking that there are so many twentieth-century writers—you know, people like Dreiser, and Hemingway, and Thomas Wolfe—whose fiction is really a kind of recovery of their own life experiences. And I was wondering, when your biography is written, are we going to see your novels in those terms?

WP: Oh, I guess some of it, but not in the current sense of a roman à clef. Not because I think there's anything wrong with it, but I mean the American vogue of writing a roman à clef to me is a big bore. It's no fun. The fun comes in transforming experience, taking something that's happened to you, something you might imagine that happened—or I'm talking to you and I could imagine something that might have happened to you—and putting the pieces all together; that's where the fun is. This business of American writers—and I've even heard them say that they go out and have experiences with drugs, girlfriends, and so forth in order to write novels—that's a bad number.

JK: Which of your novels do you think is the most autobiographical?

WP: Well, I guess all and none. I'm a little like Binx in *The Moviegoer,* but I'm also like Kate. I think any novelist worthy of his salt—and this is a Jungian idea—that what you do is, you project a piece of yourself into all of your characters. What you do is use your own experience, people you know, or you project yourself—I imagine what I would be like if I were you. So I'm like Binx, although I never sold stocks and bonds, and I'm like Thomas More because he was a doctor—but I never had an encounter with the devil and never had a lapsometer. That Thomas More lived in a place kind of like Covington. Will Barrett comes from a place and has a family history a little bit like mine. Binx Bolling's Aunt Emily is very much like my uncle, William Alexander Percy.

BF: What about *Lancelot?*

WP: *Lancelot?* Yeah, how'd I blank out on that? (laughs) That was written after I spent a year at LSU. I don't know; there's not going to be too much autobiography, to answer your question.

JK: I noticed in the *New York Times* interview [June 29, 1980] you used the expression "making up stories," as if it really was a process of fabrication rather than disguising.

WP: Well, I think I probably used Flannery O'Connor's expression. She more or less constantly referred to her work as "making up stories." But you know, you don't make it up. I was stuck with these two people, and it's funny, once I get stuck with them, I see it through; it took me four years. I had to find out what happened to them. I didn't really have to make it up—they made it up. Certain things had to happen; nobody knows how this works, but if you start making it up, or making something happen, it often doesn't work, and you have to back up, tear up a hundred pages, and if you're lucky, something happens that does work.

BF: You have to tear up many pages?

WP: Oh yeah, all the time.

BF: Jerry and I were talking about that in the car, about the Kennedy assassination.

WP: That's true.

BF: So many pages that had to be . . .

WP: That was *The Last Gentleman;* I almost had to start that over again.

JK: Did any of that get back into the novel?

WP: One section, one paragraph.

JK: Where Sutter writes in his diary about . . .

WP: Yes, one paragraph about John F. Kennedy.

JK: The novel as we have it now was mostly written *after* that?

WP: That's right. The assassination happened in the middle of the novel, and I got very upset by the assassination and thought I might work it into the novel, but it didn't work at all.

JK: You still have it?

WP: No, I threw it away. I burned it.

JK: I got fascinated with that idea because the business of Will's disorientation—although there were immediate, personal reasons for it—was also characteristic of the way people felt in the aftermath of the assassination. And I had the sense that even though you took most of it out, there was still a lot there, under the surface.

WP: You're quite right. You know, it was an indelible experience. He was almost exactly my age, same birthday almost, mine's May 28, his was May 27. And I identified with him very closely—not that I always agreed with him—but I really felt a very close relationship. As Sutter said, he was not sentimental, he was extremely cool . . .

JK: Derisive.

WP: Derisive, that's right. So it was a bad thing to happen for that novel.

BF: I'd like to ask just one more question, about literary influence. You've mentioned Hopkins somewhere in an interview. Is he a poet you read often?

WP: I guess as much as I read anybody. If I were to read a poet this afternoon, it would probably be Hopkins. It goes back to the question you started with—metaphor. Hopkins had an extraordinary sense of metaphor. You see him using words, metaphors, which are like and yet very different from what they signify. He loved nature and he loved nature-descriptions, and he would use the strangest metaphors to describe, for example, clouds: rafts of clouds, slivers of clouds, shafts of clouds. He would go out of his way to distance his metaphor. Sometimes he overdid it, but he was very much aware of what he was doing.

JK: What's going to be in *Son of Message in the Bottle?*

WP: I'll tell, you Jerry, I haven't the foggiest idea.

JK: The question of semiotics that you're working on right now, are these new problems you're working on, or are you coming back to the things . . .

WP: I would like to use the same theories and apply them more. Because some people say, "Well, yeah, this is how you say language is acquired and this is what you say the symbol is." I would like to demonstrate it and I'm thinking particularly in terms of what happens in media transactions. What happens to people who watch television six hours a day for twenty years? It'd be nice to take this theory and come up with something because right now nobody has any idea. We don't know how to think about it. I would like to apply it to the thing we were talking about before, the exhaustion of language. We know something like that happens, but we don't know what it is.

BF: Do you think it's new to the twentieth century, the exhaustion of language?

WP: Probably not.

BF: Or does this happen in every man's lifetime—he wears out the words he grew up with?

WP: Maybe so. But why is it that in Elizabethan times all of a sudden there was a tremendous explosion of language? Was it because there were a few great poets that hit onto it, or is there a cycle of exhaustion and revewal or what?

JK: Derrida's got an essay on metaphor and the wearing-out process, and he cites a metaphor that Nietzsche uses about a coin that eventually loses its inscription, loses its image, loses its sign-bearing nature and simply becomes a piece of metal again.

WP: I'm sure I've read that. It's a very good description.

BF: But metaphor doesn't have to wear out. I mean, we do read Hopkins' poetry.

WP: Well, how many people read poets? Something very strange is going on. I get manuscripts of poetry and I don't know anything about poetry. But apparently thousands of young people are writing poems. They try to get them published, and I don't know that many people who are reading poems. I don't know whether they read each other's poetry or what. That's one thing: even if I were a poet, could write poetry, I wouldn't, for that reason, because people don't read poetry. And yet people will read novels. As Joyce said, you have to use all sorts of deceit, and guile, cunning, every ounce of cunning at your command, to attract the reader. It's possible to do it with the novel because of narration, as I mentioned earlier. Narrative is a very seductive form.

BF: Is it because it's more in the vernacular; we all speak in narrative, think in narrative. But we don't necessarily speak lyric poetry to ourselves. Narrative is closer to the ordinary processes of memory and thought.

WP: It's also closer to childlike thought; I remember Caroline Gordon telling me that in one sense a good novelist should never be over six years old. And that Hemingway actually never got any older. That was what caught on.

JK: That was his secret.

WP: I know exactly what she means, you know. I can remember my father reading stories like *Treasure Island.* He told a story: "Once upon a time something happened." That's almost an irresistible act of communication, transaction, and that way you can get readers, you can sell books, and you can make a living, and you can also do other things in the novel. You can do all kinds of subversive and polemical and satirical things. You can also overdo it and get caught.

BF: You know, I've noticed that my son—he can't read a book of course—that he'll turn each page separately and . . .

WP: How old is he?

BF: He's twenty months. He will go from beginning to end and then start at the beginning. And there's a kind of narrative progression in that; of course there's no language.

WP: My grandson will do the same. If he walked in right now, he would say—he can only say about five words—"book, book." And he'll go get a book and want to sit right here and look through it. I don't know exactly what it is, whether it's the narrative, or associating pictures with things and words or . . .

JK: It's amazing too how quickly they will pick up the line that completes a rhyme or something like that. They just have a kind of innate sense of closure, they want to complete the utterance that you begin. So all you have to do is give them the beginning and they can fill in the end of it, already anticipating the ending.

WP: And even more curious is the fact that they love repetition. It can't be repeated too often; whereas it can with us—we get bored, bound to get bored. There's an almost inexhaustible vigor and freshness of language at age two, three, four, and five, and then something happens. That's another thing I want to investiage in *Son of Message.* I looked up the word "bored"; did you know "bored" is a new word? It goes back only about a hundred years. But why is it that the very children who are so excited by words, language, story, later get bored? Of course they don't get bored with the tube, no matter how often they watch it; the original seductiveness of narrative is still there—which is why people still buy novels.

A Frenchman's Visit to Walker Percy

Gilbert Schricke/1981

From *Delta*[Montpellier, Université Paul Valery], 13 (Novembre 1981), 21–26. Reprinted by permission of *Delta* and of Gilbert Schricke.

It was a long journey. Walker Percy had told me over the telephone to be at Bechac's Restaurant around one o'clock. From Métairie I drove across the shoreless Pontchartrain Lake, and then found myself in Mandeville: a town-hall without a town, a city scattered in the woods. I turned right to the Lake-store (the Lake *had* shores after all) and eventually found Bechac's place, parked my car and met Walker Percy at once. We sat down in the restaurant, waiting for his friends to arrive.

I don't know how Boswell did it with Dr. Johnson, or Eckermann with Goethe, but I find it hard to set down what he said in his own words. The first thing he said was this: he was ever shy of going and meeting famous people:

> "I remember when we were driving north with a friend through Faulkner's country. My friend told me: why don't we stop and call on him? I didn't dare go and disturb him. My friend stayed two hours with him, while I slept in the car. They had the most wonderful conversation and I missed it, because of this absurd fear. And another time, when I was a medical student, I crossed Thomas Wolfe on the steps of the University building. There he was with his huge figure, you know, he was a very tall man. I could have addressed him. I didn't dare. And when Gabriel Marcel came to speak at Loyola University, one year before his death, I went to speak to him after his talk. But there were so many people around him, and then I completely forgot what I wanted to say to him. You know, sometimes you find yourself quite dumb in front of people you want to speak to."

I know exactly what you mean.

When I told him I was to give a talk on Gabriel Marcel at le Moyne College, Walker Percy said: "Apart from the Russians, three French

245

writers had the greatest influence on me: Camus, Sartre and Gabriel
Marcel. I have studied them a lot."

Well, I read three plays by Gabriel Marcel on the plane from
France and they make good reading.

"I don't like reading plays. You have to see them acted. Take *The
Seagull* for example. I don't enjoy reading it, yet Tchekov has influenced me a lot. What I like in your French writers is their clarity,
their purpose. Take *La Nausée,* when Sartre, looking at his own
hand, discovers what 'l'existence' is. It is viscous, repulsive . . ."

I don't feel 'l'existence' that way at all.

"Neither do I. But there is a purpose, there is a purpose. . . ."

Then the other guests arrived: three painters and a young writer,
Bill Borah. When I mentioned that Gabriel Marcel, during the first
World War, had found the burial place of dead soldiers through the
use of a wooden "planchette", the conversation drifted to psychic
phenomena, which left Walker Percy skeptically interested, and
somewhat amused. Then he spoke of some of his fellow writers: Styron ("his first novel, *Lie Down in Darkness,* is the most forceful"),
Saul Bellow and his extraordinary culture, and one writer (whom
we'll leave unnamed) who secured his commercial success by going
personally to see each bookseller in the State to make sure they had
his book. "A commercial traveller," I said. "Ah now, Graham Greene
would call that a commercial traveller. We call that a travelling sales-
man." Then we spoke of Kerouac and the well-known American
urge to move, to wander, to go *elsewhere.* "They say that Kerouac
wrote his stuff on rolls of toilet paper, he just kept unrolling and writing away . . ."

After lunch, I followed Walker Percy's car through a maze of tree-
lined roads, to land eventually at a lovely French-built house of the
last century, surrounded by lawns and trees, and whose porch over-
looks a bayou; nothing but trees all around, with the ghostly Spanish
moss hanging down from the branches, and the peace of the green
water.

Sitting on the porch over a glass of iced tea, looking at the bayou, I
listened to Walker Percy:

I love Richard Strauss, *Rosenkavalier* and *Arabella* most of all. Not Wagner. When I was at school in New York, my uncle took me to *Tristan,* with Flagstadt. I was bored. But I'll never forget Lotte Lehman in the Marshallin. She was making her farewell to singing and to the stage, just as the Marshallin in saying farewell to love, youth and Octavian. It was incredibly moving—I'll never forget it. In New Orleans they think the public wants mostly Italian opera, you know, Rossini, Verdi, Puccini. And last month they had a Gallup asking what composer they wanted to hear at the opera. Guess who it was?—Mozart. Do you sing? I don't but I always dreamt of being a tenor, a Helden-tenor you know, with my voice making the ceiling shake. . . . To come back to the French, I find Robbe-Grillet the most impressive writer in the Nouveau Roman. What I like in your French writers also is their ability to look at themselves critically, to be critics and writers at one and the same time. But sometimes they can overdo it. For example, I heard Robbe-Grillet speak about his novel *Jealousy.* Robbe-Grillet said he didn't say a word about jealousy in that book, that the work was merely a structure of geometrical lines. Well, he was lying, he was LYING! Your French journalists also got on Saul Bellow's nerves. Saul Bellow was very lucky, you know, at the time of the Six Days War: he was in Jerusalem to give lectures, and the war started. He had to stay, he had to stay, and thus became war-correspondent. But when he spoke to French journalists of what he had seen, there they were, knowing all about it, and they had never *been* there! Deduction, they did all by deduction. 'They know better.' You deduce, you French people, you deduce all. It's your Descartes who is responsible for that. You know sometimes a writer has a kind of encounter. He meets with a book that sets his mind working. Recently I have read a book, you must read it: *Zen and the Art of Motorcycle Maintenance* by Robert Pirsig [Walker Percy wrote this on my pocket diary]. I had been put off by the title a long time, but then I started reading it, and it certainly set me thinking. There are books, you know, even if you do not admire them, they give impetus to your mind. In that book the hero makes Aristotle and his logic responsible for all our evils—I personally make Descartes responsible—and has a nervous breakdown, which he overcomes by running and maintaining a motor-bike. Then again he finds peace in sailing a boat. None of that scorn of intellectuals for mechanics and trivial technical details, so ease for an intellectual—You must read the book. . . .

After a pause, Walker Percy said this:

You know, I sometimes wonder if I should stay down in the South instead of going north and live in a community of writers. Look at Faulkner. He was the greatest of us all. He ended up in drinking because he had stayed alone in the South. I went some time ago to New York, and there were

Styron, James Jones, William Morris [sic] and others, all talking together, meeting one another. Do your French writers now meet like that? I sometimes think that the literature of the South is a thing of the past . . ."

But look at the wealth of contemporary writing here! Have you seen the anthology, *Stories of the Modern South,* by Ben Forkner and Pat Samway?

"Not yet. But I cannot see any writer under forty who will carry on—When you telephoned, I was stuck on the novel I am writing now. Every time you think: now I am going to put everything into it, *everything.* And I felt stuck. I have been at that novel for two years now. I feel like a pregnant woman and the child is not coming out. Perhaps the fetus is dead, perhaps there never will be a child . . . It's about two amnesiacs. One is travelling on a Greyhound bus, and suddenly along the road he sees a row of poplar trees. And this reminds him of something important, very important. He *must* stop and go back. He must go back home. So he tells the driver to stop. The driver answers: 'My next stop is Atlanta, this is a through bus, I cannot stop.' The young man starts shouting at him, threatening him. And I got stuck there!

As I rose to take leave, Walker Percy showed me the French translation of *Love in the Ruins* and a Japanese translation.

"The Japanese, you know, are thorough, hard-working people. The Japanese translator came all the way from Japan to ask for the precise meaning of a swearword . . ."

And he added, with his ironical smile, that does not dispel the sadness of his eyes: "how is your Japanese"?

As I looked at the first page of the French translation, finding that the translator had succeeded in rendering the strange beauty of the style, Percy said: "It took me two months to write that first page. The beginning of a novel is so important, it starts the reader."

I feel as if I had stolen the fire. It was a long journey, from Nantes to Paris, to Chicago, to New Orleans. A hard time I had of it. I would be glad of another theft.

Walker Percy

John Griffin Jones/1983

From *Mississippi Writers Talking*, II (Jackson: University Press of Mississippi, 1983), pp. 3–45. Reprinted by permission of the University Press of Mississippi and John Griffin Jones.

What do you ask a man who once wrote, in response to the lack of creativity on the part of his interviewers, an article entitled "Questions They Never Ask Me: A Self-Interview"? Obviously he'd already asked, and answered, many of the questions pertinent to his fiction. Undaunted, I appealed to him in early 1980. He kindly consented to be interviewed, and his letter said to meet him at a restaurant in Mandeville, Louisiana, on the shores of Lake Pontchartrain, for lunch, and then we would drive to his home in Covington for the interview. Because the spring floods of the Pearl River had covered my rural route to the south, I had to double back through Jackson, which made me an agonizing hour late for our appointment. When I ran up to the restaurant, he was the first person I saw, talking quietly with a group of young people. Too late to feel nervous about intruding on their conversation, I introduced myself. I was greeted warmly—especially by Percy, who wore a nylon parka over a white shirt, corduroy trousers, and running shoes. He was taller than I'd imagined, with the quick, nimble movements of a boy. We had a light lunch of gumbo and bread, and when someone noticed it was three o'clock, the regular group promptly dispersed. Outside, he pointed to his little blue pickup and warned me, "You better stick to my tail if you can. I drive pretty fast." He did, and in no time, it seems, we were on the back porch of his house—overlooking a stretch of bayou—drinking iced tea and talking.

Jones: This is John Jones with the Mississippi Department of Archives and History. Dr. Percy, I wanted to start off with your giving us a little of your early background if you would.

249

Percy: I was born in Birmingham, Alabama, May 28, 1916. My father was named LeRoy Percy. He was a first cousin of William Alexander Percy. He married Martha Susan Phinizy from Athens, Georgia. His father was a Walker Percy, one of the three brothers— Walker, Senator Leroy Percy, and William Percy from Memphis. They all started out in Greenville. LeRoy, Senator Percy, stayed in Greenville, and William and Walker went to seek their fortunes elsewhere. Walker went to Birmingham, which was a new city.

Jones: Right. And William Alexander Percy says in *Lanterns on the Levee* that the three came back together during the Senator's race against Vardaman.

Percy: Right. I think they did.

Jones: Did you ever come to know or did you ever meet the Senator?

Percy: Once. It was very brief, but I remember it very distinctly. I don't think either one of my brothers recalls ever meeting him; maybe they didn't. I remember once he was passing through Birmingham. He was a great friend of my father; they got along well. Uncle LeRoy and my father were great hunting companions. They both would come down to New Orleans and play poker at the Boston Club and go hunting at the Lake Arthur Duck Club. It must have been shortly before my father's death, which was in 1929. This must have been the late '20s—'26, '27, '28. Senator Percy was passing through Birmingham, and I remember very distinctly going down with my father to the L & N railroad station. I remember exactly where it was. The train only stopped for a few minutes, so there was only time enough for Senator Percy to get off the train and stand on the siding. We talked to him a few minutes before he got back on the train. I'm trying to figure out where he'd been and where he was going. He was dressed in a very light tropical suit. He was very fit and small, smaller than I expected. He was a very handsome and trim figure of a man with a white mustache, very erect and rather imperial looking. He stood on the platform and talked to my father. I can't remember what we talked about, but after a few minutes he got on the train and went on. He must have come in from Florida going back to Greenville, but how? I don't know. The L & N—maybe he was going to Memphis. It couldn't have been long before his death. I've forgotten when he died, '27, '28?

Jones: Christmas Eve of '29.

Percy: '29. Hm. So it must have been '28.

Jones: It's always been my idea and one of the reasons I started this project, that if the Senator had been successful in the election—that Will so skillfully described in *Lanterns*—that maybe we would have been saved from the tradition of the demagogues.

Percy: Well, maybe so, but I doubt it. I can't think of a state where it happened, where comparable people were successful. I think it was probably a historical tide. The quasi-populists, a funny combination of populism and racism, were bound to win. I don't see it so much in personal terms as that. I think the same thing happened in Alabama; the same thing happened in Georgia. I think if R. E. Lee himself had been running, it wouldn't have made that much difference.

Jones: I know Shelby Foote has said that growing up in Greenville the Senator was for his people the shining knight on a white horse, but that now he's not even sure that Bilbo didn't have the people's interests closer to heart.

Percy: Well, it depends. In a way Bilbo was a populist, I guess. Maybe he did; although as a populist he was corrupted and finally totally corrupt. Uncle LeRoy maybe had a streak of paternalism in him, not only as applied to black people, but also maybe to white people. But within that framework he wanted to do what was best for what he called "his people." It certainly was not in the liberal framework that we're familiar with. God knows Vardaman and Bilbo were not either. But I would disagree with Shelby saying that the Senator did not have the best interests of his people, as he saw it, in mind. Maybe nowadays we look on that as being too paternalistic. We would think maybe he was too much of an aristocrat who thought he knew what was best for blacks and whites, poor whites. But I think he was out to do the best he could within his own lights, within his own frame of reference.

Jones: Right. Do you feel that the planter, the aristocrat, is the one to blame for the way that things developed in the Delta and the South? Do you think he was the real villain feeding the people false information and leading them on with the promise of upward mobility if they performed well and were good like him?

Percy: You mean black people?

Jones: Whites too. Do you see the planter as the scamp?

Percy: No more so than other white people. I don't necessarily indict them so much as think they were the victims of history, the victims of bad luck. That's the way I like to think of it. I think the bad luck came to pass when the cotton gin was developed and cotton became profitable and therefore slavery became profitable. You had this tremendous profit motive. When you say aristocrats, you know, that's a very tricky term. Who's an aristocrat? In the South it means somebody who's had the plantation more than a couple of generations. It was bad luck. You had these people who were making a lot of money and, you know, considering the human condition, the temptation was too much. It was too easy to make money. Slavery was profitable here, not in Massachusetts. It meant that whoever could get slaves got slaves. After the thing started, here again the temptation was too great. I remember my uncle Will Percy defending the plantation, the sharecropper system, saying it could work out very equitably. After the Civil War the blacks had nothing; the whites had nothing except the land; so therefore the white planters proposed to share their land and share half the produce. It sounds very good except that what with the human condition, it depended on a man being a good man for it to work out justly. Some people were good, and maybe most were not. It meant that it was too easy, too damn easy to exploit the blacks. When it's that easy, you do it, most people do it. I don't single out the planter class as being any more exploitative than any other white class, except that they were in a position to do it. Of course, traditionally it was the middle class, white middle class, who were rougher on the blacks than the planter class. It was Simon Legree's class . . .

Jones: The Snopes.

Percy: . . . you know, who were always tougher on the blacks than ole white massah.

Jones: I know in *Lanterns on the Levee* that Will says his father became one of his chief delights after he learned a little sense. Do you remember any of the stories that your Uncle Will might have told you when you were growing up about any of those old battles?

Percy: Well, to tell you the truth, I've got the stories so confused in my mind with *Lanterns on the Levee.* The stories that he used to tell us are the same ones that you read in *Lanterns on the Levee,* about the famous confrontation with Bilbo in the—I think it was in the coffee shop of which hotel in Jackson, Robert E. Lee? During the campaign. I think it was my grandfather who came into the hotel with my uncle and Senator Percy and saw Bilbo sitting there and referred to him as "that no-good son of a bitch," or some such words. I can't remember, as I say, if I read this or remember the story which he told several times, that Bilbo never looked up from eating his oatmeal. He went on eating. I think Shelby has been seduced a little bit by the romanticism of populism. He likes to think of Bilbo as a man of the people. Bilbo was, as my grandfather said, "a no-good son of a bitch!" If you want to record this for your history, you can do it. He was totally corrupt and didn't give a damn about the people. Maybe at the beginning he did, but, unlike Huey Long, who did care about the people in the beginning, I never really saw any signs that Bilbo did.

Jones: "A self-accused bribe-taker," as Will Percy said.

Percy: Yes.

Jones: I think one of the interesting things that turns up in your work is something that, again, Will had in *Lanterns on the Levee* concerning the Senator's attitude after he lost the Senate race in 1912. The Senator said in a letter he wrote to a fellow in Winona that shooting for the stars has always been pretty poor marksmanship, it seemed to him, and he came later in his life to decide that a man had to be as good a man as he could be in his own little postage stamp corner of the world.

Percy: Yes.

Jones: I know Will Barrett in *The Last Gentleman* tells Sutter after Jamie dies that he ought to come back to the South and make a contribution, however small. Did you draw that parallel consciously? Did you have that in mind?

Percy: Yes, I had it in mind. That's pretty close reading. Nobody, I think, has ever picked up on that before.

Jones: Well, I think it turns up in other places too.

Percy: Yes.

Jones: Tom More in *Love in the Ruins* has the secret to save the world with his lapsometer, and yet he is determined to stay with his three girls in the hotel in Sunnyside. And even at the end he is staying with Ellen in—is it in New Orleans?

Percy: No, he's over at a place like this, a place like Covington. I hadn't thought about it, but I guess there is a parallel there so that he's a little like Candide who was cultivating his garden, a small garden, you know. He's not totally given up, but partially giving up the grandiose idea of reforming the world, reforming the fallen condition of man by his lapsometer—what he calls angelism-bestialism. He's now fairly well content to live with Ellen, I guess her name is, a lusty Presbyterian wife on the bayou down in the slave quarter, which I thought was a good place to be, and running his trotline. There's a fellow out here who has a trotline right across that stretch of bayou right there. He's had it here for fifteen years. He checks his trotline every afternoon and every morning. Maybe that gave me the idea. I thought it was nice for Tom, after all that crap about the lapsometer and curing angelism-bestialism, which, of course, is the disease of the twentieth century—he was right about that; he was just wrong about thinking he could cure it or isolate it and cure it, to isolate it and cure it by a device. But his instincts were good in finally being better off under the bluff in a little cottage in the slave quarter and catching a—he caught a—gaspergou, I think.

Jones: Yes. Do you remember the first time you ever saw your Uncle Will?

Percy: Sure. In fact, I described it.

Jones: Right, in the introduction to *Lanterns on the Levee.*

Percy: Yes, in that introduction. I remember that very distinctly. I don't know whether you want me to say the same thing I said in the foreword.

Jones: I was interested to get you to describe for the tape how you came to live in Greenville and how he came to offer that invitation.

Percy: My father had died in Birmingham in the summer of 1929. It was a death by suicide. My mother had nothing to do but to take us three boys, my two brothers and myself, to move back to Athens, Georgia, with her mother, my grandmother Phinizy. It was a big house on Milledge Avenue in Athens. Well, you know how kids are— they don't take that sort of thing too seriously. You don't think too much about it. It was very pleasant living there in Athens. Looking back on it now, it must have been extremely traumatic for my mother. I remember I went to Athens High School as a freshman. I think I was thirteen. I spent one school year there. Then my Uncle

Will shows up, I think in the spring sometime. I remember him very distinctly. The first time I ever saw him was when he came into my grandmother's house. He was a very striking-looking man, as I described him in that foreword. He must have thought of this for some time, but it was his proposal that we come and live with him in Greenville. So, again, at thirteen it didn't seem unusual, you know, why not? It seemed like a good idea, so we did. I think we moved down before the school started in the fall of 1930 and we moved in with him. He had this huge house. His mother and father had died; as you point out, his father had died about a year earlier. You say Christmas Eve, '29, huh?

Jones: Yes.

Percy: So. And his mother had died and he had an empty house, and we all moved in with him.

Jones: Your mother too?

Percy: Yes. My mother, who was not well, died about two years later. She was in an automobile accident. That happened in 1932. The household consisted then of my uncle plus these three boys. I was fourteen by then, my brother Roy was twelve, and my younger brother was seven or eight. So there we were, three boys and a bachelor in this house in Greenville, which no longer exists, by the way.

Jones: Right. I've always found it hard to fathom that here was a globe-trotting bachelor, a sensitive poet, lawyer, and planter who had all these concerns. Why in the world, what kind of commitment did he feel strong enough to take on three young boys?

Percy: That's a good question. I'm not sure I can answer it.

Jones: Was he that concerned with his family to go wherever there was suffering in it?

Percy: I think he was drawn in two directions. On the one hand he was a poet. He was a great lover of foreign places, particularly Greece, the Mediterranean—Taormina, Sicily, was, I think, his favorite place—and the South Seas. In fact, when we first saw him he'd just gotten back from living in Bora Bora for six months. But on the other hand, he always had a very strong sense of commitment to his region. I think this had to do with the very complicated and strong bond with his father. He felt the sense of carrying on his father's commitment, which you spoke of earlier, to make one place a little

better. In fact he had been very active in flood relief in 1927 under
the Hoover Commission, so he knew what it was to contribute to a
local community. And he had a very strong sense of family. He was
very attached to my father, and his father was, too. I think maybe he
had the notion of giving us the benefit of exposure to him and of a
good education, of giving us advantages that maybe we wouldn't
have had otherwise. But there was always a sense of conflict. After
all, it was a crushing responsibility for somebody like him to take on.
I'm always amazed at the fact that he did it.

Jones: He ended up adopting you three, didn't he?

Percy: He adopted us, yes, after my mother died.

Jones: Tell me something about growing up in his house. Did he
push on you any ideas of academic excellence, or was he a
domineering parent?

Percy: No.

Jones: What type of household did he run?

Percy: It was a strange household. He was the standard stopover
for anybody who was traveling around the South, you know, that
wanted to make a tour of the South. His house was one of the standard stops. All sorts of people came by to visit or spend the night.
Dave Cohn came to spend a weekend and stayed a year. I don't
know whether you know Dave Cohn's work?

Jones: *God Shakes Creation.*

Percy: Yes. And there were psychiatrists like Hortense Powder-
maker and Harry Stack Sullivan. He came for three weeks and sat in
the kitchen and drank vodka martinis. He was supposed to be studying the race problem. He thought it was a good place to go, and he
probably was correct.

Jones: Talking to the cook.

Percy: Yes. Sure. And nobody had ever heard of vodka martinis in
1939 or '40. Carl Sandburg and the Benets, poets, and all sorts of
people like that. Who was the fellow who did *A Southerner Discovers
the South*—from Raleigh, you know? [Jonathan Daniels]

Jones: Roark Bradford?

Percy: No, but Roark and Dave Cohn came up. Raleigh—a newspaper man. So we were exposed to all manner of folk like that, and
his own friends around Greenville were all sorts and classes of whites
and blacks. It was an unusual sort of experience to grow up in a

household like that. I guess the most important thing, you mentioned education, the most important thing was he thought it was okay for us to go to Greenville High School, and it was.

Jones: You were the only one of you three to graduate from there, weren't you?

Percy: Right. That was because my brother had difficulty with Latin, so he got shipped off to Episcopal High School.

Jones: Didn't Will go to Episcopal High School?

Percy: He went to Sewanee.

Jones: Did he try to encourage you to go?

Percy: No, he thought it was a good idea, and it was, to go to Greenville High School, which is a good school. I was always glad I did. That's where I met Shelby [Foote]. And just yesterday my friend Charles Bell came by here. I don't know whether you've heard of him.

Jones: The poet?

Percy: The poet, yes. Charles was in my same class in high school—we were talking about that—and Shelby was in the class behind us. So I wouldn't have met Charles Bell or Shelby if I'd gone to Episcopal High School.

Jones: I know you've said that your Uncle Will made available to you a vocation, and, I believe you say, a second self that, for better or worse, wouldn't have otherwise been open to you. How would you say he influenced you in terms of your studying medicine and later turning to writing?

Percy: He didn't, as far as medicine. He put no pressure at all on me as far as choosing the law or any education. I think what happened was I felt obliged to go into a profession. I didn't want to go into law. It's like a hangover from the old Southern tradition of "what do you do?" Maybe it goes back to the English or the Europeans. Certain vocations are open to you, you know. What is it? Law, medicine, army, and priesthood. I got it down to medicine, which is a hell of a bad reason for going into medicine. No, he had nothing to do with that. That's an interesting question. I wonder what would have happened if I had said to him I wanted to be a writer, if I'd said, "I think I'll just take off two or three years and just travel around." I wonder what he would have said. Of course nowadays it's much more common for a young man to do exactly what he likes and to

get away with it, which is good. The pressure didn't come from him;
it came from me thinking what I was supposed to do, what one was
expected to do, or maybe what he expected me to do. These things
get internalized, you know. It's not what your parents actually want
you or tell you to do; it's what you think you're supposed to do. How
do you account for the fact that Greenville in that ten or fifteen years
produced so many writers, you know, people interested in writing
and poetry and music? Most people think, and I think Shelby would
agree, that it was Uncle Will. He had this extraordinary capacity for
communicating enthusiasm for beauty. He had this great love which
I'd never seen before, which was unusual and is even now to see
somebody who actually gets a high delight, great joy out of listening
to music. I'd never seen somebody put on a stack of records of Beethoven's Ninth Symphony or Brahms' First Symphony—in those
days they came in seventy-eight shellacs; you put a whole stack of
them on this big Capehart, and then they'd drop down, you know—
and listen to that with great pleasure. I didn't know what he was up
to, you know; it was a phenomenon, like "What is that all about?"
The first time I heard it, I couldn't make head or tail of it. He would
just say, "Well, just listen to it." I can remember experiencing the
breakthrough. After you listen to it, all of a sudden it's like a door
opening; all of a sudden you are aware of what's going on. The same
thing went for music, poetry, Shakespeare. Those were his big ones.
Reading aloud, he could communicate that there was something
here, which is something that you rarely get in school from a teacher.
But he had this extraordinary capacity for excitement. It was unique
in my experience, seeing somebody truly excited and experiencing
real pleasure at reading Shakespeare or listening to Brahms or Edna
St. Vincent Millay. Well, she was about as modern as he got. He
didn't get much past the end of the nineteenth century. He ended
mostly with Matthew Arnold. I don't think he had much use for—I
can't remember any modern poets he liked. Millay—as I recall he
liked some things of hers. To answer your question, that was the gift
he gave me. He gave me the excitement of reading. Writing? No, I
don't think that ever crossed his mind or mine that I could take up
writing. On the contrary, I remember one time we had a poetry contest at Greenville High School, and he, poor man, got suckered into
being the judge. I won the contest, even though the entries were

anonymous and numbered, and he said, "Well, I'm sorry you won, but you needn't be happy about it because it was the worst bunch of poems I've ever had occasion to judge." That was the end of my poetry writing. They were very bad. I think Shelby was in that same contest.

Jones: He has said, "Walker and I had some poetry in the Greenville High School *Pica,* and you can go back in the files and find them, I'm afraid."

Percy: Yes, I was writing a poem the first time I saw Shelby. It was in the study hall. I don't know whether he told you this or not. I wrote a poem and had it typed, and he was sitting next to me and said, "What are you doing?" I said, "I'm writing a poem," and he looked at it and read it. It wasn't a very good poem. It had never crossed his mind to write anything either. So shortly after that he began to write some poetry which was actually, although he would deny it, no better than mine, which is to say they were terrible. So, yes, we wrote some poetry in high school.

Jones: Do you think your poetry writing was part of an effort to show something to your uncle, to get closer to him?

Percy: You know, I have no idea, because I didn't show it to him. Maybe I thought since he was a poet and I had got some notion of what he liked in poetry that it might be fun to do. I never showed it to him. It was something to do.

Jones: At that age in high school, were you reading modern fiction or poetry?

Percy: Not really. I was more interested in science. I wasn't thinking about literature. In high school the only literary experience I can remember offhand was reading *Gone With the Wind.* When did that come out? It must have been the early '30s.

Jones: Thity-six, same year as *Absalom, Absalom!*

Percy: I remember *Gone With the Wind* and *The Brothers Karamazov,* which is a pretty strange pair when you come to think of it; one of them a really great novel and the other, you know, a very good pop novel. I can remember the great reading experience of beginning to read *Gone With the Wind* and taking it to my grandmother's house and sitting on the front porch—we went back to visit her—sitting on her front porch in Athens and reading the whole thing in about three or four days, and doing the same thing with *The*

Brothers Karamazov in Greenville. Also, my uncle put me onto a
book he liked a lot called *Jean Christophe,* Romain Rolland. That
was a very exciting experience. As the kids say, "I really dug that. I
got on to that." How I got on to Dostoyevsky I don't know because
he was not an admirer of Dostoyevsky.

Jones: He wasn't?

Percy: Not that I recall, no. I got that from Shelby. Shelby was
always a very precocious reader, a good reader. Shelby might have
got on to him before I did.

Jones: You two were close all the way through college?

Percy: Yes.

Jones: This is a question that I've asked everyone in this project. I
understand that Greenville had only one farce of a lynching, one bad
lynching . . .

Percy: It did?

Jones: They lynched the wrong man.

Percy: Hm.

Jones: And that the Klan never gained control of the local politics
and that Hodding Carter could come there and write freely his type
of journalism. And I have learned in doing this civil rights project that
I told you about that among those people Greenville was known as
the country club of the Delta, less lethal.

Percy: Less dangerous, yes.

Jones: . . . that all of this is directly attributable to the atmosphere
that Will and the Senator created in Greenville. Do you think it's as
simple as that, or do you know of any other factors?

Percy: I've wondered about that. I don't think that you can trace it
back to just one or two people. It must have been that there was
some sort of a humane tradition there. I think there must have been
other people involved. They were the ones I happen to know about.
Of course it was extremely important that my uncle and Dave Cohn
were instrumental in getting Hodding Carter up there in the '30s and
put him in business with the newspaper—and the roles that my
brother Roy and his son played. I think that was extraordinarily important. I feel very strongly that a newspaper sets the whole political
climate of a place. And Hodding went through some very tough
times; he had a hard time. It wasn't as easy as some people like to
imagine. He suffered several indignities of having garbage dumped

on his lawn and such like. So yes, I know my uncle was very important and Uncle LeRoy. It was certainly important for Uncle Will to
have gotten Hodding Carter there. I hope that the cycle hasn't come
to an end, because I understand that the Carters have sold the paper
to a southern California newspaper chain, which doesn't sound so
good. I'll have to wait and see. It would be very sad for that paper,
that tradition to come to an end and Greenville to lose its
uniqueness, because the whole time I was there and knew anything
about it, it was not like other Mississippi towns. To answer your question, I would have to give these names: Uncle LeRoy, Uncle Will, my
brother LeRoy, his son Billy, the Carters.

Jones: Can you think of any other factors that you remember
growing up there that might have contributed to its liberalism?

Percy: Hm. I'm not really sure how liberal it was. All I can think of
is that my uncle's house was open to all sorts of people, black and
white. Langston Hughes came there once and spent the night. That
was funny because my uncle, being the idealist and liberal that he
was, introduced him at a meeting by saying, "Now here's a man
who's black and a poet and who has risen above the issues of race
and ideologies involved in being a black activist and who's now become a poet." Whereupon Langston Hughes got up and read the
most ideologically aggressive poetry you can imagine. I think my Uncle Will expected a little too much for a black poet in the 1930s to
have risen above the matters of race. For me it was my uncle, Will
Percy, and the Carters, the paper, who were the main influences. My
uncle was absolutely fearless. He wasn't afraid of anybody. That and
the newspaper being very influential among people of character, plus
the fact that the Carter newspaper bought out the other newspaper
and became the only newspaper, was a very powerful influence on
the way Greenville was.

Jones: I wanted to pick up on something that you said. You said
your uncle wasn't scared of anybody. You know, nowadays when
people bring up the name Will Percy, especially young history professors and such, he seems to have a Blanche DuBois reputation. I
heard James Silver giving a talk on civil rights down at Millsaps
[College] saying that he and Dave Cohn were investigating the possibilities of integrated dinners as early as the late 1930s, "while,"
quote, "while Dave's friend Will Percy bemoaned the passing of the

days when blacks displayed good manners." I've always thought that was unfair because he was something else again in his day.

Percy: Yes. He addressed himself to that whole issue in *Lanterns on the Levee,* and I talked about my feelings about it in the foreword to it. There again we're a victim of our own times. It's easy to look back now and say that he was a segregationist or paternalistic, and maybe in a sense that's true. It was also true that in his day he was regarded as a liberal, a dangerous liberal, by his friends and contemporaries in Greenville. It's easy for somebody like Silver, who is a comfortable academic liberal, to denigrate what Will Percy did in the 1920s and '30s. All I know is that he repeatedly got himself in trouble with the sheriff's department, with the police, for attacking them in public for police brutality. I can remember black people coming to the house who'd been imprisoned and beaten up, and he would take them in and defend them and attack the sheriff's office or the chief of police, in public, and was branded as a "nigger lover" and such. It's very easy to look back and criticize from our comfortable liberal perspective now. It's very easy to be a liberal in Mississippi and Louisiana these days; in fact it's downright chic. It wasn't then!

Jones: I know his house was kind of a boarding house for the passing literary figures, but can you tell me something about his friends in Greenville? Who was he close to there?

Percy: I'm trying to think who his close friends were: Ada and Charlie Williams, two old family friends; the Shields brothers, Tommy and Arnold Shields; Rufus Mock and his wife. It was not a particular class. His friends were not limited to, quote, "the upper classes." He had friends on all levels, and black friends. I remember one black guy who was more or less off the street. He'd walk up and down the street at night and talk to people. One black guy came in one Sunday and played the blues on the harmonica for several hours. But who were his best friends? My brother Roy would remember those people better than I. I don't know if you asked him the same question. He's been there all his life and I have't been there since 1945.

Jones: When did you leave Greenville for good?

Percy: After he died in 1942. I only came back to visit my brother, so I guess it was '42. After that I was either in medical school or—I contracted tuberculosis working as an intern at Bellevue Hospital doing autopsies on TB deaths. For two years I was, quote, "taking the cure," as we said, at Saranac Lake in New York, and also working as a doctor up there, which was the best thing that ever happened to me because it gave me a chance to quit medicine. I had a respectable excuse. For two years I could read anything. I read for two years.

Jones: Yes.

Percy: After my scientific education I had time to read.

Jones: Yes, I want to talk about that some more, but let me ask you a couple more questions about your Uncle Will.

Percy: Yes.

Jones: Were you at home when he died, or were you taking the cure?

Percy: No, I was interning. I was at Bellevue.

Jones: Did you come home?

Percy: Yes. I came home twice; once when he got very sick, I went back to Bellevue, and when he died, my brother called me. He died suddenly. I think he died in April of '42.

Jones: January, I believe.

Percy: Well, that could be. I was with him when he first got sick. *Lanterns on the Levee* had just come out, and he was enjoying the reviews. We were at Sewanee. I went to Sewanee with him and his driver David, David Scott—I think it was David. It was in the summer. *Lanterns on the Levee* must have come out in May or June of '41. It's funny; it came out the same month, the same year, and from the same publishing house as *The Mind of the South.*

Jones: W. J. Cash.

Percy: It's strange. There couldn't be two more different books about the South, and yet both are very valuable in their way. We were staying at Brinkwood, his summer place at Sewanee. He was enjoying himself very much because he loved to get letters, fan mail, and he was writing responses. One of his close friends was Charlotte Gailor; in fact, she was one of the people he dedicated the book to—it's to Ada, Charlotte and Tom, and to me, Roy, and Phin. We went to see Charlotte Gailor, who was the daughter of the Bishop Gailor there at Sewanee, and there were some students visiting there too. They were having a meeting, three or four students. He was talking, and all of a sudden what he said didn't make any sense. I had just finished medical school, so I had sense enough to know what had happened. It was an aphasic response, and probably he'd had a small stroke in the area of the speech zone, of all places to hit him, because he was very good, very articulate with language. He loved to talk to young people. He could talk very well. All of a sudden for this to happen and for him not to be able to say what he wanted to say; he was very much aware of it. He was aware of what was going on and what was happening and the fact that he was aphasic and couldn't make himself known, so he grabbed me by the arm and said in effect, "Let's get out of here." I knew what had happened, so I took him home. I didn't have as much as a blood pressure apparatus with me. I called old Dr. Kirby-Smith the next day, from the old Kirby-Smith family at Sewanee, and he came out and took his blood pressure. It was some ungodly reading like 280 over 150 or something like that. It was malignant hypertension. He recovered from that particular episode. He regained his speech. I took him to Johns Hopkins immediately. Another great friend and also a distant relative was Janet Longcope—Janet Dana who married Warfield Longcope who was head of the medical division at Johns Hopkins. That was the best place I could think of. I took him up there and stayed with him for about a week or so. They did all the diagnostic tests and diagnosed him as having malignant hypertension. In those days there was not much you could do about it. Now you can treat it. There were very few drugs you could give. There wasn't too much, Longcope didn't offer too much, so I brought him back to Greenville. He got a little better. He never regained his strength really. I remember being there for the Christmas holidays. My internship didn't begin until January, so I was home for the month of December. He was feeling better, was up and around and could talk. I can remember him coming out on Sunday afternoon, December 7, 1941. Of course, you know what that was.

Jones: Pearl Harbor.

Percy: Everybody who's old enough can remember exactly where they were at that moment. I do. We were in the sun parlor of the old house and Uncle Will came out at two o'clock in the afternoon. He loved Japanese kimonos. He had a black Japanese kimono on. He kept all of his stuff in his sleeve. He came out in a big hurry and said, "The Japanese have attacked the fleet at Pearl Harbor." He was delighted, because he'd wanted the United States to enter the war long before. For him this was, in a sense, good news. It meant we were in the war. He would've gone to war six months before that. In fact he tried to.

Jones: Yes, Roy told me that. Do you need to stop?

Percy: I want you to meet my wife. (Whistles)

Jones: I'd like that.

Mrs. Percy: Hi.

Jones: Hi. (Tape off while introductions being made; pick up with conversation among Jones, Dr. Percy, and his wife Bunt)

Percy: I left to pick her [Mrs. Percy] up at three o'clock in the afternoon, and I said, "The war has started," and she said, "What war?" I said, "Like the world war." I don't think you took it in. So we went out to the levee with a .22 and shot at things, and somebody stole your purse. Everybody remembers where they were on Sunday afternoon, December 7, just as you probably remember where you were when Kennedy got shot.

Jones: Yes. I wanted to ask you something about Kennedy's assassination. I read where you said that the assassination cost you a year's work on *The Last Gentleman*.

Percy: It was a long time. I don't know how long it was.

Jones: Did you know about Phinizy's connection with John Kennedy?

Percy: Yes. Sure.

Jones: They were commanders in the Navy together or something?

Percy: No, they were lieutenants on the PT boats at Guadalcanal in 1942. Things were very tough. In fact my brother, as he will tell you—or maybe he won't, I don't know whether he wants to talk about it or not—he was in the same squadron as Kennedy and he was in the boat behind Kennedy when Kennedy got rammed by that Japanese destroyer. He'll tell you the story if he wants to. You can ask him about it.

Jones: Yes, I will. To return one last time: your Uncle Will did contract aphasia right toward the end of his life?

Percy: I don't know, I guess he did. I don't remember. I remember that particular attack. I know Miss Charlotte Gailor . . .

Mrs. Percy: He had exactly the same thing my mother had, and it followed about the same pattern.

Percy: That's true, and she was about the same age.

Mrs. Percy: Right, they were exactly the same age and they were both dead within six months.

Percy: Well, he was born in '88 [actually he was born May 14, 1885] and died in '42; that would make him fifty-four, wouldn't it? He had the arteries of a man eighty years old.

Jones: What would be the cause of that?

Percy: Well, they call it malignant hypertension. That's not a diagnosis, it's a description. They still don't know the cause of that.

Mrs. Percy: Some people just have terrific high blood pressure that never comes down.

Percy: Except that now they can treat it.

Mrs. Percy: I'm not so sure they can treat it.

Percy: Well, they can treat a good deal of it.

Mrs. Percy: What did they use to treat Mr. Will with, do you remember? I don't remember what they used to treat my mother. They were giving massive doses of garlic.

Jones: Garlic?

Mrs. Percy: Yes, and then something else.

Percy: Tell John what you thought of Uncle Will the first time you saw him.

Mrs. Percy: Oh, I was terrified of him.

Jones: Are you from Greenville?

Mrs. Percy: Yes. I was a technician and the doctor came by—I was dating Walker and Mr. Will knew that I was, I'm pretty sure, because I got teased a lot. Huger Jervey was a great friend of his. Have you come across Huger Jervey's name at all?

Jones: I know Gervis Lusk.

Mrs. Percy: No, Huger Jervey was a great friend of Mr. Will's. He was—I don't know whether he was head of the law school at Columbia, but he would come down and visit for long periods of time. He was a great tease, and when Walker would come to see me, they would say, "Bye baby bunting, Daddy's gone a-hunting." My name was Bunt. I knew him because Walker told me these little funny stories and I was just terrified to go over there. The doctor came in and said, "We have to make a house call." That just meant you went on a house call to take a blood sample. When I got in the car and found out where I was going, I was even more petrified. I remember walking in the house and right through the study and then, I think there was a step-up to his bedroom. He had on a green Japanese coat, I guess you would call it, with big sleeves. He was very impressive looking.

Jones: Was he?

Mrs. Percy: Yes, very impressive. In fact, my hand was shaking when I got down to him. You remember that bedroom off from where he was sick?

Percy: Yes.

Mrs. Percy: I had to stick his finger in there and my hand was shaking.

Percy: Why were you so afraid of him?

Mrs. Percy: I think because you had told me about Huger teasing you. Do you remember? He doesn't know anything about Huger, who was a great friend of his.

Percy: Oh, that's another very good friend of his. You had asked me about friends from Greenville. This is Huger Jervey, his great friend from Sewanee, professor at Columbia University whom I lived with a year or so after I moved to New York.

Mrs. Percy: And he would come and stay for long periods of time.

Percy: Yes.

Mrs. Percy: I think he was probably one of Mr. Will's best friends.

Percy: Yes, he was. The others were, let's see . . .

Mrs. Percy: Then we took him on after that. He came and spent time at Sewanee with us.

Percy: One of the good friends that we knew about was Gerstle Mack. Gerstle Mack is still living, incidentally. That reminds me, I got a Christmas card from him. We'll have to call him up.

Jones: Tell me for the tape how you two happened to meet.

Mrs. Percy: Same way I met Mr. Will, sticking his finger.

Percy: Did you stick my finger?

Mrs. Percy: Yes.

Percy: I wonder what I was doing. Was I sick?

Mrs. Percy: Oh, yes, you were sick.

Jones: This was when you were in med school or after?

Percy: No, I don't think so.

Mrs. Percy: This was before he went to med school.

Percy: This was . . .

Mrs. Percy: No, you came over to the clinic, and . . . some way you were at the clinic.

Percy: No, no. I was getting a job. I had six months between the end of medical school and the beginning of internship in 1941, so I thought it would be nice to go back to my uncle's house because he was sick, for one thing, and get a job at the local clinic, and I did. She was working at the clinic. She was a medical technologist at the Gamble Clinic in Greenville.

Mrs. Percy: Mr. Will told Walker he could buy himself a car, and guess what Walker bought. You're not going to believe it: a green Packard convertible. He went from a nothing car, what was it? A little old Ford?

Percy: Yes.

Mrs. Percy: To a Packard, which he kept only three months, I think, before he got sick.

Percy: True, true.

Jones: This was right after you got out of med school?

Percy: I guess so, yes.

Jones: And this was your graduation present.

Percy: He was rewarding me, I guess.

Mrs. Percy: That was after med school. But didn't I meet you right after North Carolina before you went to med school?

Percy: I don't think so—after medical school.

Jones: I think this is interesting. I'm glad you all agree to talk about it on the tape. I don't think I've ever heard that story.

Mrs. Percy: Well, I think I knew Walker for about seven years before we married. I'm going backward. I was about eighteen when I met you, and I was twenty-six when we married.

Percy: Hm. I thought it was the fall of '41 when I met you, when I was working at the clinic. When I was out in Sante Fe in 1945, that would be four years later. . . . We got married in '46, didn't we?

Mrs. Percy: Yes. I thought it was more than that.

Jones: You and Shelby went out to Sante Fe, didn't you?

Percy: Yes.

Jones: This was right after he got discharged.

Percy: Yes, I believe it was. This was after Bilbo's last campaign. He did a speech in Leland at which Hodding Carter accused him of saying something like . . . somebody accused him of being anti-Semitic.

Jones: When he said, "I like every damn Jew from Jesus Christ on down."

Mrs. Percy: Yes, I heard that.

Percy: Yes he was saying that, and I was there. Hodding Carter wanted me to sign a deposition that he had in fact said that. I signed it. I didn't live anywhere. I was visiting my brother and I got to the point where I decided to move on. I said, "Shelby, why don't we go out to Santa Fe?" So we left and went to Sante Fe. I lived on a ranch for about two or three months.

Jones: Why Santa Fe?

Percy: Always liked it, always liked it. Shelby stayed for a couple of weeks.

Mrs. Percy: Well, you still like the idea of the mountains and all that. We thought about living there.

Percy: It's beautiful, clear, high country.

Jones: And then you came back and where did you go?

Percy: I came back and went to New Orleans. She was working for a doctor in New Orleans. We married in '46, I guess. See, I was a free agent. I was at loose ends, didn't know what I wanted to do. I was out of medical school, and I don't think I've ever considered going back into medicine. I don't know whether I was thinking of being a writer by then, or a bum, or what.

Mrs. Percy: Well, you got a bad x-ray right after we got married.

Percy: So I had to take it easy.

Mrs. Percy: You started intensive reading, and that's when you were wanting to write on things you really wanted to say, but you decided nobody would read it. That's how you got into novels. You wrote that first article.

Percy: I don't remember when it was. I do remember we spent the first winter at Sewanee in Uncle Will's place where I had been a few years before with him, you see, when he first got sick. So I guess I did have to go take the cure again up there.

Mrs. Percy: You were in bed most of the time up there.

Percy: After a year there we decided we didn't want to live there. I don't know how we hit on New Orleans. How did we hit on New

Orleans? I've forgotten. I didn't want to live in Greenville, didn't want
to go back there, and it never crossed my mind to go back to a place
like Birmingham or Athens or Memphis; but New Orleans, you know,
I always liked the idea. So we lived in New Orleans another winter.

Mrs. Percy: That was kind of an interesting story. We came down
to look for a place to stay and we were just going through ads in the
paper when we came to a house on Calhoun Street. It belonged to
Julius Friend, who happened to know Mr. Will.

Percy: One of the many who'd visited the house, with Roark
Bradford.

Mrs. Percy: We had no idea who owned the house. We dropped
in on them and of course they rented us the house, left us their maid,
their furniture, their silverware.

Percy: Yes, that was a case of Jungian synchronicity. It turned out
to be Julius Friend who was a friend of Uncle Will's, and the house
was built by old man McDowell who had the place next to Brinkwood at Sewanee. It was really strange.

Mrs. Percy: I'm not sure I can believe that story, because how did
he ever get away from the mountains?

Percy: Well, I think he lived in New Orleans before that.

Mrs. Percy: He did? That story was told.

Percy: It's absolutely true.

Jones: Tell me this, Dr. Percy; when did writing become an option
for you? Were you thinking about writing first and then moved into
medicine and then from your experience with tuberculosis move
back into writing?

Percy: Well, I don't know. I enjoyed writing even back at Greenville High School for the local paper, *The Pica,* and later writing for
the college paper. But, as I say, it never crossed my mind to go into it
professionally, except that I did like to do it. When did I start seriously? I don't know. Let's see. I think somewhere in the '50s, I read
some things that excited me.

Mrs. Percy: Susanne Langer's book?

Percy: Susanne Langer's book, yes. It was a very provocative
book. I agreed with it in some things and disagreed with it in other
things, so I wrote a review of it. I sent it off to a journal, *Thought
Quarterly,* and it was published. I liked that idea.

Mrs. Percy: Yes, he liked that.

Percy: Even though I didn't get paid. They sent me back fifty reprints. I said, "This is for me," you know. Fortunately, I had enough money that my uncle had left me that I could afford to do that. I can't imagine how anybody starts writing. I didn't support myself for years. If you're not an academic or you're not a pop writer, I don't know how you do it. I went from that to writing a few occasional pieces for *Commonweal,* a liberal Catholic newspaper, journal, weekly. I did several pieces for them and got paid like twenty-five dollars. I liked that too. Somewhere along there I began to write a novel.

Mrs. Percy: You wrote for *Philosophy and Phenomenological Research* and *Psychiatry.*

Percy: I wrote some articles, yes. But I can't remember when I made up my mind that "maybe I can make a living at this," or "maybe I could make a career of it." I don't remember when that happened.

Mrs. Percy: I remember when your book got accepted.

Percy: Well, yes.

Jones: *The Moviegoer?*

Percy: Yes.

Jones: What do you remember of that?

Mrs. Percy: I was outside laying a brick patio. I think I was mad at him about something. If I was working that hard, I must have been. He came to the window and hollered out, and I forgot I was supposed to be mad at him then. He said, "It's been accepted." We were both excited.

Jones: I want to ask you something else. Talking about Shelby again: I've always been surprised at the way his early fiction has been kind of glossed-over by critics. *Follow Me Down* is a fine novel. But I suppose to read even the first few pages of his Civil War trilogy is to think that here's a guy who has found his great subject.

Percy: Yes.

Jones: What do you think of his fiction and his work?

Percy: Well, I think his fiction does not now receive its just criticism. I agree with you; *Follow Me Down, Love in a Dry Season* and *Shiloh,* maybe particularly *Shiloh,* I think are remarkable. They have been reprinted, they're back in print. It is true that he took off twenty years to write that mammoth Civil War thing, which I think is an extraordinary thing to do, requiring no end of persistence, and know-

ing exactly what he was doing and doing it very well, I think it's the
best history of its kind. It was such a happy marriage of his fictional
art and his first-class history; he's a good historian. It was such a
happy conjunction of these two faculties. It lasted so long that it
might have made it difficult for him to get back into writing fiction. I
thought the novel he wrote afterwards has been undervalued. The
critics didn't really take to it very well—*September September*. I liked
it better than most of the critics. As you know, he's got a major work
afoot now. I don't know whether he's started or not. He's been thinking about it for years. It's a very large novel.

Jones: Called *Two Gates to the City?*

Percy: Yes.

Jones: I think his achievement in that Civil War trilogy is just astounding; sentence after sentence, page after page for three massive
volumes, so skillfully written. It's just good history.

Percy: Yes.

Jones: You have a rare past for a Southern novelist and you've
broken new ground in Southern literature. Do you think it is more a
product of your unique background in medicine and your readings in
existentialist philosophy and your Catholicism, or do you think you
take this new direction because the old tradition is dead?

Percy: Well, I think it's probably all of those, a conjunction of
circumstances. One is the scientific background, which is a strange
background for a novelist, but valuable, I think. I think it leads both
to an appreciation of scientific truth and elegance on the one hand,
and on the other how the scientific method and the use of technology estranges a person: how somebody who follows the scientific
method and comes to its logical conclusion can end up as a sort of an
outsider, to be outside his own method. That's a problem that Binx
Bolling deals with in *The Moviegoer*. You got that, the scientific background. The exposure to Will Percy, who was a very powerful influence—this man, what he stood for. Also, for me to break through
into philosophy, most importantly the modern French existentialists
going back to the Russian novelists, Dostoyevsky, all the way back to
Thomas Aquinas and Augustine, and finally my conversion to the
Catholic Church. Living here in Covington is kind of between the
Catholic South and the Protestant Bible Belt. I've always enjoyed the
conflict of cultures: the scientific on the one hand, humanistic on the
other; the Catholic South and the Protestant North; Will Percy's tra-

ditional Southern culture and Binx Bolling's alienation, being outside
of it. Binx Bolling, you see, has straddled both of them. On the other
hand he comes from the typical Gulf Coast, Louisiana Catholic, middle-class Catholic background. It's a dialectical thing, I guess. It's the
interaction between these two cultures, three cultures. That's what
makes a novel work when it works. It's how these influences interact
and how they are resolved, or not resolved.

Jones: Can you tell me a little of what went into your decision not
to practice medicine? Was it an intellectual thing, or could you simply
not do it physically?

Percy: I could have done it physically. I was never that sick. In
fact, I didn't have any symptoms. I had what was called a minimal
lesion. It was picked up on a routine x-ray. I didn't have any cough or
fever or any of that. Sure, I could have gone back into medicine. I
think that period of reading and the idea of being onto something, of
reading something, reading modern philosophers and thinking, "This
man might be onto something," or "This woman, Susanne Langer,
was onto something and she lost it, she dropped it, she fumbled the
ball." I got excited by it, the philosophy of language, the philosophy
of, quote, "existentialism," what was called then existentialism, in a
way that medicine never excited me. I think that there may be a kind
of a—I don't know what they call it—a hope or a conceit or a conviction, or the idea that, well, if she missed it maybe I can pick it up.
There was something here. There was something there to be found.
There was something worth looking for. That was valuable. I think
the best I could have done in medicine would have been maybe in
psychiatry. I was thinking of doing that. But I was lucky because I
wouldn't have had the—I didn't have nerve enough to set off to
become a writer from the beginning. I was lucky to have gone
through medicine and gone through a place like Bellevue Hospital,
and that old-fashioned sanatorium like Thomas Mann's *Magic Mountain.* I think I was better off doing that than doing, say, what a—what
would one do to become a writer? People always ask me that, "What
do you do to become a writer?" I don't know. I guess I would have
majored in English some place, North Carolina, then what, taken a
Ph.D. in English, then what?

Jones: Some writers say that absolutely the worst thing that could
happen to you as a writer is to be on a college campus.

Percy: Yes, not too much good comes off college campuses, not in

the way of writing, which is not to put down college campuses, because I taught a couple of times. I don't see how anybody could
teach and write at the same time. It's hard work.

Jones: Will says in *Lanterns on the Levee* that it taps the same
reservoir.

Percy: I think it does. At least if you're conscientious it does.

Jones: I wanted to ask you how you came to decide on the novel
as the way to express your philosophical concerns?

Percy: Well, three ways. One was that I soon discovered that nobody read philosophical articles, not even academics, especially
when not written by an academic. Maybe academicians read each
other, I don't know, but they didn't read mine. I don't think I ever got
a letter from anybody who'd read one of those articles in a
philosophical journal and said anything about it. One reason was
there was no audience. It was like dropping a message into a void—
no response. The other was that there was no money. The third thing
was about that time I discovered the French facility for combining
philosophy and art, or the novel or the play, which the French do
very well. It's done often by people in different professions: in the
profession of diplomacy or government, people like Claudel,
Mauriac. I was excited by what Marcel and Sartre and Camus had
done by having very strong ideas about the nature of things, the
nature of man, and transmuting this into fictional form without somehow falling victim to pedantry or ideology, although Sartre ended up
doing exactly that. I saw that it was possible to be excited by ideas,
even philosophy, and not only to combine that with the novel, but to
use it in the novel, to actually put it to good use, which the French
had been doing and the Americans had not been doing too well, or
even trying to do. The American novelist traditionally had been
thought of as an adventurer in the concrete, particularly in the
South—somebody who traffics in lore and history and stories and
conversations and family sagas and so forth in the good old Faulkner-
Welty tradition. It had not been a discovery of American literature to
do what the French had done. Of course in this country you had the
novelists over here and the artists here and the musicians and com-
posers here and the businessmen here and the professors here and
the philosophers over here. So it was quite a revelation to me to see
somebody like Sartre, even though in the end I disagreed with him.

Maybe one of the most influential novels I ever read was *Nausea*.
That was a real revelation. It's funny how something can be that
important and influence you that much and be that valuable to you,
and yet you can diametrically disagree with it. It has usually worked
with me that way. I may be mostly indebted to people with whom I
have the deepest disagreements. They are the ones I owe the most
to.

Jones: Right. I've read where you said, "You can be sure I didn't
learn to write sitting on the front porch listening to old folks tell
stories."

Percy: That's correct. That's right.

Jones: But there again I know that when you read Walker Percy,
and his philosophical concerns are very valuable, original, and
unique, what you are admiring of and what makes his work such
sheer joy is his prose style.

Percy: Right.

Jones: I know the existentialists influenced you most in terms of
the construction of your ideology, but who influenced your narrative
style most?

Percy: Narrative style?

Jones: Yes, your prose style.

Percy: I think Dostoyevsky, Camus, and Sartre. Dostoyevsky in his
idea of people obsessed with—these characters who're obsessed with
some idea or something, or find themselves in a certain situation, a
terrible predicament, and behave accordingly. Camus for the style,
the sparseness, the laconic brevity, and precision of his sentences.
Sartre for catching on to the value of being a twentieth century outsider, man who is outside of it, and Sartre being able to use this and
to see the value of it. Psychiatrically it would be considered as a
pathology, a symptom. Literarily I saw that the great value of what
Sartre had done was to take the outsider and use his very out-
sideness as a way of seeing things in a different way. Who else? Well,
from the Americans I'd have to say Mark Twain.

Jones: I was going to ask you about Twain.

Percy: Yes. Mark Twain and Hemingway, and I guess Faulkner,
although I was scared to death of writing like Faulkner. That's curious, though. Even though I've gone out of my way to avoid Faulkner, in spite of my—because of my—admiration, nevertheless, I find

myself thinking, "Oh God, that sounds like him," you know, when I
write it. Faulkner is at once the blessing and curse of all Southern
novelists, maybe all novelists.

Jones: Because he so delineated the style?

Percy: Well, he's so good, and he's so overwhelming, so big, and
also so seductive, not necessarily in the right kind of way. His very
faults are seductive. That involuted syntax is seductive, and not necessarily good either. You find yourself falling victim to it—that is, using it in a lazy kind of way, using it as an excuse not to be precise the
way that Camus would be precise. It's so damn easy to fall victim to
that.

Jones: And it probably makes for the worst type of literature if
done badly.

Percy: That's right.

Jones: I was going to ask you about Mark Twain because it has
always seemed to me that there was some connection between you
two, especially as seen in the article you wrote for *Esquire* on bourbon.

Percy: Oh, yes?

Jones: I haven't laughed that hard at something I read since "The
Literary Offenses of James Fenimore Cooper."

Percy: What was it that reminded you of Twain in that?

Jones: Well, just the humor.

Percy: Oh, just the approach?

Jones: Right. Kind of looking at it sideways.

Percy: I hadn't thought of that.

Jones: It was really funny.

Percy: Well, maybe, yes. That's true, Mark Twain's humor. I find
humor very valuable.

Jones: You're very good at it.

Percy: Well, I discovered that the use of humor is not to be funny.
I only found out later what Kierkegaard said, that humor is the most
serious thing of all. Humor is not the opposite of being serious. He
said that humor is the last stage, in going through the stages of life—
he called them the aesthetic and the ethical and the religious—he
said humor is the last stage before the religious. I thought that was an
extraordinary statement. I just discovered that humor is a valuable
technique in fiction. There's some strange quirk in the modern con-

sciousness, the contemporary consciousness, so that one is more accessible, the reader is more accessible, and that there is some sort of communication that goes on between writer and reader which is facilitated through humor. I don't know exactly how that works except that it's just been given various names, like black humor—you know, humor used kind of perversely or sick or whatever. It does have a valuable function which I haven't quite identified.

Jones: Shelby Foote says that every page of great literature has at least some element of humor in it.

Percy: Yes.

Jones: So you steer clear of gin fizzes as you said in the *Esquire* article?

Percy: Oh, yes. Yes, that really happened to me, that gin fizz thing.

Jones: You and Dr. Tom More.

Percy: I guess. He had it too, didn't he?

Jones: Yes. You said it made your lip stick out like a shelf, like Mortimer Snerd.

Percy: True, true.

Jones: Oh, yes. Let me ask you this too, to kind of make a bow toward this other project that I'm doing on the civil rights movement. Early on in your career you expressed at least a sympathy with that movement and its objectives, but by the time of *Love in the Ruins* and *Lancelot* you had taken the sentiments of those movement people and kind of satirized them. Lancelot makes fun of his NAACP connections. Do you think that the movement got kind of misdirected toward the end?

Percy: No, I don't. I use that purely as a means of drawing the character of a particular person in a novel. The satire comes in view of a person who thinks he can find his own course in life through liberal causes. The NAACP was admirable, the civil rights movement was admirable, but it was also a way of avoiding one's self. One could give one's self the civil rights movement and escape one's self for the next ten years, both for the very serious, idealistic young, and for a man like Lancelot who was middle-aged, cynical, who nevertheless came off as a liberal of sorts who wanted to do the right thing, quote, "the right thing" about the interracial thing. Also, for him it was a little cynical. He was doing it maybe to irritate his neighbors. I guess that is a legacy of the existentialist tradition. Marcel always talked about being wary of mass movements or causes. There's always a danger of taking up a cause, of being too much identified with a cause. Also the political thing is that the civil rights movement has won, in a sense. It has won as much as any political movement has won, so that the blacks, I think, have made their point to a degree, which is not to say, God knows, that there aren't still serious areas of injustice and brutality and racism. They've won to the extent that a young black man can do pretty much what he wants, or he's a lot closer to it than he was twenty or thirty years ago. Also there's a danger from a novelist's point of view of taking on a liberal cause. There's no greater danger to fiction, I think, than ideology. I can't think offhand of any good novel which has been animated by the desire to oppose segregation, either from the black point of view or from the white point of view. If you set out to write a novel and your main motivation is the abolition of segregation or racism, it's almost fatal. God knows how many bad novels have been written by both blacks and whites, passionate novels which indict racism. I can only think of one or two that survive, and they survive despite the passionate ideology. I'm thinking of *Native Son,* Wright's novel, and what's the other one?

Jones: Ralph Ellison's *Invisible Man?*

Percy: *Invisible Man,* right.

Jones: Yes. It's a curious thing that Mississippi in ten years, or really from 1964 to 1970 when desegregation came about—I was in high school and it was largely peaceful—that Mississippi did a complete about-face in terms of history in an incredibly short period of time. I'm sure that you'll agree that that will have some effect on Mississippi being a spawning ground for writers.

Percy: Sure, right. And that's the good thing about at least the partial victory of the civil rights movement: that they won thanks to, mainly, to Lyndon Johnson of all people—Martin Luther King and the activists, and then Lyndon Johnson. The good thing about that is that now you can address the middle-class black reader, or you're beginning to be able to, and you no longer have to be bothered about, "Well, racism is bad, and there's no way I can write for you because you have to achieve the middle-class American success before—you have to know how much trouble we're in before I can talk to you." There's no way you can write in good conscience to a per-

son who's deprived of the ordinary means of life, who doesn't have
what everybody else has. The single greatest change that happened
in this country in the last fifty years has been this extraordinary revolution that you're talking about in Mississippi: the rise of the black
middle class. Now you have a generation of blacks who are in as
much trouble as affluent whites, and God knows that is a lot of
trouble!

Jones: They didn't know what they were getting in for.

Percy: That's right. Now they know!

Jones: So Mississippi is no longer the land of, as you put it,
"good-looking and ferocious young bigots." That was in the article
you wrote for *Harper's* called "Mississippi: The Fallen Paradise."

Percy: I remember writing it, but I've forgotten what I said.

Jones: It was in '65.

Percy: Yes.

Jones: You wrote about how the proud tradition of the Mississippians involved in Pickett's Charge was being prostituted by those
students at Ole Miss in '62.

Percy: Yes.

Jones: Well, I've just got a couple more questions. The only review of your work that I've ever read that was less than all-praising
was written by John Gardner in the *New York Times Book Review*
about *Lancelot.*

Percy: Yes.

Jones: Gardner said that while you adumbrate—I learned that
word from you—the woes of modern society and, as you put it, the
"malaise" in the modern world better than any other modern fiction
writer, that you don't take us across the river, you don't show us the
fruits of the search. Do you see that as your role?

Percy: No, that's not my role.

Jones: He said that art today, in his opinion, ought to "stop snivel-
ing, go for the answers, or shut up."

Percy: Yes, that's true, he thinks that art should be edifying, and
that's not bad—edifying in the best sense. It should be, in the best
sense. But I would agree with Kierkegaard there; he would say that
art functions at the aesthetic level. Let's face it. We're limited. The
most we could hope to do as artists, and that's what a writer is or
what he hopes to be, is to point out certain home truths. Faulkner

said it too. He called it "the motions of the human heart"—to say
how it is, how it is to be alive and how we find ourselves and what's
there. Kierkegaard said himself—he said, "I am not an apostle." In
the aesthetic phase you can talk about how it is on the island, see,
how it is in a certain time and a certain place in a certain culture,
even a Christian culture, but what you can't do is you can't speak
with the authority of an apostle. That's what Kierkegaard would say.
He said himself, "I do not have the authority to tell you that God
came into history and that therefore you should believe in Him."
Now that's not for me to say. That's not for the novelist to say. The
novelist can say how it is for a man in a certain state whether he's
Christian or non-Christian or whatever—sinful, always sinful. But
Gardner, I think, is confusing the aesthetic and the religious stage, at
least in my mind. Maybe he can do it, but I can't. That's why the
main criticism of my novels is that they all end indecisively, which is
very deliberate. They'd be in big trouble if they ended decisively.

Jones: Am I right in saying that the search that you discuss in all
of your novels is the important thing, rather than what's at the end of
it?

Percy: Well, that's open. That's an open question.

Jones: Only in *Lancelot* is the search clear, and there, I suppose,
the search is for the unholy grail, to find the reality of his wife's sin.

Percy: Yes.

Jones: Would you care to comment on the nature of the search in
your other novels?

Percy: Well.

Jones: I know that's a hard one.

Percy: Yes. I think if the novels have found any response it's because anybody who has any sense at all finds himself in this culture
in a state of confusion; that is, as Guardini would say, we're living in
the post-modern world. The world has ended in a sense. We're living
in one of these times that hasn't been named yet. Looking back on
history, we can talk about the fall of the Roman Empire and what
happened after that: the Dark Ages, the Middle Ages, High Middle
Ages, the Renaissance, Reformation and so forth; something has
happened now and we are not into it far enough to know what it is.
We're living at the end of modern times. The end of modern times

will be the end of Christendom as we know it. No one has named this period yet. We don't know what it is. So I think the normal state for a man to find himself in is in a state of confusion, spiritual disorientation, drawn in a sense to Christendom, but also repelled by the cultural nature of Christendom. To answer your question, the common thread that runs through all of my novels is of a man, or a woman, who finds himself/herself outside of society, maybe even in a state of neurosis, psychosis, or derangement. This last novel has a man and a woman who are psychotic in different ways. What I try to do is always pose the question, "Is this man or woman more abnormal than the 'normal society' around them?" I want the reader to be poised between these two values, and I want the question always to be raised as to who's crazy, whether the psychotic person is crazy, or the outside person—Binx Bolling, the king of laid-back, cool outsider; or Will Barrett, who's a much more disturbed outsider; Lancelot, who's downright violent; and the rather shadowy priest, who is kind of the mirror image of Lancelot. The reader is supposed to recognize the outsider in himself, and to identify with the alienated values of these characters. Maybe I try to design it so that it will cross the reader's mind to question the, quote, "normal culture," and to value his own state of disorientation. You say the search. I think the search is the normal condition. I think that's the one thread which unites all of my characters, that they're at various stages of disorder, and are aware of it, and not necessarily unhappy about it, not altogether unhappy about it.

Jones: Yes, not victims of the worst type of despair.

Percy: Yes.

Jones: I read the short story, the excerpt that you had in *Harper's* from your new novel. I see that you're returning to Will Barrett.

Percy: Yes, that's Will Barrett twenty years later.

Jones: Why Will Barrett?

Percy: I don't know why Will Barrett. I started writing this novel and it wasn't Will Barrett. He had a different name. After hundred pages or so I realized it was Will Barrett; at least with a couple of changes I was able to make it Will Barrett very easily. It couldn't have been anybody else, so I became aware it was Will Barrett.

Jones: Is Will Barrett closer to your own condition?

Percy: I don't know, not necessarily; no closer than Binx, no closer than Thomas More, or even Lancelot, or even the priest. I don't know. Or even Kate. Maybe Kate's closer to me than any of them.

Jones: Talking about Kate, have they ever considered making a movie out of *The Moviegoer?*

Percy: Well, Karen Black bought it, but nothing ever happened. She hasn't made it.

Jones: I can't see her as Kate.

Mrs. Percy: I told her that. It shocked her.

Percy: I made the mistake of saying, "Karen, which secretary are you going to play, Linda or Stephanie or Sharon?" She said, "I'll have you know I'll be playing Kate." She'd be a much better Linda.

Jones: She probably hasn't ever done anything with it because, playing Kate, she couldn't get anybody else involved.

Percy: Well, she had her a leading man lined up.

Mrs. Percy: A great leading man!

Percy: Yes, he would have been all right.

Mrs. Percy: Sam Waterston.

Jones: Yes, Sam Waterston.

Mrs. Percy: He would really be good.

Jones: He'd be a good Binx.

Percy: You know him? He played Nick Carraway in *Gatsby.*

Jones: Yes. I've seen him in other things too.

Percy: No, what happened was she split with her husband, and it was her husband's screenplay. I think she was doing it to help him out, doing it to be nice to him. He was the one that liked it. She didn't care much one way or another. I think, when they split, that was the end of it as far as she was concerned.

Jones: Has anyone else approached you about dramatizing any of your novels?

Percy: Yes.

Jones: *Lancelot?*

Percy: Yes, somebody has an option on *Lancelot.*

Jones: Good. One final question. I met you down at Mandeville where you were meeting with some fellow artists and writers. In a '68 interview I read, you said, "I have a couple of friends who're writers, but I don't talk to them very much." Do you think that it is important that writers communicate with each other?

Percy: Not particularly.

Jones: You remember Cowley said that if Faulkner had had some friends of like intellect to discuss things with his fiction would have been better.

Percy: No. No, if I thought that, I'd be living in New York, or living up in that Connecticut area where Styron and Updike and Cheever live. I don't think that's too important. In fact, I don't think they see too much of each other, to tell the truth.

Jones: Well, we've talked for a couple of hours and I know you're tired. I just wanted to say that I appreciate your talking with me and having me down.

Percy: Well, it's been a pleasure, John.

The Reentry Option: An Interview with Walker Percy

Jo Gulledge/1984

From *The Southern Review,* 20 (Winter 1984), 93–115. Permission to reprint by Jo Gulledge.

One reviewer called Walker Percy's sixth book *The Second Coming* (1980) "a work full of sharp, quirky perceptions, vividly achieved small scenes." But Percy's latest book *Lost in the Cosmos* (1983), a satirical commentary on the horrors of the post-modern era, has defied any pat critical summation. Reviews of *Lost in the Cosmos* range from one that condemns it as "self-indulgent priggishness" to another that praises the book for speaking in a "beguiling and civilized" voice unparalleled in American literature today.

Within the framework of existentialism and semiotics, Percy covers such topics in *Lost in the Cosmos* as religion, promiscuity, history, and travel. He does it so honestly that at times he may be self-indulgent, but never dull. Applying his semiotical methodology, he approaches the self on a triadic instead of dyadic plane, seeking "reentry options" that will fill the "everydayness" that his novelistic characters have attempted to avoid. While the book may be called "pontifical" and "irritating," Percy himself smiles slyly; after all, this is his intent.

In *Lost in the Cosmos* Percy says, "The painter and the sculptor are the Catholics of art . . . and the writer is the Protestant. He works alone in a room bare as a Quaker meeting house with nothing between him and his art but a Scripto pencil, like God's finger touching Adam. It is harder on the nerves." Percy's art touches the nerves of his readers. While some "wish he would stay with writing novels," Percy's friend, novelist and historian Shelby Foote says, "*Lost in the Cosmos* is funny . . . the best book Walker has written. I'm pleased he got away from novel-writing for a while."

The following interview with Percy examines some of the criticism of his latest work, his previous non-fiction *The Message in the Bottle,* and, in retrospect, *The Moviegoer,* his 1962 National Book Award novel.—JG

JG: In a previous interview, you indicated that your next book on language would be similar to your collection of essays; in fact, you gave the tentative title as *Novum Organum.* Why did you decide to write *Lost in the Cosmos,* a half-serious, half-satirical approach to language, semiotics, and the problems of pure science?

WP: The intermezzo in *Lost in the Cosmos*—a primer on the semiotics of the self—is, despite its offhand tone, as serious as can be. I have never and will never do anything as important. If I am remembered for anything a hundred years from now, it will probably be for that. The thesis is radical and the evidence is there. The thesis is nothing less than a semiotical account of the emergence of man in all his contrarieties from the collision of atoms in the Cosmos and the interaction of organisms—something that evolutionists have failed to do and the religionists have copped out on by placing it all on God, a sure enough *deus ex machina.*

I wrote it as a primer and in a light tone to make it accessible and to avoid academic portentousness. Readers, I have discovered, are not much interested in heavy works on semiotics. Nobody reads academic semiotics but semioticists, and I sometimes wonder if they do.

JG: Yet I've found lately more and more people are interested in linguistic theory, even the lay reader. Even you said that the sales of *The Message in the Bottle* have picked up recently. And look at the number of critical articles that have been written on that book. Even if you don't want to be taken seriously by the academic community, I wonder why this light, pop-attitude?

WP: Well, look at Kierkegaard's first and best selling work, *Either/ Or.* It's a similar sort of potpourri of bits and pieces of novels including "The Diary of a Seducer," along with snatches of philosophy, all this together, and yet it works. It's regarded as one of his best works and was his only best seller. And yet he is still taken seriously by serious readers. So why can't you do both? If I write an article for an academic journal, it's read by maybe forty academics . . . about as many as read each other. *Lost in the Cosmos* is intended to be both comic and deadly serious. And sure enough some readers laugh and others get angry. If it's true and if it's any good, I've observed, sooner or later people will take notice.

JG: But that's what you're saying you care the most about as of right now—not selling a large number of books.

WP: Well, I have to make a living. But I think all this semiotics stuff comes out in the wash eventually. Maybe no one will read it now, but if it's any good, it's going to be read later. In fact I think the structuralists have got themselves up a tree and are going to be looking for help, even from novelists. So, I hope to do more in semiotics. One reason I don't is laziness; it's hard work, and particularly hard when you realize that very few people are going to read it. It's tough enough to write with expectation. You know, most of us, even Faulkner, write with the expectation of being read.

JG: A major criticism of *Lost in the Cosmos* seems to be what reviewers consider a hard line approach on homosexuals, and that's a difficult topic to deal with. Do you think you're going to get any feedback from that?

WP: Well, I don't recall being any harder on homosexuals than I was on anybody else, or heterosexuals. I mean, where was I unkind or uncharitable to homosexuals? Are you talking about the scene in Donahue where the gay promiscuous cruiser goes to Buena Vista Park for his five-hundreth encounter? There is such a thing, after all, as a promiscuous homosexual. But look at the next guy—a promiscuous heterosexual. The next guy is a business man who is a connoisseur of the "lunch-hour liaison." He's heterosexual and sure doesn't come off any better than the homosexual. And what about the two male Nobel Laureates who are heterosexual and propose to benefit millions of women by distributing their sperm and their genes to a gene pool? There's such an organization, you know, in southern California.

There are millions of women who are, according to the two Laureates, suitable candidates but intellectually inferior, and their willingness could upgrade the human gene pool. Clearly I don't find that attitude admirable. Maybe homosexuals are more sensitive, but they are not getting any rougher treatment than heterosexuals or Nobel Laureates or astronauts or whoever, I think. In that book everybody, especially the author, is in trouble, right? What does a writer do but write from his own predicament?

JG: It is a humorous book to read and I'm sure was difficult to write considering that your subject is serious. But most reviews found the space odyssey, with one man and his three women, to be a weak section of the book.

WP: I wouldn't have minded one woman and three men, but off-

springs were important. It happened that it worked out better in the
various groups who tried out for the space odyssey. It's a commentary on the post-Christian age: marriage as more or less kaput. And
it's a satire, after all. And how can you please all women? What do
women want? Yes, it's true by the tone of some letters I received
from women about this book, though many sane women loved the
book. What I was trying to do was a satire on florid sexual behavior
of late twentieth-century man . . . and woman. Look at different
possibilities for the accommodation of astronauts—if you're given a
choice for the best space team, check one: two lesbian women, a pair
of straights, an unmarried man and woman, two male Nobel
Laureates, a pair of homosexuals, a lapsed Catholic and a Germaine
Greer type, and various other combinations. Not a married couple,
and not a live-in couple, which is a commentary on the difficulty
people have living together these days, both married and not married. But, the point is, at the end of the book, what happens? You
have a choice of going to New Ionia or beginning anew in Lost Cove,
Tennessee. In New Ionia, there's the Captain, with his wife who's
sulking, and the two girl friends. They are starting a new life in a new
world (recall Dr. Aristarchus Jones's proposal) without the People of
the Book, unlike the Pilgrims, who *didn't* leave it all behind. No more
Jews, no Protestants, no Catholics, no Moslems and no more religious wars. That's all gone. We're making a fresh start, without all the
cruelties, inhibitions, and sectarian infighting. We're going to have a
combination of kind of a Skinner-Walden II and a Jungian group
session. It's going to be a new world to work out our problems in,
and God what a depressing place it is! Come to think of it, Skinner's
Walden II is probably the most depressing book written in this century. The alternative is Lost Cove, Tennessee. There's the Captain
sitting on the hill overlooking the cave, with a Mass going on below
which includes the abbot and a few ragtag Catholics; there are a
couple of Protestant services going on. Nearby the Jews are arguing
about what kind of temple they're going to have. The Captain's sitting up there drinking whiskey, wonderful golden moonshine which is
pretty good stuff. And so he finally says, "I've got to go back to Jane;
she will be expecting me; I have a pig on smoking and it's time to
come off." So in the end he's monogamous and happy with it. A
triumph, sort of, of monogamy. Right?

JG: And in the same sense, the ending of *Love in the Ruins?*

WP: Yes, that's right. Except that was Thomas More's second wife, but this is the Captain's same wife, and he's sixty-five years old. So the idea is that he's given a choice, and which is better? Then when all is well, one of the "covites" from Carolina, Kluxers of the future, (where else but Carolina?) tries to start it up with the Catholics, Jews, and Blacks. The Captain starts laughing. Jason McBee, the bootlegger, says, "What are you laughing about, Captain?" and he says "Jesus Christ, here we go again." In other words, it's going to be the same thing. You have a choice: new world without all that stuff, without all the evils of religion, and you have polygamy, pot, drugs, and Skinner. But I'll take the world of Lost Cove, Tennessee, with all its nuttiness because there is joy there. And there ain't no joy in New Ionia or Walden II.

JG: Your women characters never fare well; in fact, they are criticized for being so stereotyped—the female psychiatrist on a lecture tour in New Orleans, for example, with her *Favorite Recipes* for the best ways to live/love. You show her hypocrisy by setting her in an angelism/bestialism situation.

WP: You regard that as a slur on the feminine gender?

JG: No, only in that the situation *itself* is pretty vicious. You attempt to reject the standard world of Will Percy, woman as either lady or whore, but in actuality you embrace the standard traditions of his old order more than he *ever* did.

WP: It certainly could have happened to a male psychiatrist, but I've only heard female TA psychologists. What about the male scientist on the next page who masturbates and then wipes out ten million people? He's not exactly a charmer. How come women are so sensitive? I don't hear men complaining. I hadn't intended to be a sexist . . . maybe I'd have been perfectly happy to make the psychologist a man except that using a woman was a better way to bring out the demoniac spirit of sexuality, the lack of which irritates me about the naive blandness of TA, or the usual psychotherapeutic attitude toward sexuality. Their sexuality is at best playing, nurturing, loving, or caring, a mutual relationship between two people and so forth, which is fine; that's the good part of it, but there's the demoniac side of it, too, which they overlook.

JG: Aren't you confusing, then, the term *passion* with *demoniac.*

WP: No, I don't think so. A good deal of the ambiguous pleasure of sexuality derives from the demoniac component. This is not something that I made up. On another Donahue show, or some talk show, I heard a woman analyst or some sort of psychologist who did a survey asking women their most commonly experienced dreams, sexual fantasies in their dreams. It was being assaulted. I mean bodily attacked. Not raped, but a handsome stranger coming in, and she, the dreamer, experiences violent sexuality which I call, half-seriously, the bestial-erotic. The thing is real—the data comes from women like Nancy Friday. Quarrel with her.

JG: It isn't a quarrel—only an observation. But that's the point— the data comes from women *like* Nancy Friday. You have to question the survey itself and also consider the audience of the Phil Donahue show.

An article in *Time* (May 27, 1983) mentioned that in the last twenty years data kept on patients that have sought help through psychotherapy indicates at least half of those who have been under treatment have not recovered as well as the ones that did not receive formal treatment. Interestingly, there are more cases of suicide in the ones that received help.

WP: That's one of the first questions of this book: why is it that there's only one theory of pneumococcal pneumonia, and yet there are sixteen schools of psychotherapy, sixteen theories or views of the personality, and a patient can do just about the same in each of the different schools? One works as well as the other.

JG: Or leaves them just as badly off. So what's the point? It's a science that can't be pinpointed.

WP: The point is that we don't know very much about the psyche, not much more than Plato. The point is I was also trying to lay the grounds for triadic theory. My feeling is that the only way to get a hold of any "science of the psyche" is to approach it through triadic theory. Most traditional psychology, all science, tries to explain things dyadically, interaction, secondary causes, function . . . which is a strange thing in a way, because here's a triadic creature, Einstein or B. F. Skinner or whoever, explaining the universe, the cosmos, on a dyadic model, where he himself is a triadic creature making dyadic theories about a problem which works fine for oneself or for the cosmos, works fine for explaining the solar system or black holes or quasars and pulsars; the whole cosmos is a dyadic system. But it doesn't work fine for explaining *other* triadic creatures. It doesn't work *at all* for explaining consciousness, language, poetry, other triadic activity, e.g., uttering a sentence. Ask a scientist what a sentence is. What is it to assert a sentence? You'll get some strange answers—as strange from Chomsky as from Skinner. Fifty years of strenuous attempts to teach "language" to chimps, apes, and dolphins and not one sentence has been asserted. So that's what's peculiar. When a triadic creature tries to explain triadic activity, he can't presently do it. What he can do is try to set it forth on a dyadic model, either a Skinnerian stimulus-response model which they've tried for fifty years; or a formal linguistic model, a structural linguistic model, where you can explain it as the transformationalists do by sentence rules, S $\rightarrow$ NP + VP, and by phonology as a system of binary oppositions. This is *purely* formal: here's two things, they say, two formal structures either in opposition or in a sentence; the other is Skinnerian behaviorism, scientific dyads, but suppose someone took Charles Peirce seriously and tried to start a triadic science. How would that work? You would have a different set of variables, which I tried to explain in the chapter on semiotics. It's a whole different world. All of a sudden as soon as people start entering into triadic behavior, you have a world, *welt* as opposed to *umwelt*. If you say *welt* or "world" to a scientist as opposed to *umwelt* or "environment," you get a blank look. He doesn't know what you're talking about. You might have uttered a word in Sumerian. My triadic primer is theoretical, but not so technical that the lay reader can't get through it. As a matter of fact, it's lots of fun. That's the reason I keep harping on it: the only way to get at the psyche is through a study of triadic behavior. The key notion is *placement* in a *world*. Say *placement* in a *world* to a dyadic psychologist and you get another blank look.

JG: In one sense, you have an appreciation for the scientific study of language through linguistics, even to the point of remarking that you wish you had taken up the formal study of linguistics. You seem to be at odds, in general, with the academic linguists. One example that comes to mind is "Walker Percy's Theory of Language: A Linguist's Assessment" (*Delta*, November 1981). How valid is the article's argument that there is a misunderstanding on your part toward "comparing and evaluating" the implicit assumptions of the behavioral school?

WP: It has been a while since I read it, and I don't remember it too well. As I recall, my main objection was that it did not address the thesis of my article. The article proposed a theory of sentences. Transformational grammarians do not have a theory of sentences. They have a rule of sentence structure:

$$S \rightarrow NP + VP$$

This works very well as a formal description of declarative sentence utterances of two words or more. But what does the TG linguist make of the child's one-word utterances, especially the naming behavior so dramatic in the second and third year of life? They don't say. Chomsky has professed a monumental indifference to empirical data of language acquisition. Both the TG people and structural linguists in general have had very little to say about the fragmentary utterances of children. Indeed, what *is* there to say once you are committed to an analysis of text, e.g., two or more words, as a theory of language?

But what do you make of the event Peirce described: a man pointing to a balloon, his son seeing it, the father saying *balloon,* the son nodding and repeating the word *balloon?* Clearly there has occurred a naming sentence, not an NP-VP assertion, but an assertion that that round, red, inflated object, a percept held in common, "is" a *balloon,* that odd sound.

I was attempting to devise a rudimentary formula to encompass both the early naming sentences of childhood as well as the conventional, well-formed NP-VP utterances. A theory of sentences must account for more than textual items, e.g., it must also account for indexical signs, percepts beheld in common, the status of the copula, uttered or unuttered, in naming sentences as well as NP-VP sentences.

I recall that the article made great fun of my use of Wittgenstein's dictum that a sentence means whatever it is used to mean. This is easy to do. As the article states, one can hardly use the sentence *Today is Wednesday* to mean *My back hurts.* But of course I was using it in the context of language acquisition in children. Thus the utterance *baby chair* (Brain's example) can mean any one of several things accordingly as the child uses it. The mother has no trouble deciphering the meaning-use within the child's behavior. Thus, it might mean: *I want my baby chair, There is a baby chair, The baby is in his chair,* etc.

You know, I think a lot of this confusion came to pass when the structuralists after Saussure turned him upside down. Saussure said that linguistics is a branch of semiotics. Thus, the above semiotic theory of sentences accounts for purely linguistic sentences . . . as well as non-linguistic (naming, art, etc.). But once the structuralists turn it around, adopt the linguistic model as primary, to which semiotics must conform, then you've got all the problems the structuralists ran into: inability to account for the data of L-acquisition, the confinement of the semioticist to the strait-jacket of the *text* and textual analysis. And you end up with some rather silly structural analyses of such things as fashion, even cooking, which is made to fit into, of all things, the phonological model of binary oppositions.

JG: You once said that you hoped that this next book would be a radical approach (or an important standpoint for you in studying the human consciousness) in trying to establish a new model of theory about language and how humans interact and assess their predicament. Do you feel you've done that in this book and are you, at least, satisfied with your own approach now that you've been writing about, thinking about, language for nearly thirty years—since you compiled the first essay, "Symbol as Need" (*Thought,* 29, Autumn 1954), which seemed to be a starting point for you in 1954? I assume all of this came about from the discovery of your daughter Ann's deafness—around 1951 or 1952.

WP: I had been interested in the process by which sound utterance gets to mean things, the combination of the two, the sound uttered, the object referred to, and the transformation of the sound part by the meaning part of it. What I was interested in doing here which is new in semiotics, and I'm sure that many semioticians will thoroughly disapprove, is to focus not on the text, not on the sound utterance, not on binary oppositions, but on some new way to derive the self semiotically. Mention the word "self" to a structuralist or a deconstructionist and you get not only a blank look but a dirty look. However, we all are stuck with our selves, even structuralists. Structuralists like Lévi-Strauss and Foucault aim for the exact opposite; to get rid of the self. My interest is this: Is there any way you can approach the self from a triadic theory, from a semiotic theory? So that's what I was interested in doing in the chapter "A Semiotic Primer of the Self." I simply start from a word construed, and named, and understood in its totality. So I'm involved in it as a *world,* but categorized and articulated by sound patterns, words, sentences, meanings, the whole issue, with one exception: the self. The self is forever an unknown. That's the point of the comic opening where it asks, "Why is it that, when you are shown a group photograph in which you are present, you always (and probably covertly) seek yourself out? To see what you look like? Don't you know what you look like?" Are you worried when you see yourself in a home movie? Does it make you a little uneasy? I probably should have used a second epigraph at the beginning, following Nietzsche, from St. Augustine: "God, give us the power to know ourselves." (The paperback will have it.) The point is you're always worried about what you look like. That's because you don't know, really. And it, the self, is a moveable piece. You can't pin yourself down.

JG: It's important how others perceive you.

WP: Yes, so we're all trying to fit into the way they're going to see us.

JG: Yes, so therefore you want to fit a mold of how you think you look.

WP: True, but the point is that you don't know, and the point is that sure enough *you* are different from all other people. But, you perceive yourself as utterly different and that's intolerable. All the other people you know fit into more or less a category; they even fit their names. In your perception, you don't fit your name; you don't fit anything at all. Therefore sometimes you're way up; sometimes you're way down. I call it being existentially freed-up: you're an unguided missile in the Cosmos; you're on a sliding semiotic scale from minus infinity to plus infinity. Look at the two sentences at the beginning of the book: (a) "You are extraordinarly generous, ecstatically loving of the right person." In other words, you are, or I am, potentially the most sensitive person, the most loving, understanding person the world over; or (b) "You are of all the people in the world probably the most selfish, hateful, etc." Or, I am the bloodiest, the

most envious, treacherous, disloyal person imaginable, and so forth.
Now suppose you read these two sentences to people and ask them
which one applies to them. The answer from most is both. So what I
was trying to do is figure out how to get at the self. Triadically, semiotically. After all, the self has been in limbo for two thousand years—I
mean ever since Plato. What would happen if you asked a current
academic psychologist, "What is the Self?" What would he say?
Probably something about how you arrive at your *self* through role
modeling or trying to perceive others and how they perceive you and
all that stuff. So, I was trying to arrive at a semiotic explanation of the
peculiar predicament of the self. I did it by showing that the *self* is
that unknown entity in the whole world which it understands and
knows the least about.

JG: But to understand the book in this way, you have to read the
chapter on semiotics and then go back and apply it even though you
challenge the reader to skip the chapter.

WP: And what happens when the reader gets to that point?

JG: It makes you backtrack. If you understand the book clearly on
that level, you have to apply it to what you call the satirical question-
naire.

WP: You don't really have to read the semiotic chapter. The Taos
chapter, the Reentry chapter, are intelligible without it. I'm curious to
know how that worked, especially that brief page that says you don't
have to read this. Some tell me they took it as a dare and therefore
said, "I'm going to read it." Most of them did, at least the ones I
talked to. Some of them were put off and put the book down. Some
of them skipped it, but I think most of them read it. Well, they read it
through at least. It does help to understand the rest of the book,
which has to do with how the twentieth-century self lives in a post--
religious age, you know; it's post-cosmological, post-mythological,
post-Oriental, post-Christian. You're the self and the world, with God
more or less omitted these days. The self is in orbit. It either tran-
scends the world through science and art or it tries to reenter. And so
the book is about the reentry option, different ways to get back in the
world. It's not going to make any sense unless you understand
"What is this thing orbiting the earth?" That's the self, the self of the
twentieth century in a peculiar situation vis-à-vis the world: he's/she's
abstracted from it, and always with a reentry problem. How do I get

back? How can I get back to feeling real at 4 o'clock on a Wednesday afternoon? How can I get through this? Maybe I go see a great movie. Then what do I do?

JG: That's a kind of escape in a way.

WP: It's not an escape to try to live. Do you believe it's an escape to listen to Beethoven's Ninth Symphony? Maybe it's an escape to read *The Brothers Karamazov,* but it's also an exhilaration. The problem I was interested in is what to do afterwards, both for yourself and for Dostoyevski and for Faulkner. Maybe it's an escape to be von Frisch and study bee communication for forty years. He's happy. The only happy people in the world now are, generally, scientists. Serious scientists usually don't have reentry problems. You know why? They're in permanent orbit; they're thinking about science all the time. Look at Barbara McClintock.

JG: Once you forget about it, you lose the continuity of it, and then you're back out again.

WP: Back into your life. Or else you have the two main options now in the post-religious age: the transcendent option and the immanent option. The transcendent is obvious; scientists are the princes of the age, I say, because they're having the best time of all. Einstein could think about the general theory of relativity for twenty years and be happy. He's ambling around in a daze, not thinking of anybody, but he's perfectly happy because he's getting warm, getting close to finding something out. That's the transcending option.

JG: And he looks the most abnormal of anybody.

WP: Yes, he looks the part of the absent-minded, strung-out professor. But the other option is immanence. This is where I get criticized. When you're not a scientist and you're not an artist, or science-lover or music-lover, you cultivate the immanent world. For example, you take courses in parenting, go to TA groups, to group encounters or consciousness-raising groups—all to cultivate the various things open to you: you go to the best plays, only watch the best TV; so those are your two options. What I was interested in (where I had the most fun) was doing the reentries. We all get into orbits of transcendence, right? You get excited about something you're writing, or reading (you don't have to be a writer), or a good movie, or anything creative . . . then what happens when you go home? That's where the problem comes; it's a universal problem. That's why there's so much drinking, so many drugs, eight hours of TV, so I'm talking about the problem of sorting out the reentry options. What are the various modes? The fun was deriving it, deducing the options, from semiotics or semiotic theory; deduce the theoretical options, then see if you can match them up with the way people actually behave. For example, the travel option: people travel so much; some can go around the world and still not be satisfied. I know a lady who goes around the world every year. I think I had ten options of reentry. It was fun deducing it from triadic theory and then looking around like Mendeleev who did the periodic table theory of elements. His delight was in compiling the periodic table just by the way it ought to be and then looking around for elements to fit in. And there are still some gaps in his table. And mine, too.

JG: As you say, people get in a rut, are bored, subject to depression, suicide. But why is it that when you throw people out of their routine, they become even more depressed? People go on vacation looking for something; they want out of their rut, but when they're out of their realm and have expectations of what their vacation is supposed to be like, and they're actually looking for something, they're thrown off by their everyday schedules?

WP: It depends on the person; some people just get tranquilized in a rut of their immanence. They do travel the same sort of way. They buy a certain trip tour. Remember, I have three kinds of tourists. One does the routine tour of Mexico and is happy. Okay, the bus breaks down like it does in *Night of the Iguana,* and the first tourist gets very unhappy. "This is not what I paid for. You promised to take us to the Cancun Howard Johnson or the Yucatan Hilton." He or she is happy only if the bus sticks to schedule. Okay, Tourist B: what about him or her? She's/he's happy with the breakdown; this is something off the path, off the beaten track, he's or she's exhilarated. They put up at an old abandoned monastery converted into a hotel. This is just as exciting. You know the kind of traveler I'm talking about. They'll come back and tell you this story: "Guess what happened to us. We were on this regular bus tour, the bus breaks down, and we went to this old monastery and the walls were a foot thick and it was really interesting." Then there's Tourist C who knows all this like Joan Didion and takes the tour anyhow as a kind of antic exercise.

JG: Half-jokingly, you were going to subtitle *Lost in the Cosmos:*

Why Carl Sagan Is So Lonely . . . a statement obviously directed at scientists in general who try to "dissolve the uniqueness of man" and make him like all other species. This brings up the problem again and again of the doctrines of evolution and creationism. While the evolutionists don't pretend to see their view as the "eternal truth," scientists, like Carl Sagan and others, see the status of evolution as a logical theory—even though it is not provable in a traditional scientific method. While he can't be proved wrong, your book points to some of the holes in his theory which caused Sagan to write and ask about *Lost in the Cosmos*.

WP: Yes, he wrote me he'd read somewhere that I'd written a book in rebuttal to his writings and questioning the fact that he's left God out of the Cosmos. He said if I could show him any cited evidence that God was ever there or ever in a being, he would have to consider it. He just said he'd like to read the book. He reminds me of a pathologist who finished an autopsy and said to his students: "Where is the soul?"

JG: So he hadn't read the book yet.

WP: No, he hadn't, so I sent him a copy.

JG: Most reviewers come up with the idea that it is a rebuttal of Sagan, but it isn't against him personally. It only mentions Sagan one time.

WP: I only mention him in one question and one footnote. People like to latch onto something, and the two most obvious names are Donahue and Sagan. They're featured in different parts of the book. But you know where the loneliness comes from? It comes from a triadic creature, scientist, whether it be Einstein or Darwin or Sagan, who tries to explain the whole world by dyadic theory and mostly succeeds. Darwin was trying to do it—thought he'd succeeded. Darwin's theory of evolution is purely dyadic. Organisms compete, then small, accidental changes occur, which survive through adaptation and survival of the fittest. But notice that there is a curious movement taking place while you're explaining the whole world by dyadic theory: you yourself are getting more and more removed from it. There you are sitting making up these theories, but how do *you* fit in? So you feel a little isolated and so end up with these fanciful notions of ETI's and talking chimps. Sagan wrote books which appear to explain not only the whole Cosmos but the human condition,

how humans get to where they are, through his theories about the
reptilian brain and cortex brain as computer and so forth. But why is
Carl Sagan so anxious to find an ETI (extra-terrestrial intelligence)?
Because the triadic scientist gets lonely. If everything gets put in the
sphere of immanence, the sphere of dyadic interaction, one gets
more and more isolated. Where does one fit it? Then he has a problem of reentry. How does one lead his life? Well, one way to do it is
to communicate with extraterrestrials. If one is a great scientist like
Einstein, one simply does science. If not, then one starts longing for
encounters with extra-terrestrials. What people like Sagan don't
realize is that humans are far more mysterious than any extra--
terrestrial they've yet imagined. It's a fanciful idea of Sagan having
explained the whole Cosmos and the human position, then trying to
find an ETI to tell it to, to communicate with.

JG: You, on the other hand, seem to find a way to live in the
Christian culture with Catholic dogma. Once, you remarked that
"dogma . . . signifies belief in the central Christian mysteries, for example, the Incarnation." Fiction is your own means for exploring the
mystery of human existence?

WP: Yes, it's important to the novelist, at least to *this* novelist. I
have never felt constrained by my own beliefs; but, on the other
hand, a good number of writers I know are paralyzed by belief in
nothing, in abstract freedom. Orthodox Christian belief is congenial
to my vocation, which is evident, I suppose, in the peculiar pilgrimage of Binx Bolling, the old moviegoer.

JG: Now that *The Moviegoer* has been out for over twenty years,
and considering its success, we can now focus on the character of
Binx Bolling as a survivor as Lewis P. Simpson would call him—not
just in his own family and his own place—but in *history*. Why do you
think that Bink has become part of our literary history?

WP: It may have to do with the fact that it was one of the first
times that an American novel did what the European novels had
been doing for many years—talking about alienation, talking about a
man, a young man, who has everything materially, has a noble family
history, and has his needs basically satisfied, but he feels out of it. In
the same sense that we think of Russian characters, like Raskolnikov,
or an extreme case—Meurseault in *The Stranger*. Of course, both
those novels excited me, and they were not in the American tradition

that I had read, not in the tradition of the southern novel, not in Faulkner's tradition. The main difference is that Binx Bolling, being American and southern, is more easy-going and good-humored . . . like Huck Finn.

JG: It goes back to something we've talked about before—while someone like Shelby Foote, who has a Jewish ancestor, has a need for the southern tradition and tends to strive toward it, you, on the other hand, are always going in the opposite direction; you *have* the traditional southern heritage in the strictest sense and always tend to steer away. Why?

WP: I did my "southern apprentice" novels, but they were imitations of Thomas Wolfe and Thomas Mann. I hear southern writers talking about writing—people like Faulkner and Welty saying that it all comes from a very family-oriented tradition, of storytelling and family histories. Of course, all Faulkner's novels are deeply rooted in this or that tradition, whether it's degenerate or not. And you're very much aware of his looking back to the Civil War and beyond; in fact, he makes a great point of tracing historical ancestry. Well, that doesn't interest me in the slightest, except . . . well, maybe that's unfair . . . it interests me as a backdrop to something more important. What happens when it's all over—when you find yourself in the second half of the twentieth century with all this history behind you? Then what? I think a time comes when you can spend too much time ruminating over family sagas and epics, defeats, and the lost war. And then a time comes when you have to figure out how to live in the here-and-now. I'm kind of a maverick; that is, I don't fit into the southern pattern. On the other hand I couldn't be other than a southern writer . . . I write with all that in the backdrop. All my characters, whether from Binx Bolling to Will Barrett to Thomas More and the others, find themselves in a here-and-now predicament. And the whole backdrop is this historical scene which is drawn so well by Shelby, Eudora, and Faulkner. It's *there* all right, but my character is looking in the other direction; he's not looking back. And that's why I've always felt more akin to Faulkner's Quentin Compson than to anybody else in his fiction because he's trying to get away from it. He is sick of time, because time means the past and history. So he tears the hands off his watch. He's wandering and wanders around this godforsaken Boston suburb, and the last place he wants to go is back to Mississippi, to time and history. When he says to his Canadian friend, "I don't hate the South, I don't," he protests too much.

JG: And he has to get away from it to like it . . .

WP: If he likes it at *all.* So, I suppose, I would like to think of starting where Faulkner left off, of starting with the Quentin Compson who *didn't* commit suicide. Suicide is easy. Keeping Quentin Compson alive is something else. In a way, Binx Bolling is Quentin Compson who didn't commit suicide.

JG: Because of the character Binx Bolling, *The Moviegoer* is taught in numerous college fiction courses, as was Salinger's *Catcher in the Rye* in the sixties. Do you think Binx will remain a cult figure?

WP: Really? I'm surprised that it is used that much. I wouldn't think Binx had reached that stature.

JG: You underestimate the book's popularity. After all, it's been eight years or so since you've taught on a campus.

WP: Yes, it's probably a good novel to teach; it's open to being taught because academics, after all, are interested in ideas, and this is a novel of ideas as well as, I hope, a good novel in its own right. And, of course, that's a trick . . . in effect what I was trying to do. It's a teachable novel because it's in the European tradition, not the American. I was very much aware of the ideas floating around in my head when I wrote the narrative . . . the ideas came from Kierkegaard, among others, and being raised in Birmingham: being in a predicament. Being raised in a country club subdivision is very different from being raised in an old Mississippi town. I was very much aware of trying to do what the Europeans did—Sartre, Camus, and Marcel, while keeping hold of hard-headed, Anglo-American empiricism. Hence *Message in the Bottle* which is a bridge between the two. At the time I'd been reading Heidegger . . . what at the time was called *existentialism,* which is a bad word. I don't know what it means. Mailer does. To him it means acting on impulse. So it has gotten a bad name. But generally, I suppose it meant exploring man's predicament, exploring that part of oneself which cannot be encompassed by scientific categories. So, I thought what better way to do it than in the novel form rather than doing a complicated, philosophical examination of what Heidegger called the "existentialia" . . . things like the inauthentic fallen state, which very few Germans, let alone Americans, had read. Why not explore it novelistically because that's where philosophy and art come together in the so-called European existentialist novel. It was, for me, a very happy fusion of the two; in the first place, I wasn't equipped as a philosopher to express my ideas. My essays on the subject were amateurish, but this, novel writing, seemed to be a wonderful way to explore it. And what could be more fun than to take someone I had made up, partly from myself, partly from the South, partly from other people I knew. That's where the South comes in, because without the southern backdrop—Mississippi, Louisiana (New Orleans)—the novel doesn't work—it doesn't work at *all*. Try to imagine Binx Bolling in Butte, Montana. There has to be a contrast between this very saturated culture in the South, on one hand, whether it's French, Creole, uptown New Orleans, or Protestant. It's a very dense society or culture which you need for Binx to collide with.

JG: A review article of *The Second Coming,* "Fiction and the Private *Life"* (*The Ontario Review,* Spring-Summer 1981) made the comment that "Walker Percy is likely to remain a cult figure, since one doubts that his preoccupations will significantly broaden; but like other Southern writers—Flannery O'Connor, for instance—he will continue to command respect for his power to communicate a deeply private, often unsharable world-view with such impressive skill and feeling." He's right when he says that your concerns will remain the same, but explain what he means by a "private world-view." The *everydayness,* I suppose?

WP: If it's all that private, it's not going to work. Art, after all, is a public phenomenon. I'm not sure what he means by the term, "world-view," but I know what *I* mean. I know that the parts of the novel that people like best are the parts where I manage to communicate a certain attitude or feeling which *I* certainly have and is shared by the reader, which hasn't been covered before in fiction— not the usual attitude found in fiction. I use various words to describe it: one is "upside-down-ness," another is a particularity of Wednesday afternoons, when you're supposed to feel good and you don't. I'm talking about the commuter in East Orange, who has everything he thinks he wants in life, yet he feels bad. And I describe how he feels bad, and, of course, the whole of *The Moviegoer* is about Binx's malaise, and everybody picked up on the *malaise* because that was something that hadn't been written about, at least not by most

American novelists during that period. So, it's the sort of thing, judging from the letters I get and the response I get, that people say, "Yes, that's the way I feel, but I didn't know anyone else felt that way," or "Yes, that's the way it is; that's what it's like for me."

JG: Your critical reputation seems to grow as we find numerous quarterlies devoted to the study, not only of the fiction, but essays, as well. There's something to be said for *imagination,* but you seem to attempt to get at reality without encasing it in a "period vacuum"— time becomes transcendent, and Binx is the best example of a character who expands beyond; he's in a very fluid circumstance. Do you agree with that?

WP: Do you think that someone like Binx would have been understood in 1862?

JG: I think so—this was a transitional period in history, with the scientific and industrial revolution. This was the problem Hardy had; his characters Jude Fawley and Sue Bridehead were among the first of what I would call the "alienated," lost characters of literature.

WP: The question arises whether Binx expresses a universal situation of the human condition now or whether he and the other characters express a situation confined to a particular period of time and a relatively few number of people. In other words, maybe an English professor likes it, and other novelists like *The Moviegoer,* and a few readers, because it's a commonly shared neurosis. Maybe only a few people are screwed up in the same way, because I also get letters from people who don't know what the hell I'm trying to get at. They say, "What's the matter with this guy? Why the hell doesn't he straighten up? Why doesn't he get with it? Why is he so out of it? What is this malaise? He's just neurotic." It *still* remains open whether Binx is pathological or whether he's expressing an authentic mood of the time. It's an open question. I would like to think that he's an embodiment of a certain pathology of the twentieth century. There are a great many people who would say that he's a nut, he's abnormal, he's neurotic, he's a goof-off. After all, it was his aunt who told him off in proper style. She said, "Why don't you do research or make something of your life?" Binx is not buying this. He is holding out for more. He senses a kind of despair in his aunt and at heart is hopeful.

JG: Lewis Lawson in a recent article ("Time and Eternity in *The*

Moviegoer," *Southern Humanities Review,* Spring 1982), defines two modes of time in the novel: (1) time of the here-and-now, the concreteness of money as time, and (2) Binx's time spent as the moviegoer, that is to say, a universal and eternal timelessness. Within the "eternal" time, we find Binx standing, as he has for the past ten years, in front of his aunt's mantelpiece trying to understand the expression, which he cannot name, on his father's face in the portrait. "He was commissioned in the RCAF in 1940 and got himself killed before his country entered the war. And in Crete. In the wine dark sea . . . with a copy of *A Shropshire Lad* in his pocket." What is Binx's conception of his father's "time" as he searches the eyes, one at a time, and finds the "ironical"—which, in a sense, is a clue to his horizontal search—of time of the past? It's in the same way he searches for an answer by reading *A Study of History:* a solution to the problem of time. Could you add the other, a time of the past, as a third definite mode of time?

WP: Sure, and also the time of the search—the horizontal search—as a different mode of spending time from the others. Most of his time past, his *a la recherche,* is recaptured in that very mode of romanticism and science—both of them. In fact, I think when he's lying on his mother's dock on the bayou sleeping, and the last thing he thinks before he goes to sleep (he might have jotted it down in his notebook, I forget) is, "You know, there's a connection between science and romanticism." Both of them have a way of dealing with the world. And you come to an end of it, and then what do you do?

JG: And that's where he it right now . . . at the end of the past.

WP: And what very few people have noticed in *The Moviegoer* is (they understand about the southern romanticism and the Stoic tradition of his aunt, which goes all the way back to Marcus Aurelius, Walter Scott, and the good soldier. His father was very much overtaken by that—the idea of dying in the "wine dark sea" with *A Shropshire Lad,* which is, after all, strictly southern cavalier, half-ass English romanticism); science is also in the same mode—it's a parallel mode. Kierkegaard placed them together, which nobody else did. Science has a way of dealing with the world, and it works fine, and then you have the problem of how to live after you've done both: you can construe the world romantically or scientifically; but neither is enough. For Binx it didn't settle the problem of how to live out his life . . . on an ordinary afternoon. Hence, his horizontal search, which is what the novel is about—for God, if you will—he starts out having exhausted both science and romance, that is, the southern "good-pagan" tradition. So, he's starting out on his own odd quest. The action of the novel takes place in the horizontal search, except he kids himself along the way with his moviegoing, playing at "rotation" and "repetition." Binx plays games to give himself the illusion of a sort of reality. His moviegoing is a way of escaping into a kind of universal time. The other mode would be what Kierkegaard would call the aesthetic, the love affairs with his secretaries, which didn't work with Kate because she was onto him and because he loved her. And the romantic escapades or rotations, which happen on the Gulf coast, finally didn't work. In the end he wanted to make a life with Kate.

JG: Kate was so much a part of him, the female part of him. She wouldn't let him fool her—she saw through him every time.

WP: That's it exactly. Remember how he would play his little tricks on his secretaries, posing as Gregory Peck or whoever, and they would always fall for it? Kate even saw through his moviegoing, which was his secret weapon. The others never saw through him.

JG: Especially the first one, Linda, who doesn't even appear in the book. She's happy being wined and dined.

WP: She doesn't want to go to the movies—just wants to go to the Blue Room instead. But Kate paid him the ultimate understanding when she says, "I know what you're doing." When they went to the movies together—and he took her to the movies deliberately, *knowing* that she would know what he was doing, and she had had a *real* anxiety attack—and he took her to eat some oysters, then to see *Panic in the Streets* on Tchoupitoulas Street. And this is where, I don't know, maybe luck comes into play, but for me this worked, and a few have noticed it. But this is where it makes it a good novel to teach because a student always understands this—that the movie was made in New Orleans, around Tchoupitoulas Street, so they go to the movie house in the same place. But Kate knew the little game he was playing. You can call it "certification." And it wasn't so much that the technique itself worked to get her out of her anxiety attack; it was the fact that they were communicating. He knew that she knew what he was doing. She says in effect, "I'm on to you," but it works anyhow.

JG: And they could admit to each other that they knew each was a self trying to escape itself?

WP: Sure. It was a way of saying, "We know something . . .

JG: about each other . . .

WP: and other people don't."

JG: They had an understanding not to talk in the movies.

WP: Right, so that way Binx is not now existing in Lawson's time—the pure universal—he's using that as a way of communicating with Kate, so he's existing in a very personal mode of time. He's got this girl next to him whom he loves and who is in desperate shape, but who understands him perfectly and depends on him in a very scary way. And in the end, I think, he depends on her. So you *have* Lawson's term—universal time—moviegoing or whatever—but you have it used as a means of something going on between two people, and it has nothing to do with touching her—he doesn't touch her in the movies. Unlike most novels, sex between them fails, and even the failure works. And that gets back to what we were talking about earlier about communicating unspoken feelings that people have which don't ordinarily get written about in novels. But it's strange, everyone, mostly kids, understands that particular episode—what was going on when they went to the movies—what was going on between them.

JG: Do we have the same expansions of time—the here-and-now and the eternal timelessness in, say, *The Second Coming?*

WP: Allie is the one who does the time-tripping; she's the feminine Binx. Will Barrett is a man who has missed his life. He asks somewhere, "Is it possible to miss your life like you miss a plane?" But he's very much aware of the problem of time; he's aware of the universal twentieth-century problem of Western culture, namely as in, I was telling you earlier, this new novel I was thinking about—where Tom More comes back and in looking at all his patients begins to see the one thing they have in common. He begins to develop a question: "Where are you; why aren't you here—*here* in the present?" Because most of the people are, as far as time goes, either casting ahead: "My God, what's going to happen, what am I going to do? I'm worried to death about what's *going* to happen." Or else, "My God, what's happened, what have I done?"—impaled. This guilt of their past, this worry about the future. So, he's thinking, "Where are

people now, where are *you* now?" So that's Will Barrett's problem;
all of his life he has relied on somebody—at the beginning, what he
thought were experts, the psychologists. Then he depends on Sutter
to be the expert, and Sutter declines the invitation and says, "I'm not
going to be an expert . . . I'm not going to tell you anything. If I did
you'd simply take it as yet another psychological input." Will's whole
career consists of what he thinks he's *supposed* to do: first, he
thought he was supposed to take up with Sutter and be the disciple
to the proper kind of guru; then, to marry Kitty and get the right kind
of house in a suburb. Instead, he changes his mind and decides to go
to law school. Then to shift to a northern scene: he's a successful
lawyer, marries a rich lady. Then he thinks he should move back to
the South and live a good life in the perfect house with the perfect
view. Having done all that, he still has the sense of missing his life,
which gets back to John Cheever's quotation which I use in *Lost in
the Cosmos:* he said this poignant thing in talking about his own
friends . . . who have been to Harvard . . . in other words, the best
and brightest in the northeast, and had the best education and the
best economic advantages. Do you know what their main reaction is
to middle age? Guess what?

JG: That they have done all that they were *supposed* to do but
not all they *wanted* to do?

WP: Yes . . . the main emotion was disappointment. This was
done very well in different style, in an old kind of style, by the novelist John Marquand in *So Little Time, Point of No Return* . . . about
the point of no return being passed by disappointed people.

JG: Binx is often disappointed by what he thinks he's supposed to
do, too. In other ways, he experiences disappointment in the expectation of a pleasant experience which then only leads to his despond-
ence. His only happiness is in the *unexpected*—I find the same trait in
Will Barrett. The expectation of meeting Kitty in the summer house,
and being "lost in a cloud," is an experience which is a repetition and
only a sensual pleasure to him now, leaving Will *lost* out of touch.
But his unexpected encounter with Allie and the coming together
gives him more than temporal happiness.

WP: Most people cannot conceive planning or initiating a course
of action which would truly be an exercise of freedom. Although
maybe they ought to. Most people are *thinking* of or are *waiting* for

something magical to happen. And this is the kind of magic that coin-
cides with the low point in Will Barrett's life. Remember that he's at a
kind of end of his life; he experiences an affair which is halfway
comic because he falls down after hitting a great three-wood . . . or
makes an eagle and falls down in a sandtrap. His perspective of the
world is from this topsy-turvy position. It was designed to be a "confluence of influence," namely, living an ordinary life in a certain aspect of time. It's a pretty desperate kind of life—as it may be lived in
an affluent resort in North Carolina, which can in itself be a life of
despair. But it's more than the literal falling—he sees a bird, the blue-
dollar hawk, and all of a sudden, the past comes back. He hadn't
thought about his father for thirty years. So he's overwhelmed by the
past and, at the same time, he slices out of bounds—"out of bounds"
is important, out of bounds of one's ordinary life—and there is the
sunlight shining on this girl. So he has the confluence of three things
at once at one point: the old life, the life of despair; his present life,
which is going nowhere, falling down; now all of a sudden, a literal
ray of hope. The sunlight actually breaks through the pine trees and
he sees the girl, whom he *thinks* is a boy. Well, it's kind of grace in a
way; after all, you don't plan on grace. You try something. Then
something happens to you, you fall down, you get lucky.

JG: Before Will, Allie divides time into good and bad: the nights
and the mornings are good, but the afternoons—"late afternoons
with nothing to fill in the void of time between working and eating
and sleeping," are bad.

WP: I don't remember any of her good times, except fixing up her
bed and moving the stove.

JG: Well, that's a quote from the book. Is this void a repetition
that leaves a blankness every day, which is to say, meaningless, leaving one left over? Of this period, Allie tells her dog that "this time of
day is a longens. . . . In this longitude ensues a longing if not an
unbelonging." Because Allison has no past, so to speak, to turn to, is
this the cause of her despondency? She doesn't have this kind of
past that Will can lose himself into at times.

WP: Of course, she's in a position *opposite* Will. He has his whole
life behind him, somewhat of an unfortunate life which seems to him
a sadness. She has a life in front of her, but that's because she rejected the way she started out because she didn't like it. Clinically,

she'd be called schizophrenic, I suppose. After all, her mother found her curled up in a closet, and she didn't do anything right: she flunked out of school, she messed up her concert, didn't make her debut, didn't get married, didn't take up a profession, didn't go to graduate school, just ended up back in the house which, to a certain kind of family, is the worst thing that can happen to a girl or a parent. The story of Allie in that novel is a quest for a life. She's saying, "I'm not having any of this; this is not life." She says, of the life she had with her mother and father, "I'm wiping that out." The shock treatment was good in the sense that it helped her do that, even schizophrenia is a way of doing that. So she chose to live in the present time.

JG: Will's own thoughts bear resemblance to William Alexander Percy's comment in the chapter "For the Younger Generation" in *Lanterns on the Levee* in which he says, "At the intensest peak of our emotions, lying at the bosom of the one we love, or lost in a sunset, or bereft by music, being then most ourselves, we dissolve and become part of the strength and radiance and pathos of creation. When most ourselves, we are not ourselves, and lose our tragic isolation in the whole." This seems to me the condition of both Binx and Will; when they should be the happiest, in the most comforting situation, then neither is himself.

WP: Yes, but in the same passage, I also got a sense of the terrible loneliness of Uncle Will. Recently, wasn't it *The Lonely Crowd* which mentioned that the twentieth-century disease is loneliness? And, in spite of all the emphasis on interpersonal relations, and how to get along with people, love better, and all the self-help books, the fact is that people are, by and large, probably lonelier than ever. And one of the best things that ever happens in my novels is when the loneliness is bridged. There's a quote in the beginning of *The Last Gentleman* that talks about the end of the modern world—how the world will be stripped bare of all the old togetherness, even of love. But as bad as it is and as lonely as it is, it's going to be *honest, clean,* no bullshit, and there will actually be a possibility of one lonely person encountering another one, *really* encountering another one and perhaps even God in a way that hasn't been possible before, even in a culture which sets every value on togetherness, groups, and relationships. And that, to go back to what we were talking about earlier, is where *Lost in the Cosmos* ends up.

A Conversation with Walker Percy about Thomas Merton

Victor A. Kramer and Dewey W. Kramer/1984

This previously unpublished interview is presented by permission of Victor A. Kramer (1984).

This interview was conducted at Walker Percy's home in Covington on the afternoon of 1 May 1983, when Kramer, coauthor of a reference guide about Percy's work, had arranged to take him a copy of that book. Earlier correspondence had informed Percy that Kramer was compiling an oral history about Thomas Merton, someone with whom Percy had exchanged correspondence in earlier years. That oral history project had been designed as an archival record, and there were no plans for immediate publication, but when the transcript of the Merton talk was approved by Percy, in the summer of 1984, plans were already underway for the gathering of all significant Percy interviews into this book. Percy suggested that this "Merton talk" might be included in such a gathering because it covers material not available elsewhere.

The transcript records the last forty-five minutes of a three-hour conversation in which Kramer, Dewey Kramer, his wife, and Percy conversed about a wide variety of subjects. A friend of the Kramers, Bernard Cleary, was also present. Percy drew everyone into the conversation. Memories of Germany in 1934; life in New York City; discussion about the contemporary church; comments about the Cistercian monastery at Conyers, Georgia; religious orders; memories of Caroline Gordon; and comments about Flannery O'Connor, as well as Merton, filled out the conversation.

The afternoon began on the deck of the Percy's new cottage, and continued there for almost two hours. The group almost forgot that they had agreed to tape comments about Merton. As the light began to change, they reluctantly decided to go into the living room to make the tape. The comments transcribed here document the last part of an intense, but paradoxically very relaxed, afternoon.

Comment: So, why don't we just start.

Answer: Sure.

Question: And I'll ask what was your association with Thomas Merton?

Answer: Well, I've met him only once and the connection was unusual. I had been asked to be on the advisory board of an obscure journal called *Katallagete,* which means in Greek "let us be reconciled." It was organized, edited, and published by two friends of mine, one being Will Campbell, who is a very interesting Baptist preacher, theologian, civil rights activist and his friend Jim Holloway who was the editor, I think. So, Will asked me to be on the board. And he said that he had all sorts of Protestants and he had blacks and he didn't have a Catholic. So I (laughter) was his token Catholic, I guess. And he had Merton. I don't know why he needed me if he had Merton. (VAK: He needed a lay Catholic.) That's a nice way to put it, a broken-down lay novice Catholic, right. So I don't mind doing that because being on the advisory board means you don't have to do anything. I had no particular duties and the idea was that we would meet at a different place every year. Well, I've only been to one meeting and the only reason I went to that was that Will called me and said, "We're going to meet at Gethsemani Abbey this year. We're going to meet at Merton's place." So that was a chance to meet Merton, which turned out to be very fortunate because I think that was either the year or the year before he died, before he went to Burma. So, we all converged on Gethsemani. I think I flew up to Louisville and was met by somebody, maybe Will, and we drove to the Abbey. And we drove up the hillside to Merton's; Merton had a little cinder-block cottage about a half-a-mile or so from the Abbey.

Question: So you went directly to the Hermitage?

Answer: We went directly to the Hermitage. And, I'd been curious about what the connection was between Merton and the Abbey and the Abbot. I'd heard the strangest things about Merton. One that he was schizophrenic, and another was that he had left the Church or he had broken his vows or he was living with a couple of women, you know, and all sorts of things. I was amazed at the number of intellectuals who admired Merton and who could not tolerate the idea that he could be an observing Trappist monk for twenty years. And I wanted to see for myself, well, what he was like. But as I say, I think I corresponded with him. (VAK: Because you were corresponding when you were in process of writing *Love in the Ruins*.) Right. And I think he wrote me about *The Moviegoer*. He had read *The Moviegoer*, and he was interested in *The Moviegoer*. But I just remember finding ourselves sitting on the front porch of this rather rude, but pleasant, cinder-block cottage overlooking a little swale, a little meadow. And Merton, Merton surprised me. He was much more robust than I expected. Now that I look back on Furlong's book, she talks about him being sick all the time, you know. You would think after reading the book that he was an invalid. Maybe it was true, that he was always complaining about this or that, usually a gastro-intestinal thing. But I'm sure it was true. But he was very husky, and I think he was dressed in—he had jeans and I don't know whether it was a T-shirt. I have a recollection of something like a Marine skivy-shirt, something like that and a wide belt. And as I say very, very healthy looking. A pretty tough-looking guy. And very open, outgoing, nice, nice and hospitable. And he fixed everybody a drink. He poured me a nice bourbon and water. (DWK: Tavern at the cinder-block.) (Laughter.) Well, we were right in bourbon country, you know. In fact driving from Louisville, I remember seeing all these huge places where they stored the liquor.

Question: Can you describe Merton's face? Can you remember?

Answer: He had a ruddy complexion and a healthy, unlined, not particularly distinguished face, in any particular; I mean, if you met him in a crowd, or on the street you wouldn't pick him out as being extraordinary looking. I think maybe thinning hair. But, well a sturdy, outgoing, well-met fellow.

Question: Had you read many of his books?

Answer: I had read most of them. Not his poetry particularly. I don't read much poetry. I don't have a gift for it. But I'd read most of his prose works.

Question: And so when you were there at that meeting did you talk about the magazine mostly? Or did you have a chance to talk about other things?

Answer: Well, I don't remember. It was very casual, I think. There was a lot of bantering, kidding around, you know. I mean not very serious talk. And I remember I was left alone with him for maybe a half hour. And I was a little uneasy about what to do, and I think he was uneasy with me. You know, what do two writers say to each other? And what do you say to Thomas Merton? And there were a lot of things that I wanted to ask him, But I didn't. Well, I remember thinking what to call him. So I called him Father Louis. He didn't say otherwise; I called him Father Louis. I didn't want to ask him.

Well, I would have wanted to ask him things like: "What's going on here? I mean, what's your relationship with the Abbot?" Maybe I should have. Maybe he would have answered. Well, I, you, just don't do that with . . . obviously I didn't do it. So we made polite conversation. And I think I remember the only thing I remember him talking about was I asked (meanwhile we had had a meal. We had gone down to the refectory with the other monks and it was the usual. . . . (VAK: So did you eat with the monks?) Yeah, once. We ate there; it was good, it was very nice and the monks were very nice. And we went back up the hill, but I don't remember Merton being with us when we ate with the monks. I don't remember whether he came down there or not.) I asked him what he thought of the future of the monastic movement in this country. I wasn't particularly, really interested in that; I wanted to ask him about himself but, I mean, I didn't. Oh, incidentally, he had a lot he was into, he was doing—he had a camera. And I think he'd seen Griffin in the meanwhile. And Griffin had been up there right before then. In fact, there were photographs by Griffin of Merton, big, big, almost poster size—showing Merton just as I saw him in his jeans and. So that's exactly how I saw him, the way Griffin photographed him. And I think Griffin had just been there, we just missed him was my impression. And Griffin had gotten him interested in photography. And he was taking pictures. I remember him; we looked across the meadow and there were deer right at the foot of the meadow. So I asked him something about the future of monasticism in the U.S. And he said something about . . . it's amazing how little we found to talk about. How much I wanted to ask him, and didn't feel free to ask him. But he said he didn't think that the big monastery or the big abbey was going . . . was a thing of the future. He thought that there were going to be small communities, maybe in cities or. . . . And he talked about a few men living in a house, you know, somewhere maybe in Louisville or something . . . I don't know. It was a rather standard reply which a lot of people were thinking in terms of in—when was it 19 . . . ? I don't

know, what year did he die? (VAK: '68) Well, o.k. (VAK: So that
would have probably been '67 or '66, somewhere in that time.)
There were maybe half a dozen of us, one was a black guy from
Atlanta, and I've forgotten his name. He would be on the board of
Katallagete. He's a black activist. (VAK: Is he in Atlanta now? Julius
Lester is. . . .) I think that's who it was.

Question: Did you go to the Abbey after that? I mean did you
spend additional time? (WP: No.) So you didn't go into the Guest
House or anything, it was just that one afternoon?

Answer: That's right. Just a few hours with Merton.

Question: Would you like to say something about the magazine?
Do you want to say anything about the magazine?

Answer: Well, *Katallagete* is a very remarkable magazine which
goes quite a ways back and mainly reflects the thinking of Will
Campbell and Jim Holloway. But it was one of the earlier expressions
of ecumenism in a particular sense, Will Campbell being a drop-out
from the National Council of Churches. He disagreed with the social
orientation of the National Council of Churches very much believing
in Christian orthodoxy or rather Anabaptist anarchy. And yet at the
same time with a very strong feeling for . . . maybe the main orientation was racial reconciliation. And this, in the early sixties, was not as
commonplace as it is today or not as easily accepted. And he attracted . . . I'm impressed by early issues having articles by the . . .
who is a French Protestant theologian who wrote *La Technique?*
(VAK: Jacques Ellul.) Ellul. Jacques Ellul. Ellul was an admirer of
Katallagete. I don't think the magazine ever had a circulation of over
a thousand or so. And, it was chronically broke and you never knew
when it was coming out. But it's unique.

Question: You said that you had read several of Merton's books.
Do any of those books stick out in your mind?

Answer: Well, *Seven Storey Mountain* meant a great deal to me.
It was about the time I, it came out about the time that I became a
Catholic so it had a good deal of influence on me. We were coming
from the same place—shall I call it Columbia University agnosticism?
And I was interested in the fact of Merton's own reaction to it, I think
he came to dislike the book himself. Life is never as simple as you
think it's going to be, and I think he regarded his, he came to regard
his monastic vocation as much more romantic than in fact it turned

out. But that didn't make *The Seven Storey Mountain* less attractive, it was a very compelling and attractive book and the timing was just right both for me and maybe for my generation—postwar, a postwar feeling of uprootedness and dislocation. And I had powerful reasons for connecting up with it like, I guess, many people did. His background was quite similar to mine. We had both been to Columbia and I knew people that he knew. So I was fascinated with his idea of just leaving Columbia and striking out for the wilds of Kentucky.

Question: Were you surprised when he first wrote to you to say that he'd read *The Moviegoer?*

Answer: Yes, I was astonished, because I had heard from him and Flannery O'Connor about the same time. And I was much flattered, and I wrote him back. I think we corresponded a half-a dozen times.

Question: I think maybe one of those letters of his indicates he sent one of those abstract drawings of his to you?

Answer: I've got 'em somewhere. I didn't understand it, I didn't know what he was trying to do.

Question: Some of those were printed in a book called *Raids on the Unspeakable.* Do you remember that book?

Answer: No.

Comment: It's a book of essays and it has a prose elegy in it for Flannery O'Connor. It's a very nice piece.

Answer: I wonder if he corresponded to any degree with Flannery? He must have.

Comment: There's no record of it.

Answer: Really? You would think that he would have. Come to think of it, I don't remember any correspondence from her in her collected correspondence. I don't recall anything about Merton.

Comment: She mentions him a couple of times but she really wasn't excited about what she read. If you go through the index, his name is there a couple of times but, you know, she didn't spend much time with Merton.

Answer: Yeah, I think she was on good terms with the monks at Conyers, wasn't she? Didn't she go over there?

Question: Oh, yes, yes. And then also because of the Robert Giroux connection, she was very aware of what Merton was doing. and you may know, Sally Fitzgerald wrote a little piece which was

given at Columbia University where she compares Merton and
O'Connor. Have you read that?

Answer: Really? No.

Comment: It's a nice essay, it really is. And she talks about
O'Connor and Merton as having similar temperaments and living a
monastic life and being disciplined and so on. I met Bob Giroux in
November and I talked with him about Merton and he made some of
the same connections. And Mr. Giroux was saying that when he
would go see O'Connor she would ask questions about Merton and
when he would go see Merton more questions would be raised about
O'Connor. So, he was kind of the intermediary.

Question (Dewey Weiss Kramer): Well, I wonder if there was that
same lack of knowing exactly, as you were saying earlier, about what
to ask that you and Merton felt, between the two of them? What was
it you said about *The Seven Storey Mountain?* Were you already
Catholic or were you thinking about Catholicism before you had read
it, or did it just help you find your way as a Catholic?

Answer: I think it did. I don't exactly remember the timing. You
don't remember when it was published do you? (VAK: 1948.) Well,
that would be about right. I think my wife and I both became Catholics in '48. So I read it with great enthusiasm and much interest.

Question: You mentioned Columbia and your being a student at
Columbia during the same time Merton was. Would you want to say
a little bit about Columbia and New York City at that time?

Answer: Well, it would be no connection, because I was in medical school which was up at 168th Street and he was down at Columbia College. He knew people like Giroux, and his friend, Robert Lax,
and Mark Van Doren, and I knew none of those. I had not the slightest interest in English or English departments or writing. I was a medical student at P & S.

Question: So you had no suspicion at that point that you would
become a writer?

Answer: Not the faintest. No, not the faintest. In the interval I had
interned at Bellevue Hospital, had done all the autopsies on tuberculosis patients and had contracted T.B. Not a bad case, but enough.
In those days you went to a sanitorium, you know. So I was out of it
for a couple of years and then all of a sudden I read a good deal. I

had taken very, very little English literature. I'd majored in German and chemistry and so I knew more about German and chemistry than I knew about Mark Van Doren or anybody like that.

Question: But, you know when Merton finally decided to go to Gethsemani he was so relieved to leave New York City. What do you think it was about New York City that he found was so oppressive?

Answer: I don't know. I think he must have mentioned that. Well, you know, he had a political period. He was very funny talking about his first novel. He said it was a very pessimistic and ominous novel, from a left wing point of view, about Nazi bombers flying over the waterfronts of Hoboken or something. Sounded like a very bad novel. And he said it was. I think he got tired of the standard secular liberal orthodoxy around Columbia University. He was on his own spiritual quest.

Question: Right. Do you have any ideas about why Merton became such a popular writer?

Answer: Well, it had to do more with his talent. He was a very skillful writer and a very appealing writer and a very prolific writer. And also, the times—in the late forties and fifties there was a tremendous spiritual awakening or hunger in this country and in the postwar generation. The monk I was talking to you about who was a friend of mine and Caroline Gordon, Father Charles, he had been a friend of Merton's and he had read the book and he had been a tail-gunner on a B-24 that got shot-up on the Ploesti raid. I think there was a whole generation of people who had been through the war and been through that experience. And, imagine going from being a tail-gunner to a Trappist monk in Conyers. Well, it wasn't a unique experience.

Comment: Merton was very concerned about racial issues in the sixties and he's got a book called *Seeds of Destruction*. He's using the same idea as *The Seeds of Contemplation* and he writes about a novel by William Melvin Kelley called *A Different Drummer*. He never mentioned that novel? (WP: No, no.) Do you know that novel? (WP: Not at all.) It's a novel about a mythical state somewhere between Alabama and Mississippi and Georgia where all the Negroes decide to leave one day and the white folks can't quite figure out what's wrong. (Laughter.) And they leave anyway. (Laughter.) And Merton wrote this piece about that, *A Different Drummer,* talking about the moment when something has to happen. The moment that no one is prepared for and I think that is the way he thought of the 1960's as a time when things were happening that the country wasn't really ready for.

Answer: Yes. I remember another thing I wanted to ask about, but I didn't. I knew he was interested in Eastern monasticism, which is one of the reasons he went to Burma. And, I wanted to ask him more about that and didn't. I don't know whether it's an American trait, or a trait of writers but they don't really like to talk to each other much. But I had the feeling that if I could have spent the weekend with him or maybe had six drinks or something I think I would have been able to say a lot more and ask him a lot more. But there was a sense of a great deal left unsaid and a great deal that I would have liked to ask him about.

Question: Did you ever return to Gethsemani after that meeting? (WP: No.) So, you went there once and you've been to Conyers just once. Is that right?

Answer: Yes. Something else I was always curious about and wanted to ask about, and didn't feel like it. How did it work for him, for the abbots to ask him to write, produce these books. Cause, when you go to the bookstore at Conyers or the bookstore at Gethsemani it looks like a big display, it looks like a Doubleday display of Merton's works. I've often wondered how he felt about that. On the one hand, he liked to write. And maybe it didn't and maybe it wasn't a bad idea, you know. 'Cause writers often need somebody to tell them to go ahead and write. Like Dickens wrote under duress, you know.

Comment: Well, I think Merton realized that. I mean on the one hand, he would say that he would prefer not to write. And on the other, and there are records of this, he knew full well that he profited by being told to go ahead.

Answer: Yes. I had that feeling that it might not have altogether been a bad deal (VAK: That's true. I think that's true.) Although one likes to think, I mean the popular idea is "poor Merton," having to crank out all this stuff just to help the Trappists, you know. But it wasn't that, I'm sure it wasn't that simple.

Comment: No, I think he enjoyed it, I really do. And I think he found that he could, through the writing, find what the next step would be. And he learned more and more to be very disciplined. I

talked with Father Flavian, the man who was his abbot in the last
year of his life. (WP: That's the one he liked a lot better than the
previous abbot.) That's correct. He liked Flavian a lot. And Father
Flavian said that Merton was so disciplined that finally he could just
kind of stop doing one thing, maybe counseling as Novice Master,
stop talking, go to his room, sit down, and just kind of turn on the
valve and write. (Laughter.) And that he would write for a half hour
and then he would stop. And that takes a lot of discipline.

Answer: It takes a lot. And something, not all of us do either.
Some of it sounds like that. I don't think his poetry, although I'm not
a critic of poetry, ... it doesn't strike me much of his poetry is really
first rate.

Comment: Yes. Well, part of the problem there is that the *Collected Poems* is such a fat volume. He never would have republished
all that stuff. He would have selected some of it and now we've got a
great fat book which the editors just put together, and so, it'll be a
long time before people sift through all that.

Answer: I'll tell you one thing that surprised me about Merton. I
made a retreat at a, they have a Jesuit Retreat House here near New
Orleans—in Manresan on the River, you know—and they have a
tape room with different tapes. And I notice that they had a series of
tapes of Merton's "Talks to the Novices." He was Novice Master. And
they are really impressive. He really had a gift for that.

Comment: Yes, well in fact he spoke to the Community on Sunday afternoons and they started taping so that the lay brothers could
hear it also. And they did for about five years. They've got, well, over
two hundred tapes and some of them are quite good. And so those
are just a few little excerpts. But he would speak to the Community
about all kinds of subjects—ranging from monastic history and, you
know, certain kinds of questions about monastic life. (WP: You mean
during meals or. . . .) No, this is on Sunday afternoon—three or four
o'clock in the afternoon. It was, I suppose, for the novices, but it
finally became a kind of open talk for anybody who wanted to listen.
And there are some interesting talks there about literary theory.

Answer: Well, what was admirable about it was the spontaneity
and the humor. It's funny. I would think he would have been an
excellent Novice Master.

Comment: I think so, yeah. That's what everybody says.

Answer: It was hard in my own mind to square this impression of him talking in this way about the novices with the portrait that Furlong paints of a rather tortured soul, you know.

Comment: Right. I think that's true. I think that she didn't talk to enough people. We had a man named Jim Finley come to Atlanta and speak at the conference we did on Thomas Merton, and he was a novice of Merton. And Jim Finley told the nicest story. He said he had gone to Gethsemani, he was a young man, and Father Louis was. . . . (Tape ends) So, he was there as a young novice of seventeen and he was supposed to go in and talk with Father Louis. And he said he went in several times and he was just so nervous he didn't know what to say, and he just felt he wasn't getting anywhere with the spiritual direction. About the fourth time he went in and Merton realized that this young man was very, very nervous. And so Merton said, "Well, what's your job here at Gethsemani?" And he said, "Well, Father Louis, I'm in charge of feeding the pigs." And so Merton started laughing and Jim Finley started laughing. And Merton said, "Now look, from here on when you come here for your weekly conference, I want you to tell me something very specific about the pigs. And so when you come back, you tell me something that happened with the pigs that week." And so, Jim had to go back the next week and he said, "Well, I was feeding the pigs and this one big pig, kind of, pushed this little pig over. . . ." (Laughter.) And then they both started laughing, and then they laughed a lot. And Jim Finley said that was exactly what he needed, and then Merton was his Novice Master for the rest of the time, and it was a real success.

Answer: You know, I'm just remembering one thing you said about the Abbey . . . the only thing that I recall him saying about the Abbey. It was a rather hostile remark about the Trappist Monastery. He was talking about nonviolence, he was very strong on nonviolence. And he was saying how the Trappists, even the Trappists, violated this principle. And either I, or somebody, said, "Well, what do you mean? How do they do that?" He said, "Well, look at the way they exploit these brothers, these monks. . . ." I remember the expression was "They got to break their ass carrying all this cheese around." (Laughter.) I said, "Well. . . ." I didn't really buy that, I didn't really think that was doing violence to people carrying cheese around. But. . . . (VAK: I think he's probably right though.) He didn't think much. . . .

Comment (Dewey Weiss Kramer): Well, he wasn't in favor of the cheese business. (VAK: No, he thought there was too much emphasis upon cheese.) The point is the cheese, the dollar market. . . .

Answer: He didn't like that, he thought that was a commercial exploitation.

Comment: Well, in a sense it is.

Answer: Do they need that? Do they need the money to be self-sustaining, I wonder?

Comment: Well, they give their excess money away. And in fact, at Gethsemani they employ people from that neighborhood on full-time and a part-time basis. And I think the younger monks are pretty aware of, you know, of their responsibilities within the Community and so on, so I don't think it's really a problem. I don't think anybody's getting rich.

Answer: Yes. Yes. Maybe I ought to say that I went there with some curiosity about the relationship between him and his hermitage and the Abbey. And I came away with the feeling that there was, not that there was no disaffection, that they were on good terms. I mean maybe I expected to find him grousing in the woods and putting down Gethsemani Abbey. But, the only thing, only unfavorable thing, he said was the crack about cheese.

Comment: Well, I think unless you have something else that you want to recall.

Answer: I wish I could tell you more.

Index

A

Adams, Henry, 152
Aeschylus, 97
Agee, James, 138
Anderson, Sherwood, 35
Antoninus, Marcus Aurelius, 72, 152, 211, 303
Appleton, Victor, Pseud., *Tom Swift,* 5
Aquinas, Thomas, 43, 63, 120, 124, 134–35, 155, 204, 272; *Summa Theologica,* 153
Ardrey, Robert, 55
Aristotle, 135, 247
Arnold, Matthew, 258
Assis, de, Machado, *Epitaph for a Small Winner,* 15
Augustine, St., 5, 272, 293
Austen, Jane, 88

B

Baldwin, James, 18, 19, 25–26; *The Fire Next Time,* 20
Barrett, William, *Irrational Man: A Study in Existential Philosophy,* 40
Barth, John, 24; *The Floating Opera, The End of the Road, Giles Goat-Boy,* 81
Barthelme, Donald, 159, 163, 168
Bayley, John, 12
Beckett, Thomas, 15, 75
Bell, Charles, 38, 257
Bellow, Saul, 11, 49, 50, 97, 159, 163, 168, 222, 246–47; *Herzog,* 14, 29; *Henderson the Rain King,* 29; *Humboldt's Gift,* 141; *Mr. Sammler's Planet,* 50
Benet, Stephen Rose and William Vincent, 256
Bergson, Henri, 77
Bird, Scott, fn 1, 127
Bloomfield, Leonard, 137
Böll, Heinrich, 78
Boswell, James, 245
Bradford, Roark, 256
Brain, Walter Russell, Lord, 292

Brooks, Cleanth, 98, 207, 211
Brown, Roger, 132, 144
Browning, Robert, "Love Among the Ruins," 46
Buber, Martin, 119
Buckley, William, 104, fn 4, 128, 172

C

Caldwell, Taylor, 162
Campbell, Will D., and James Holloway, *Katallagete,* 310
Camus, Albert, 3, 12, 31, 42–43, 73, 75, 79, 106, 153, 164, 183, 246, 264–75, 300; *Fall, The,* 82, 146; *Stranger, The,* 42, 73, 76, 298
Carr, John, *Kite-Flying and Other Irrational Acts: Conversations with Twelve Southern Writers,* 86
Carter, Hodding, 57, 260, 268–69
Cash, W. J., 58, *Mind of the South, The,* 151, 263
Cassirer, Ernst, 106, 137
Chaplin, Charles S., 81
Chardin, de, Teilhard, 42
Chastain, Thomas, *Judgement Day,* 68
Cheever, John, 158, 159, 163, 168, 221, 222, 283, 306
Chekhov, Anton, 148; *Seagull, The,* 246
Cheney, Brainerd, 80
Chomsky, Noam, 129, 133, 137, 290–91
Claudel, Paul, 274
Cleary, Bernard, 309
Clemens, Samuel L. (Mark Twain), 88, 275; *Adventures of Huckleberry Finn, The,* 53, 76; *"Literary Offenses of James Fenimore Cooper, The,"* 276
Cohn, David, 11, 38, 57, 260, 261; *God Shakes Creation,* 256
Commager, Henry Steele, 49
"coming-to-oneself," 81, 219–220
Copernicus, Nicolaus, 223
Cowley, Malcolm, 283

321